It's a Love Story

It's a Love Story

Shirlie & Martin Kemp

MIRROR BOOKS

First published by Mirror Books in 2020

Mirror Books is part of Reach plc
10 Lower Thames Street
London EC3R 6EN

www.mirrorbooks.co.uk

ISBN 978-1-913406-36-3

Typeset by Danny Lyle

Printed and bound in Great Britain by
CPI Group (UK) Ltd, Croydon, CR0 4YY

A CIP catalogue record for this book is available from the British Library.

3 5 7 9 10 8 6 4 2

Dedicated to our beautiful Yog.
Without you this love story
wouldn't have been possible.

Contents

Foreword
by Noel Fitzpatrick

As a teenage boy growing up on a farm in the Irish countryside in the early 80s, the highlight of my week was Top of the Pops. I saved 50p pieces for the wind-up box on the side of the television so I could marvel at the glitz and glamour perched on the old sofa in our living room. I could only dream of the kind of pop star cool that Martin & Shirlie presented to the world. I saved up coupons so that I could get stickers of Spandau Ballet and Wham! to adorn the door of the pink cupboard in my bedroom.

Like many young men in the early 80s, I wanted to be Martin and I wanted to date Shirlie. Spandau and Wham! defined the pop greatness of the decade. Martin as the suave, quaffed and velvet clad bassist of Spandau Ballet was the epitome of New Romantic louche glamour and Shirlie was exquisitely beautiful in her white dress and whiter hair, with the voice of an angel as she danced and performed backing vocals for Wham! I was infatuated with both of them. I felt that I needed to go to the confessional and declare my 'love' for Shirlie and 'envy' of Martin as forbidden sins – which says all that needs to be said. They were simply magical, awe-inspiring and so very very cool.

The 80s were in my mind halcyon days for musicians, and the Kemp's are undoubtedly that era's most enduring love story; four decades on they are still obviously besotted with one another. If ever two people were simply meant to be for each other – Shirlie and Martin are those two people. They were and are each other's destiny. They radiated beauty from the stage and television screen - so how wonderful then, to find out many years later that they radiate even greater beauty from within. They're two of the kindest, most compassionate, caring and considerate people I have ever met. To see how they protect, respect and complement each other, for me at least, is life-affirming.

Their careers saw them rise to dizzying heights of stardom, selling 50 million albums between their respective bands, and with that came the trappings of success, but they have never taken anything for granted, least of all each other. Together they've faced some incredibly tough challenges, but despite life and death battles their love, passion and commitment to one another remains as strong today as ever. In an industry that can be fickle, they are two of the most genuine people one could hope to meet, always contributing goodness to the world without exception. Their integrity and truth shine brightly in their children Harley and Roman, who are grounded in sincerity, which is truly a credit to their legacy of love.

For me Martin and Shirlie are role models. Their romance is the stuff that dreams are made of and is a real-life testament to the power of unconditional love; their loyalty to each other and honesty with each other is an anchor of rare serenity and solidarity of purpose - and their profound friendship should inspire all of us to try to become the people we dream of − not just on TOTPs - but in real life.

For these two beautiful friends, the fire of their love burns even more brightly than the first light they shared with me from a TV screen in 1982 - a beacon of hope for all of us True New Romantics. To be in their company is to be in the most wonderful of places and to call them friends my truly great honour. I know that theirs is a love that transcends space and time − for it was written in the stars, which shall forever shine a path for all of us lucky enough to have shared its light and its warmth.

Shirlie and Martin, may your love shine forever.
Noel Fitzpatrick

This is a Love Story

But this is a love story with a difference. Because most love stories end when the boy gets the girl. But that's where we're going to start.

Our love story started almost 40 years ago when, in many ways, the world looked and felt very different. There were hundreds of things we now totally take for granted, and it seems weird to imagine a time without them. Yet back then, they were brand new. Like pound coins! Our love story is priceless – but it's almost exactly the same age as the round pound.

In 1983, CDs had only just been released – the idea that in the future, you would be able to listen to any music you wanted to, in any place, at any time, would have blown our minds. (To be honest, the Sony Walkman had blown everyone's minds, as well as the contents of their wallets – Wham! and Spandau fans were spending a lot of money on batteries!) We were heading for one of the hottest summers on record. Everything felt new, and everyone felt restless – as though something very exciting was about to happen.

It was a brilliant time to be making music. Boundaries were blurring, and the charts were a celebration of punk, pop, new wave and everything in between. Technology was evolving, and taste was, too – for the first time, no one had to commit to any one style or genre. You could go anywhere in the world and be anyone you wanted to be, as long as you were young and up for it. If you were talented, ambitious and liked to experiment, it was a time to shine.

Of course, it helped that we had plenty of talented, ambitious friends. Our love flourished because we knew how to bring out the best in each other, but we were also extremely lucky to know so many people who understood how to bring out the best in us. We're still close to some of the people who knew us right back in the beginning, and I think they would all say that, ultimately, we haven't changed at all.

We know how it feels to be caught in the spotlight, surrounded by buzz, and to be told we're at the centre of everything. We also know what it's like to feel crushed, lonely and frightened, caught in a maze of hospital corridors, fighting fate, as though it's just the two of us against the world. From the outside, it may look as though we've been to heaven and hell. The truth is that every moment has been heavenly as long as we've been able to create memories together. We've managed it from opposite sides of the world, and we do it best when we're side by side on the sofa.

When you live life in the public eye, people feel as though they know you well. It makes sense. Pictures of our early dates were in the papers. Our oldest friends and colleagues are household names. Seen from a distance, our life together must seem quite glamorous. But we want to show you that the glamorous bits aren't the best, or most memorable, parts of our lives.

Our love story isn't about parties and premieres – it's about singing in the kitchen, coffee in bed, long walks with the dogs... It's being with our two beautiful, brilliant children, Harley Moon and Roman, celebrating when they make us explode with pride – and loving the fact that, even though they're adults now, we can still make them want to die of embarrassment. It's making a living scrapbook of postcards, diaries, photos, trinkets and memories, creating layers of love and happy days. It's growing together, and finding the joy in the everyday, every day.

Our love story started with a flurry of headlines and flashbulbs, but it has never needed those things to flourish. Just two people who chose love, and who keep choosing to turn to the next page together…

1

Beginning in Bushey

Shirlie

Under a silver sky, a young girl skated across a frozen lake. She was small but determined, spinning and gliding, as graceful as a ballerina. She was all by herself, and even though she was moving swiftly and smoothly, there was a stillness around her. She could smell the crisp, alpine air, and feel the bracing chill of the wintry weather in her bones. Snow glistened on the tree branches, and she thought she saw a flash of red above her – a plump red robin, come to cheer her on. But she was focused, focused, focused, thinking only of the gleaming ice beneath her, as she elegantly lifted her leg before jumping into a perfect pirouette, and…

"Shirlie! My records! For fuck's sake, what are you doing? Get off 'em *right now*!"

My magical ice rink melted. My dad, a dragon, came in roaring and breathing fire all over it.

His records were his pride and joy, but he didn't have them locked away and out of reach – they were piled up, spilling out of the sliding concertina doors of the radio-gram (a cabinet with a built-in radio and record player), lying on the floor in front of it. He didn't even bother to put them back in their sleeves. To a five-year-old girl, these records weren't sacred objects – they were stepping stones to an adventure.

The radiogram was gleaming, made from lacquered wood. The only way to get to it was to use the records as skates, with your feet gliding on the vinyl. As soon as I stepped on the slippery surfaces, I was transported thousands of miles away from Bushey and into my own special world, away from the noise, drama and shouting of our house. I wasn't just playing make-believe. I was *there*. I was in that forest.

My dad's radiogram was the only thing in our house that you could polish. We didn't have anything valuable; in fact, our whole house was incredibly untidy, very shabby and dowdy. Our sofa had a hole in it, hidden with a cushion. There were cigarette burns on our carpet, and our dining table would often have a car engine sitting on it.

My mum didn't have time to be house-proud. In fact, our house wasn't one to be proud of. It bothered me a lot that we didn't have a nice normal home. I would try to do the housework but it wasn't easy trying to navigate a vacuum cleaner around whichever items were lying on the floor. And in between all the chaos, my mum and dad had lots of little ornaments that would collect even more dust. In the end, I had no idea what I was even supposed to be cleaning.

When I was little, I didn't know why my dad shouted all the time, or what made him so scary. All I knew was that only two things could calm him down – animals and music. Now, I realise that my dad was suffering and struggling, and almost certainly living with depression. He was desperately unhappy, and he didn't have any way of dealing with his feelings or understanding them. So he took it out on my mum, my brothers, my sisters and me.

For six days a week my dad would rage, shout, slam doors and find mysterious, invisible problems to get cross about. Yet, on Sundays, he'd soften. Sunday was his record-playing day, and the music soothed him. He'd play old rock 'n' roll tunes and teach me how to jive. It felt as though the sun was coming out after a thunderstorm.

After days of shouting, dancing with my dad made me glow. I still remember him fetching my mum to watch as I threw myself around the room.

"Look at her! Look at her!" he beamed as I jumped up, swivelled and twirled.

I was hypermobile, so my joints were unusually flexible – and when you're little, you don't think about what damage you may be doing to your knees or your back.

Unfortunately, everything that made me a good dancer – my energy, my imagination and the way I loved to lose myself in a good story and a good beat – meant I was very bad at sitting down quietly and staring at a blackboard. The trouble with Sunday was that it meant Monday morning was right around the corner and I had to go back to school.

In the 60s, school was no place for an imaginative little girl. These days, education has changed, and we're much better at understanding that different children need different environments to learn in. But back then, school seemed terrifying and overwhelming to me.

I'd come from chaos. I shared a bedroom, and a bed, with my big sister and my little sister. There wasn't space to work or read or think. Suddenly, I was expected to sit still, on this hard, plastic, painful chair, in a room filled with kids. There was too much to focus on and make sense of. The smell of the building, fresh paint, plaster and chalk was overpowering. I was surrounded by new faces, deafened by the slam of wooden desks, distracted by the teacher's shoes. On my first day, I couldn't stop myself bursting into tears.

"I want to go home," I sobbed.

My teacher wasn't at all sympathetic. "Don't be so ridiculous," she hissed, returning to the blackboard and filling it with the mysterious hieroglyphics that everyone else seemed to understand.

I think school might have been more bearable if I'd known how to read. All of the other kids seemed to have mastered the skill straight away, but I was completely confused and couldn't work out what was going on. Even my beautiful, brilliant best friend Jocelyn, who lived three doors down and sat at the desk next to mine, wasn't able to help me. I still remember the surprise I felt when she instinctively shielded her work, covering it with her forearm. She didn't understand that I was struggling, and I didn't know how to tell her that I desperately needed help.

Then, soon after I started school, I became very, very ill.

It started in the night. I woke up, sandwiched between my big sister Lorraine and my little sister Nicola, and I knew something was very wrong. The bedroom ceiling was sliding down the walls and onto the floor. One moment, I felt as though I was on fire, the next, as if I'd turned to ice. I tried to crawl to my parents' room, which was no mean feat, because the landing carpet was spinning like a disco ball. The next thing I knew, I was downstairs, wrapped in a thick red blanket, sobbing and screaming with pain as I was carried out of the house on a stretcher.

It was meningitis. I'd managed to get to the hospital at a critical point. I was given a lumbar puncture, without any anaesthetic – at the time, I screamed in agony, but it probably saved my life. Hospital was strange but felt much safer than school, and the thing I liked best was that it made my parents get on with each other.

At home, my mum and dad constantly argued, shouted and cried. When they visited me in my hospital bed, they were sweet, tender and gentle. They were kind to each other, and kind to me. Deep down, I think I came to a strange conclusion. Everything was better when I was sick. The world felt safer, and gentler. When I was poorly, it brought my parents together.

I'd always been small for my age. I was born premature and too little for baby clothes, and had to be dressed in dolly outfits. I was always prone to infections, and I believe the stress and anxiety of school played a part in the meningitis.

My time in hospital made my dad realise just how tiny and vulnerable I was. He was always trying to wrap me up and protect me, even buying me rabbit-fur coats to keep me safe and cosy. That's how I was given my nickname, Snagglepuss – it was something that my dad called me after seeing me wrapped up in a fur coat and hood. He would still rant and rave, but on a good day I was his girl.

So I was definitely taking advantage of his protective nature when I persuaded him to buy me a pony.

Like my dad, I'd always loved animals, and I longed for a pony of my own. When you live in a tiny council house in Bushey, and the only outdoor space you have is the mat by your front door, you're not really in a position to keep a pony. But that wasn't going to put him off. He was a builder, which meant he knew a few labouring travellers who could sell him a pony. He also knew the lay of the local land, so he found a field where my pony wouldn't be disturbed.

My pony was the first true love of my life. I didn't really want to ride him, I just wanted to love him. For me, the best thing about animals is that you can stroke them, cuddle them and look after them. I longed for intimacy. It was hard to find at home, where everything was loud, disorganised and disruptive – but it was there in that field, where I could be with my pony, daydreaming away. He didn't ask any questions, he didn't want me to read aloud, or play a noisy game, or stop hogging the duvet. With my pony, I could just "be".

Of course, even if you find a field, ponies are expensive to feed, and we didn't have a lot of spare cash – so eventually we had to find him a new home and give him to someone who could take care of him properly. It broke my heart, but something was about to happen to help it heal.

By the time I was 12, school had become a little bit more bearable because I'd made a brand new friend, Tracey. She was from a different part of Bushey, but it may as well have been on the other side of the planet. She lived in a beautiful house – she was the first person I'd met who didn't live in a council house. It was huge, clean and quiet.

To this day, I feel happy when I smell furniture polish, because it takes me straight back to being in Tracey's house. I remember the gleaming floors, the wooden staircase and the high ceilings. This was a house you could move and grow in. Everything in my home was so cramped you felt as though you always had to hold yourself in. Stepping inside Tracey's perfect, polished house was like emerging from the depths of the ocean and being given an oxygen tank. Best of all, Tracey had a horse.

Tracey loved riding and was a gifted horsewoman. There's nothing more pleasurable than watching a talented person performing, and watching Tracey brought me so much joy. I loved helping her and spending time with her horse while she competed in events up and down the country. Soon, she was winning competitions, attracting attention and being offered sponsorship. When we were 16, her parents decided to move to Sussex. They wanted to set up a restaurant and buy some land with more space for Tracey's stables. Tracey would only move on one condition – she wanted me to come with her.

If my own children, Roman and Harley Moon, had come to me when they were 16 and told me they were moving to Sussex, I would have cried my eyes out. My mum was devastated when I told her I was leaving with Tracey, but at the time I didn't understand why. I was desperate to get away, and Tracey's offer seemed like a real dream come true. I know that sounds like a cliché, but I mean it. All my life, I'd been retreating into a fantasy world, and now one of my fantasies – running away with my best friend – was about to happen.

At first, living in Sussex was everything I hoped it would be. We had acres of green space and nothing to worry about but horses. Tracey's parents were focusing on their restaurant, so Tracey and I lived like farm girls, getting up at the crack of dawn and spending all day outdoors.

Even though we didn't have much to get dressed up for, we loved glamour, and we were fascinated by fashion magazines. Tracey's big sister Beverley lived in London, wore incredibly stylish clothes and went to the best clubs. We were intrigued by her world, and we loved looking at her magazines.

Tracey would plaster the walls of her room with pictures from Vogue and Harper's & Queen. I couldn't believe how skinny the models were. Tracey was effort-lessly tall and slim, but I think being surrounded by those pictures made us both feel a little bit worried about our weight. The two of us soon became obsessed with monitor-ing what we were eating. We adopted a diet of Kellogg's Country Store cereal, with one bowl for breakfast, one for lunch and one for dinner. It wasn't even like doing the SlimFast diet, where you get a proper meal in the evening. We both became frighteningly thin, although we couldn't really see it at the time. I was using up so much energy, running around outside all day long, and I wasn't giving myself enough nutrition or fuel.

The other problem was that reality was starting to intrude upon my dream life. Sussex was stunning, but it was a little bit too remote. I was a guest in Tracey's house, which meant that, in some ways, it was just as hard to live in as my own home. I didn't feel as though I had my own time or space. If I was feeling down, I couldn't hide away or escape. I had to keep smiling and put a cheerful face on my feelings.

Eventually, I snapped. By the time I was 18, I realised that while Tracey was destined for great things, I was going nowhere. I wasn't earning any money, I didn't have much of an education to fall back on and, if I didn't get out soon, I'd be trapped. It was that gut feeling, a feeling that there was no future for me, that made me realise I needed to do something about it.

The last place I wanted to return to was my home in Bushey but I felt a strong sense, like a force, telling me I had to go back there. I knew Tracey would be upset, and I was scared I had nothing to go back to, that I was heading into the abyss. But I made the decision – it was time to go.

With no idea what I was going to do next, I moved back to Bushey with a real sense that I'd failed.

2

Made in Islington

Martin

The funny thing about growing up in London is that you see ghosts everywhere you go. When I walk around Islington, where I was born, I can be surrounded by glamorous bars and boutiques, yet still hear a faint echo of voices singing "Roll out the Barrel" and the sound of wooden barrels making their way along the cobbles, pushed by the men who used to work in the pub we lived next door to. Now, the area is full of parks and green spaces. But somewhere out there, a baby Martin is being pushed along in his old-fashioned, tasselled pram, while his big brother Gary peers curiously at the little boy inside.

As you can tell, my ear for listening to the sounds the city makes began very early on. And once, I was filming a documentary in an old turn-of-the-century Music Hall – someone had attempted to convert it into a shopping centre but had run out of money and given up halfway through – and I was surrounded by dancing ghosts. I was standing in the space that used to be the dance hall where my mum and dad had their very first date. Even though it looked dusty and unloved, you could tell exactly where the stage and the dance floor used to be.

I could picture my parents, Frank and Eileen, young, in love and utterly carefree, not yet worried about work and life or looking after two little boys while making enough money to put food on the table. I could see the ghosts of other couples too, young and old, first dates, anniversary outings, passion, celebration and joy. It made me wonder what would have happened if I'd been born at a different time and met Shirlie in that dance hall. I'm certain we would have found each other, no matter in which era we were born. I'm not sure if I believe in fate, but I do believe that Shirlie and I were meant to be together.

These days, I appreciate the friendly ghosts around me. They're just memories, really. I've had plenty of super-natural encounters in my time, and I've lived to tell the tale. More on that later! But when I was a little boy, we lived in an old Georgian terraced house that had been split into flats. My cousins lived in the top-floor flat with my auntie, we had the middle one and an old woman lived on the bottom floor. I remember the basement being filled with the most terrifying creatures imaginable. I knew about the rats and spiders, and I was certain they were the least of it.

"Watch out for the old man in the corner!" Gary would say, warningly, and I believed him. I was certain that some scary, ghostly figure was looming in the shadows, waiting for me.

The trouble was that we all shared an outdoor toilet, and to get to it, you had to go past the basement. I still remember running outside as quickly as I could, just in case something emerged from the dark and tried to grab me. Even now, I have nightmares about the place. Thinking about the dark, shadowy doorway, and the creaking pipes that used to freeze solid in the winter, makes every single one of my hairs stand on end. Gary was terrified, too, of course. But by winding me up, he could pretend he wasn't scared. Not that anyone believed him.

There was one time of year when Gary and I could just about be persuaded to face the rats, mice and monsters: Christmas time. Our parents would hide our presents down in the basement, under heavy blankets, thinking we would never, ever go down and look. But never underestimate the excitement of small children at Christmas. We were so desperate for a preview of what could be in our stockings that we'd sneak down there with our torches, trying to convince ourselves that there was nothing lurking in the shadows after all.

One year, I was thrilled to lift a scratchy corner of a blanket in the basement to discover a bright blue bike. It was beautiful. I could already imagine myself flying down the hill at a hundred miles an hour, ringing the bell. Christmas morning dawned, and I was even more excited than usual. I couldn't wait to see my bike! I saw it soon enough – under my cousin's bottom. It was my auntie and uncle who had bought the bike. My Corgi Rocket cars were a great present, but I did feel a slight twinge of jealousy every time I looked out of the window and saw my cousin pedalling up and down the road.

When you're a kid, you don't always notice the problems that make your life difficult or different. Money was always a source of worry for my parents. Mum had to give up her job as a machinist to look after us, and Dad's job in a printworks wasn't very well paid. Sometimes I'd hear the sound of muffled sobbing behind their bedroom door. Your mum and dad weren't supposed to cry. Gently pushing the handle, as quietly as I could, I'd see Mum hiding her tears from me because she couldn't afford to buy any food for tea or new shoes for us. Until then, I hadn't realised we were worse off than anyone else. Everyone I knew had to make do, and I didn't even notice that we never had new clothes – I felt happy, I was very loved, it was perfect.

Mum believed our education was really important, and she spent a lot of time making sure we knew how to read and write before we went to school. Gary fell in love with words and always had his nose in a book. I didn't mind reading, but I was at my happiest when I could play and lose myself in my own imaginary world.

When I was very young, I was painfully shy. If I saw my school friends across the road, I'd suddenly become very self-conscious. I can still remember being short enough to bury my face in Mum's buttocks – a soft, cushiony hiding place! Mum, possibly for my sake, and possibly for the sake of her bum, had a plan for us both. She enrolled us in Anna Scher's theatre school, which had just opened up over the road.

Twice a week, she found 10 pence for our Tuesday and Thursday lessons. A "theatre school" sounds grand, but it was the community centre council hall in Bentham Court. It was the place where everyone went for their bingo, wakes and wedding receptions. If I concentrate, I can still smell the cigar smoke that seemed to linger and curl in the corners of the room.

When I started there, I became very familiar with those corners. I'd hide away and hope no one could see me. But Anna was kind, wise and encouraging. She never put me on the spot, and always made sure her lessons were such fun that it was impossible not to join in. Sometimes we'd arrive and find a huge box in the middle of the room, filled with a selection of hats. You'd pick the hat you liked the best, and Anna would want to know which sort of person would wear that hat and how you would demonstrate their personality.

She taught me how to improvise by starting me off in situations I knew well. I'd begin by imagining myself waiting for a bus by the side of the road with a friend who had a secret to tell me... and away we would go. After six months with Anna, I'd left the corners of the room and was more than comfortable standing on a stage. I still think that half of my personality comes from Anna. She made me realise that even when I was playing with my Corgi cars, I was improvising and inventing.

News of Anna's school had spread, and soon TV casting agents and production people were coming to meet us, looking for kids who might be able to appear in their programmes. Gary and I were both chosen for a few bits and pieces. Usually, it was to be a young boy in a crowd scene, and we'd get the odd line here and there. But when I was 16, I was cast as Graham Black in *The Glittering Prizes*.

The Glittering Prizes was a TV series starring Tom Conti and Nigel Havers. It followed the lives of a group of students who'd gone to Cambridge in the 1950s and looked at what happened to them. My character, Graham, was a schoolboy who was being fought over by his teachers – one wanted him to focus on sport and the other wanted him to pick a more academic path. My shyness dissolved. I *loved* being on set, having lines to learn and having the chance to really lose myself in every scene I was in.

A couple of years earlier, I'd become obsessed with Elvis. *Jailhouse Rock* was on the telly on Christmas Day. I'd looked up and become fully absorbed in the story. Within an hour, my collar was flipped up and I'd pulled my hair into a makeshift quiff. I couldn't take my eyes off him. He had this indefinable characteristic that made me feel as though I was lit up inside like a Halloween pumpkin. As a young, confused teenage boy, my feelings were so intense that I even wondered whether I'd been attracted to Elvis. After a fair bit of soul-searching, I realised I wasn't gay – but Elvis had a magical quality that couldn't be ignored.

How did Elvis do it? What exactly was it that he managed to project, whenever he was on stage or on screen? It wasn't just talent, and it was more than attitude. He seemed to have a profound faith in himself. He didn't seem to seek attention or validation – he was sure of his gift and seemed to want to share it. His performances weren't all about him, but his way of making every single person in the audience feel as though they could share in his aura – whether they were in the front row of a concert or watching from thousands of miles away, years into the future.

Appearing in *The Glittering Prizes* was my first small taste of fame. I threw myself into my work, unselfconsciously, and found myself getting lots of attention. Without Anna's help, I might have hidden away, but I discovered that I adored it. Suddenly, I wasn't just the dreamy, distracted kid, the boy with the bright brother, Gary. Now, I was Martin the young actor – and I loved it.

I'd caught the acting bug, but a couple of things were about to cure me of it. One of my last scenes was set in the school shower room and required me to get naked and wee on another lad. Nowadays this would be unheard of, but in the 70s, values and standards were very different. Still, I wasn't relaxed about it – I felt anxious and humiliated. In fact, I was so anxious that I couldn't go. One of the assistant directors had to stand behind me with a funnel, a tube and a jug of orange squash!

After that day, I decided I didn't want to act again. I'd felt so vulnerable, and it was especially hard because no one on set seemed to care about my embarrassment or acknowledge there was anything weird about the scene. My shyness came roaring back. I couldn't risk that happening again.

But something more exciting was on the horizon, and it was going to make my decision much easier.

Gary's band, The Makers, was starting to do really well. He was a brilliant songwriter and, together, the boys were playing bigger venues and getting more attention in the local press. I was keen to help out, so I offered to be a roadie. Partly because the band was fantastic and I loved listening to their songs – but mostly because I was a teenage boy and loads of girls went to their gigs.

I *loved* listening to music, but Gary was definitely the talented one. I played a little, and borrowed his records – not always asking first! But music was Gary's "thing". Of course, he wanted his own path, and his own identity. He didn't necessarily want his little brother coming along and getting in the way. I wasn't going to ask Gary to be in his band, but I was so jealous, watching him up there, throwing rock god shapes to the front row. I dreamt day and night of being up there with him. I remember praying that something terrible would happen to one of the band members so I could take their place.

One of Gary's school friends, Steve Dagger, was managing the band. He is one of the nicest men you could ever meet. We were at the 18th birthday party of Steve Norman, the band's sax player.

"Martin," he said, after a few too many glasses of home brew, "I want to change the bass player. I want to take him out and I want you to step in. You can play bass, can't you?"

My mind was racing, as it was everything I'd dreamt of. "Yep," I said.

Steve continued, "I haven't asked Gary yet, but he'll be fine."

"OK," I said, struggling for words and taking another mouthful of murky alcohol, as I realised I had some work to do. At the time, I had my school punk band called The Defects, but I only knew three chords on the guitar.

Steve replied, "Right, I'll talk to Gary and the boys and you're in!"

Gary took a little persuading to have his younger brother join the band, but our mum laid down the law and I was in. And just like that, my whole world changed.

It was a period of possibility. Life in London in the 70s and 80s was dark and difficult. Everyone was broke, our families were struggling and jobs were hard to come by. Still, it was an exciting time to be a teenage boy. The future was up for grabs, and anything could happen.

I felt restless, ambitious and curious. When Steve asked me to join the band, I felt as though a huge, heavy door was swinging open before me. I didn't know what I would find on the other side, but I was desperate to find out. I was surrounded by creative people, I would find inspiration in the most unexpected places, and being in a band made me feel as though I belonged. Quickly, all of these boys became my brothers. We joked and bantered, but we were a little family and we adored each other. I had no idea that soon we'd be living our lives on tour buses, appearing on *Top of the Pops*, discovering our personalities and seeing the world together.

Years later, I'd remember everything I learnt during those early days and share it with my children. The biggest life lesson I took from that time is this:

"Breathe in the moment – don't rush, don't wish your life away, don't miss special time because you're waiting for something bigger and better."

If I could go back and tell teenage Martin anything, I'd make sure he really savoured those early days and that feeling of joy. But, as they say, hindsight is 20-20. My future looked bright, and I was desperate to meet it. I constantly daydreamed about what could happen next. Still, I never could have predicted *who* I would meet – and how she would change my life.

3

The Punky Girl

Shirlie

I sipped at my orange juice and winced. It was warm and had an acid, slightly bleachy aftertaste. *What am I doing here?* I wondered. It was so noisy. Everyone was laughing, so I forced a smile that didn't quite reach my eyes. I knew this was a bad idea. A friend of my brother told a joke I couldn't quite hear and found the punchline so hilarious that he kept pounding his fist on the table. I wished I could hide under it.

Being back in Bushey was a real assault on my senses. Everything seemed so dirty, noisy and overwhelming. I felt desperate. I'd longed to get away from Sussex, where the quiet could feel claustrophobic, but this was just as miserable in a different way.

Home was the same as it had always been – cramped, messy, full of chaos, argumentative brothers and sisters and rowing parents – and I wasn't looking forward to bumping into my old school friends, either. Nothing had evolved, no one had worked their problems out and I had the same anxious feeling being back in the middle of it all again.

In some respects, it was the saddest time of my life and I believed I'd made the wrong decision. Why on earth had I done it? I didn't really have anything to show for my time away. I hadn't made any money, or even become an amazing showjumper. My confidence was never a strong point, but that night at the pub it was at an all-time low. My idea of a perfect night out was to go to a gig and see a live band. But this pub, despite being full of young people my age, just made me feel out of place. I felt like I didn't belong here. I've never been much of a drinker, and in 1980, my local – any local – was a fairly depressing place. All I wanted to do was go to listen to music.

There are plenty of aspects of modern life that have changed dramatically over the last 40 years. My grown-up children and their friends sometimes claim that they would *just die* without certain creature comforts, such as Sky TV, Instagram, taxis and takeaways at the touch of a button. But if I really want to freak them out, I tell them about how much pubs have changed. When I was growing up, pubs had more in common with old Victorian inns than pubs today. Now, we bring our families to sit in bright, conservatory-style spaces, sipping chilled rosé, eating sweet potato fries and expecting the hand soap to come with a matching moisturiser.

In 1980, there were lots of pubs where loo roll was considered to be a luxury. If you tried to order a salad, you might have caused a riot. If you were lucky, you could buy a packet of peanuts. (And if you were really lucky, you might have seen a picture of a naked lady sometimes slowly revealed from behind the packets of peanuts.) In my mind, pubs were sad places for dads who used to go there to complain about their lives, their jobs and their families. I expected to be surrounded by middle-aged men who had pretty much given up. At 18, I was just about ready to give up, too.

So when my brother asked me if I fancied a night out, I was surprised by his choice of venue – but I was also touched that he didn't mind his little sister tagging along. After all, even I knew that I was awful company. Back then, we didn't know much about depression or mental health. You might be down in the dumps, but you'd try to cheer yourself up, or let yourself be cheered up. If you were sad and anxious, you never spoke about it. Certainly not if you didn't have anything specific to be sad about. I did my very best to act the part of a young woman having a great night. I managed about 15 minutes of acting before I decided to get up to go to the loo. *I've given it a go, but this isn't for me*, I thought. *After this, I'm going home.*

Who knew that a simple trip to the loo could change your life? Things were about to get a lot better. On my way out of the loo – which had loo roll and soap, the absolute height of luxury – I heard an unfamiliar voice say, "Shirlie?"

I looked up and saw a boy I vaguely recognised from my old school, Bushey Meads. Oh no!

As I tried to place him, I remembered spotting him on the drive home from Sussex. At school, he'd always given off a vague impression of nerdiness, but he now looked quite cool. I'd slowed down a bit to get a good look at this boy in his nice blue peg trousers, stylish stripy top, dark skin, short hair with a long ponytail at the back, and confident walk. He looked out of place in plain old Bushey. When I know someone is going to be part of my life, reality goes into slow motion. As I drove back to my mum's, I said, "I wonder who he is – I'm sure he was a boy from my school."

"Hello Shirlie," the voice said in the crowded pub, in a well-spoken middle class accent. I turned around and, to my surprise, it was the boy in the stripy T-shirt from a few days ago.

The Punky Girl

"It's Andrew," he said. "I was in Bushey Meads in the year below you. I remember you, you were the punky girl. It's so good to see you! Would you like a drink? Come and sit with us."

I remember standing there, watching this confident well-spoken boy talk to me in the middle of the Three Crowns. I was taken aback. Then a memory flashed up, of Andrew coming out of my form room after a music lesson, as the rest of us banged on the door to be let in.

"What a load of geeks!" my mates would mutter, scathingly. We loved music, but the music we were taught at school seemed to be whole galaxies away from the records we adored. Still, it turned out that the geeks shall inherit the earth.

Andrew was far from geeky. As I sat down with him, we started to talk about the music we loved, the gigs we'd been to and the bands we wanted to see. I shared everything from my old passion for jive to my love of punk.

"That makes sense," said Andrew, smiling. "We always used to refer to you as the cool punky girl at school."

At the time, I'd never *felt* cool. I loved the creativity of punk and having the chance to dress up and express myself. You could make a surprisingly sexy dress out of a bin liner, and I'd even been known to use a kettle as a handbag. But I'd always felt like an outsider. Even my

27

lovely mum, who had always praised my mad outfits, made me think that she was humouring me a little bit. (When I had children of my own, I realised that refusing to be shocked when your teen comes downstairs with green hair is actually an ingenious parenting tactic.) But when I talked to Andrew, it was the first time I'd ever been aware of someone admiring me. Of anyone looking at me from afar and thinking I was cool. I could feel a tiny seed of self-confidence start to bloom.

Andrew was in a band, and he was very keen for me to come and see him. They played ska music, which I loved, and were called The Executives. The four members included my friend David Austin, Andrew's brother Paul, and Andrew's best friend, Yog, who was the lead singer.

"You know Yog… from school," Andrew said. "George? You must have seen me going around with him?"

I frowned, as I could barely picture Andrew at school. I had a shadowy memory of a plump boy with very thick glasses, holding a violin, but I couldn't imagine him as the frontman of any band. It must be someone else.

We made a plan for me to come along to one of The Executives' rehearsals. Andrew begged me for a lift and persuaded me to stop on the way and pick up this pal of his, Yog. It wasn't hard – being in Andrew's company had boosted my spirits.

I now didn't feel like a loser who was back in Bushey and going nowhere, with no prospects beyond my childhood bedroom. Instead, I was cool, punky Shirlie Holliman, that glamorous girl from the year above, with her own car. I don't know how many luxury limousines George and Andrew were driven in over the years – but they treated the passenger seat of my little Austin Mini Estate as a hallowed space for VIPs.

George lived on the other side of town, in posh Radlett. I'd thought my friend Tracey's house was lovely, because it had been so clean and so quiet. But Radlett was something else entirely. The only way I can describe it is this…

Imagine being in a noisy junk shop, where everything is cramped, chaotic, dusty and messy – and then walking into the homeware department of John Lewis. It's not just that everything is clean, calm and bright. The air feels different. It smells different. The tension seeps out of your shoulders, and you know you're in a safe space. Walking through George's front door for the first time, I could actually hear myself think. His parents were kind, hardworking and extremely house-proud. The scent of beeswax polish takes me straight back to the moment when his mum, Lesley, opened the door for the very first time. The most astonishing detail of all was that George's house had white carpets. This was a family with three teenage children, and Lesley was able to keep these beautiful carpets clean!

"Shirlie," said George. "It's so good to see you. I'm so glad you're here!"

Something had happened to the plump, bespectacled boy. He was the person I remembered from school – the boy from the violin lesson. Yet he had somehow become a different person entirely. I'd never met anyone like this before – a teenage boy with genuine charisma and confidence.

Looking back, I realise that George had an astonishing relationship with his gift. He wasn't a pop star yet, but anyone in a room with him could *tell* that something huge was going to happen. He was ambitious, but without being remotely arrogant about it. He had a gentle, generous spirit. You could see it in his relationship with Andrew, and he immediately treated me as the missing member of the gang. It was best friendship at first sight.

The Executives were a good band, but even when I went to see them rehearse in a dark damp basement, it was clear that the end was in sight and things were starting to unravel. George's talent as a performer was unignorable, but I could see that being a band was too frustrating for him, and there was plenty of petty squabbling among the band members.

It happens all the time – when you have a load of teenage lads getting together to make music, some are going to take it a bit more seriously than others. Some are under pressure from their parents to get a job, or spend more time on their schoolwork, and some want to spend hours standing around arguing about the Beatles versus the Stones instead of actually playing any music. As I remember it, The Executives' split wasn't acrimonious or dramatic. George was very excited about making his own music and working on songs and ideas. But if the boys were serious about anything, it was about having fun.

At the time, pop music was going through a kind of evolution. We'd all grown up with punk, which was about protest. The point of punk was to call out the establishment and call for rebellion. The Sex Pistols, The Clash and The Damned had a message for us. We didn't have to live the way our parents did – we didn't have to accept their values, we could be individuals, push for progress and change the world.

George and Andrew had a unique, tongue-in-cheek take on punk. They both felt that the most rebellious thing a person could do to the establishment was laugh at it. And as unemployment rose, opportunities became scarce and the political establishment increasingly favoured a wealthy elite, George came up with a radical proposition. If you wanted to inspire your generation, and piss off the people who were holding you back, you may as well do it by going out and having fun.

Long before Wham! were famous, we were living the Wham! lifestyle, which meant we were embracing hedonism and refusing to worry about the concerns that made life so hard for our parents' generation. I'd seen it first hand. My parents got together when they were very young. They had an unhappy marriage and became even unhappier trying to provide for children on a low wage, without any time or space to do anything they wanted to do. We didn't want to waste our youth. There would be time for responsibility later, but there was no point rushing into the adult world.

Looking back, I'm not quite sure how I managed for money. With George and Andrew, I felt like my teens would never end. Who needed responsibilities? Not us! We never thought about growing up or worrying about money. As long as we could afford petrol and a McDonald's, that was all that mattered. Whoever had the money on them would get the strawberry milkshake and chicken for me. George and Andrew had their root beer and hot apple pie.

Getting mega-rich didn't cross our minds – being together and having fun was our currency. Mum said she didn't mind where I worked or when I worked, as long as I could give her 10 pounds a week for the housekeeping. Other than that, I guess my only real expense was petrol for my vintage beige Mini Clubman.

The three of us spent every second of our spare time together. We'd go swimming in Watford Leisure Centre, mainly because our friend David was the lifeguard there and would sort us out with half-price tickets. We would do anything in the pool to make David blow his whistle, so we would pretend to drown. We were just innocent teenagers. And we were constantly being told that we should live in the moment. I can honestly say that during that time I lived day by day, not looking forward or back. It was real and it was fun, and the boys were my friends and my heartbeat. We'd dance, non-stop, in George's bedroom, and sometimes we'd go out to clubs and dance there. It truly was a happy time.

We were starting to attract attention to ourselves. George and I had a special chemistry when we danced. It was funny. Most of the time, I still felt shy and extremely self-conscious, but when I danced with George, those feelings melted away. I was five years old again, jiving with my dad. We were either so great or so bad that everyone cleared the floor! The other clubbers would stand around watching, as we performed all of these routines we'd made up in George's bedroom.

It was the dancing – not the audience – that I loved. George was an incredibly gifted dancer, and he liked to hold my gaze while we danced. I quickly realised how much he calmed me down. If I paid too much attention to all the people who were watching us, I'd freak out. But if he looked straight at me, I could match him move for move. It reminded me a tiny bit of working with nervous horses or being with a slightly anxious puppy. He had a way of reassuring me that went beyond words, where he simply helped me to find the quiet, calm place within myself and lose myself in the music.

Looking back, I think the magic of Wham! came from the fact that it wasn't just about being in a band – we really knew how to have fun. Obviously, George was an astonishingly gifted singer and songwriter, and was always going on to greatness. But when you're in a band, it can be difficult to get the balance right between being committed to what you're doing and taking it all too seriously.

It helped that Wham! seemed completely organic. It was a true extension of what happened when we all went out and had fun. Also, Andrew and I both knew that George's talent was so immense that it was impossible for any of us to let our own egos get in the way. Perhaps that made it easier for George, too. There was no tension between us, so we could focus on expanding this special project that seemed so much bigger than the sum of its parts.

And we *were* getting bigger. George and Andrew were taking the business of fun very seriously. Even though we seemed to be spending all of our time dancing, laughing and driving between Bushey and Radlett, George and Andrew were working very hard on their music. They were both talented, but George seemed to have magical powers. The songs just poured out of him. His voice was so good that he could sing along to an advert on the radio and make it sound amazing – and he was coming up with lyrics that managed to be funny, heartbreaking and wise all at once.

I wasn't surprised when George and Andrew were offered a record deal with Innervision. It was fantastic news – I knew it was what they wanted most in the world. I could have exploded with pride. I felt just as joyful as I did when my friend Tracey was given her big showjumping sponsorship deal.

The boys had been waiting anxiously, hoping someone would sign them, but I knew they were too talented to fail. It was only a matter of time. Yet what George said next surprised me.

"They want us to come and do a PA in a nightclub," he said. He looked as though he was still working out whether he felt excited or terrified. "Would you come along and dance with us?"

"Sure, of course," I beamed. I'd do anything to help out my friends. "But, er, what's a PA?"

I soon learnt what those letters stood for. Wham!'s first Public Appearance would be happening in a nightclub in Haringey.

"It would be good if we had another girl," suggested Andrew. "We could do more of a routine."

By then, Andrew had become my boyfriend. Looking back, it's difficult to explain the relationship, because I don't really remember how it started, or how it ended. The connection between us was pure and joyful, but never romantic in the way it was with Martin. It seemed more of a way to make our friendship official. And we never went anywhere without George.

The three of us were a solid unit. Occasionally, Andrew would claim that his boyfriend status meant he should be sitting at the front of the Mini with me – but we never went out on proper dates. We were just kids having a great time. Still, the suggestion of bringing in another girl made me feel slightly uneasy.

I knew Andrew was right. The song and the routine would look much better if we were two boys and two girls, and this was a big deal. If everything went well, they could have a record in the charts. But the three of us were so close. If someone else turned up, how would we explain all of our inside jokes, silly expressions, and the stupid voices we'd put on for each other? She'd think we were a load of weirdos.

After me moaning about how bad the pub was, it was a great surprise that this soon became our favourite place where we would meet every Friday night. Going into the Three Crowns, we would hang out on the right hand side of the bar.

In the end, we asked a girl called Amanda, an old friend who also used to come to the pub. She was a pretty blonde, who also loved dancing and she thought that the PA sounded like great fun. After some hasty rehearsals on the white carpet, we piled into my car and drove up to Haringey.

Weirdly, I wasn't nervous. Well, I was a little bit anxious about making sure we did a good job for George. I knew once the routine got going, the rhythm would take over and I wouldn't feel self-conscious at all. But when I peered out into the dark, looking at the clubbers, I remember thinking, *They're going to hate us.* They were having fun on a Saturday night, dancing to amazing soul music, and suddenly these kids were going to turn their music off and interrupt their night with a dance.

It took me a little while to work out why there weren't any other women in the club. Our audience was almost all men, all dressed immaculately. I'd never been to a gay club before, but I relaxed instantly. If there had been other young women watching us, I'd have worried they would have been a bit catty and critical and judged my outfit, my dancing or my hair. These men looked as though they were interested in what we were about to do – they weren't standing around with their arms folded, thinking, *What a load of rubbish!*

The music started up for 'Wham! Rap', followed by 'Young Guns Go For It'. We did our thing, and I threw myself into the routine, thinking, *I may as well have fun with this!* As always, I looked for George on stage, making eye contact, feeding off his energy, trying to reassure him that it was going well. Suddenly, we'd finished – and the audience loved it. They clapped, cheered and screamed for us. I was completely stunned.

"What? Seriously?!" I said to the others, who seemed just as shocked as I was.

Best of all, we were taken to a table and told we could order free burgers, chips and as much Coca-Cola as we could drink. I've been lucky enough to go to some truly fabulous restaurants all over the world, but that's the meal I'll remember forever. Burger and chips, washed down with gallons of Diet Coke.

As we were tucking into our burgers, the club's owner came over to chat with us. He was a lovely guy called Norman, and one of Wham!'s first big supporters.

"I love you guys! I want you to come back and do this again," he said, enthusiastically.

So we did.

Amanda decided that the PAs weren't for her – she was working as a hairdresser and she didn't have time to do both. The record company suggested that the singer Dee C Lee joined us. She had an amazing voice and was always very focused and professional. She was there for the start of Wham! but eventually she left to pursue her own creative passions. She's a hugely talented singer, and I think she knew she'd never have room to sing as much as she needed to in the band.

When she joined us, I knew something had shifted. We weren't just three kids from Bushey (well, one of us was from posh Radlett) – we had a job to do.

The PAs had been going really well, until we were asked to get out of our comfort zone, away from the Watford nightlife, and put on our show at the world-famous London club, Stringfellows.

In 1980, Stringfellows had just opened in Covent Garden, and it quickly became *the* place to be seen. I never dreamt I'd ever get to go there, but I'd often imagined its glamour. It was packed full of celebrities, drinking nothing but champagne. And not only were we going to the hottest club in the country – we were performing there. This was the most exciting opportunity we'd ever had.

So once again the four of us climbed into my tiny car and drove all the way into town. Stringfellows looked glossy and glamorous, but it was a little bit smaller than I was expecting. I squinted into the dark, searching for celebrities, but I couldn't see anyone I recognised. In fact, I couldn't even see a stage for us to perform on.

"Just do your dance here," said the booker, pointing to a small patch on the shiny, slippery floor.

Just a few bars in to 'Wham! Rap', I started to worry that it was going very badly. What if the audience *hated* us? It must have been a shock for everyone to see these young kids in the middle of this sophisticated club. I was peering at the audience, trying to work out whether they looked bored – or worse, looked as though they were about to boo.

Still, slowly, they seemed to warm to us. At one point, George gave a high kick, and his shoe – a white espadrille – sailed off his foot and into the crowd. I beamed at him, trying to keep him calm and stop him from panicking. George always wore towelling socks, and I was a bit worried he wouldn't be able to keep a grip on the flooring – he'd just slide onto his bum. Before too long, he got his shoe back – someone had thrown it back across the crowd. I noticed it out of the corner of my eye, before it hit him on the head!

Morale was pretty low when the music stopped. The boys were gutted. Dee and I were gutted. What had we done wrong? Did we not work as a group outside Watford?

We were thinking of sneaking out and driving home when a woman approached us. She seemed quite business-like, serious and suited.

I remember thinking, *I wonder what she's doing in Stringfellows. She looks as though she's never been to a nightclub in her life!*

But to our surprise, she smiled and said, "That was brilliant! I thought you were all wonderful! I work on *Saturday Superstore*, and I'd love to have you on this week's show."

Just seconds earlier, we'd been about to call it a day. I'd been thinking of calling Amanda and asking her if she thought I'd be any good at hairdressing. Now the group was going on TV. I could feel my heart beating with excitement and relief. It wasn't all over.

But George burst my bubble. "If we're going on TV, maybe we should get professional dancers," he said, thoughtfully.

It was as though I wasn't there at all.

For a moment, I could have cried. It wasn't that I wanted to be on *Saturday Superstore* – I didn't even want to be famous – but I wanted to be with my best friends. I'd been there for George and Andrew for every single moment of their journey. I'd spent hours and hours dancing, practising, supporting and encouraging them. Now, I was cold with fear. The two of them didn't need me. They could carry on without me. And I felt angry, too. We had chemistry. I *knew* George needed me on stage with him, that I made his performance better. Did he really think he could have that kind of chemistry with a dancer he'd just hired?

Andrew was usually in favour of any schemes that could make the band seem more professional, but even he looked a bit shocked. I think George could tell how crestfallen I was, and he said we'd stay as we were.

"But you'll have to practise really hard," he added.

Filming *Saturday Superstore* was great fun. I remember being enchanted by how orderly and organised everything was. So much was going on. It was so busy, but everyone moved with purpose and knew where they were supposed to be. It meant a lot that George's mum made a point of telling him how well I'd done.

"Shirlie looked really, really good on TV," she told him, giving me a secret nod. I think he'd said something to her about getting some trained dancers in, and she'd fought my corner.

Still, nothing could have prepared me for what happened after the programme went out.

Every Saturday morning, Mum and I had a bit of a ritual. We'd watch telly and then I'd drive her to Watford High Street, where we'd potter around the shops and stop for a sandwich and a cup of tea. I never bothered with any make-up or putting on a special outfit. I mean, this was *Watford!* I didn't think Betty at the caff needed to see me with lipstick on.

We were chatting about what we'd have for tea, ambling down the high street, when I heard shouting.

"Hey! Aren't you that girl on TV?"

I looked around, trying to see who was behind me. Was Selina Scott in Watford?

Another voice piped up. "It's her! You were on *Saturday Superstore!*"

I could feel my chest getting tight and I was finding it harder to breathe.

My mum was beaming, oblivious to my discomfort. "Yes, it's her! She's my daughter." She grinned at me. "I'm so proud of you."

I didn't feel proud of myself at all. "Can we just go home now?" I begged.

At least I had a baseball cap with me. I jammed it over my head, hiding my bleach blonde crop. I was terrified. The strangest thing was that everyone was shouting and staring, but no one was actually talking to me. I don't think I'd ever felt so vulnerable. It was as though every single movement I made was magnified. What if I'd been picking my nose or had a spot on my chin?

This was my first real taste of fame, and I hated it. I learnt to live with it, but it was the first sign I had that I was different from George and Andrew. This was something they could tolerate – and sometimes even enjoy. But this wasn't something I was destined to do, and I certainly didn't want to pursue it.

All I wanted to do was dance and spend time with my friends. And with friends like George and Andrew, I could understand that the world wanted to spend time with them, too. But that day I realised my ego didn't need that kind of attention – and from then on, I never left the house without a hat and a pair of Raybans.

4

Blitz Kids

Martin

If half of my personality came from Anna Scher, I think the darker half came from the Blitz nightclub.

In 1978, when I was 16, I went with Gary and Steve Dagger to the most amazing club in Soho. It was called Billy's, and it was an extraordinary place. A new side of my life that was exciting, subversive and dangerous.

When I close my eyes and picture the dingy, smoky, overheated room in Soho, I see bright young things, all dressed as though they'd fallen out of a dark fairy tale; something straight out of a Tim Burton movie. I followed Gary around the club, awestruck, my eyes like saucers. This was different from the soul clubs and punk clubs I'd been to before. This was out there on its own, like a solitary planet spinning in the galaxy, and I loved every second of it. It was such a shame, because that night was the last night that

Billy's ever opened. But before too long, Steve and Rusty who ran Billy's opened up a new club – the Blitz.

During the 70s, punk had been a big part of our lives, but the mood was changing. Punk needed somewhere to go. It was all about nihilism and destruction, so it made sense that the next big movement would be a reaction to that. Being part of this Blitz scene meant focusing on colour, ambition and, most of all, the future.

The Billy's crowd – now the Blitz Kids – were all art school students. Back then, there were two separate schools, the Central School of Art and Design and the St Martin's School of Art and Design. They merged at the end of the 80s – but the Blitz happened to be located just where the students met in the middle, figuratively and literally.

People didn't just get dressed up to go to the Blitz. They wore costumes, like sculptures. Everyone was androgynous, and no one was hung up on sexuality or gender identity. You could be anyone, as long as you were being creative. We saw people in Elizabethan ruffs or with their faces painted like Pierrot dolls. Gary and I were in our Space Cowboy looks. I'd bought a shirt from an amazing shop called PX, in Covent Garden. It was a thrilling, slightly intimidating space, but, back then, new clothes were expensive. I'd have to save up for one thing from PX, and then supplement it with home-made clothes and things from charity shops. Luckily, I'd found the perfect leather jacket in Oxfam. I wore it with these electric blue pegs, my favourite trousers. (I think those eventually found their way onto a few Spandau posters.)

When we arrived at the Blitz, the queue was enormous, already stretching all the way down to Drury Lane. We were in theatreland, but the real theatre was happening on the pavement. I saw ballerinas, preachers, space cadets and beekeepers. It was the most exciting group of people I'd ever seen. Steve Strange was on the door, deciding who was hip enough to be allowed into the hallowed space. Sometimes, he would point a mirror in their direction and say in a muffled voice, "Would *you* let you in looking like that?"

It's an overused expression – but Steve was a legend in every sense. Growing up in Caerphilly, Wales, he used to organise local gigs for some of the biggest punk bands of the 70s, including the Sex Pistols and the Stranglers. He came to London and worked for Malcolm McLaren, and formed a band with Chrissie Hynde, who went on to form The Pretenders. Steve went on to form Visage, and even appeared in the video for David Bowie's song 'Ashes To Ashes'.

Steve Strange was the maddest, coolest person I'd ever seen. At the time, he was usually dressed in bottle-green velvet, a cascade of kiss-curls escaping from his peaked green hat. He was Robin Hood, making life richer for the

47

broke, bored teenagers who'd been living with poverty and disappointment throughout the 70s. But would he let me in? Would I pass the test?

"Oooh, hello!" said Steve, as I made my way in, my money sticking to my sweaty palm. "Wait for me inside!" He gave me a theatrical wink over his black contact lenses that covered his eye.

Was he flirting with me? I'd never had another man flirt with me before. It was cool, and Steve wanted me in his club. Steve was one of the great loves of my life. From that day, he became one of my very best friends – but he *never* stopped trying to move in on me.

Walking through the swing doors of the Blitz felt like entering a saloon in a Western. This was a space where anything could – and would – happen. I was the stranger coming to town – but here, everyone else was a stranger, too, and being strange was something to celebrate. Even though the club was dark, the space seemed luminous. Everyone's sequined, glittering outfits spun and shone like silver stars in the night sky. I looked at the long bar on the right-hand side of the room and had my first sighting of one of the club's most famous regulars, Barry the Rat.

Barry wasn't in much of a costume – more a leftover from a punk club – but he didn't need one. Nestling into his trademark mohair jumper was his huge pet rat – the

Roxy. As I walked in, Steve's DJ Rusty Egan put on one of my favourite Bowie records, 'Boys Keep Swinging'. Nothing could have been more perfect. I felt alive. I felt like I belonged, right here in this club, with this music and these weird and wonderful people.

That night, I tried speed for the very first time. To be honest, everyone in that room was on so much speed, talking and dancing faster and faster.

"This place is fantastic, it's brilliant, it's me!" I kept saying to Gary, Steve, the boys from the band and anyone who would listen.

It felt as though we'd been in the club for half an hour when the lights went on and it was chucking-out time. Gary and I had spent all our money on expensive Schlitz beer, so we walked the three miles back to Islington. By the time we made it home, it was just starting to get light. The blackbirds had started to sing, creating a kind of "a cappella" accompaniment to the ringing in my ears. The soles of my feet were burning, and every muscle in my face was aching, especially my jaw.

The Blitz club took over our lives. Everything revolved around Tuesday night. It would take us several days to recover, but by Friday we were starting to think about putting together our look. It wasn't just about dressing up – or rather, it was, but it was opening up our minds to what was possible.

The Blitz was the crucial ingredient in the formation of Spandau Ballet. The club was the band's womb and our sixth member. Being around these exciting, creative people made me feel as though life had no limits. I'd always wondered how to reconcile my dreams with real life. But maybe I didn't have to. As a child, I'd seen how hard my parents worked – they'd toiled and struggled for no reward. They were talented, but they'd never had a space to realise that talent. Now, I was seeing a new kind of energy developing. I was around people who were prepared to take risks, and live their lives in a way that served their creative spark. Possibility was in the air, and that was what allowed Spandau to fully come to life. Everyone we met at the Blitz was determined to blur the boundaries between dreaming and doing.

Growing up in the 70s could be difficult, dark and gloomy. I think the seeds for the scene at the Blitz were sown during the Winter of Discontent, from 1978 to 1979. Across the country, public sector workers were on strike. Their pay rises had been capped, as part of a government attempt to control inflation – but this meant many people were trapped financially and struggling to look after their families. For normal people, it was difficult to make ends meet – let alone have a little bit of luxury and fun. This dismal state of affairs wasn't helped by the fact that the UK was facing one of the coldest winters on record.

I was incredibly lucky to find the Blitz. It happened at a time when I was surrounded by people who wanted to open the world up to me and help me to forge my own path. This magical club was a spark of light for so many of us, a space where the grey world turned technicolour. For Gary and me, I think it was our art school. But we were both incredibly lucky to be supported so generously by our mum and dad. The generation that came before ours was shocked and confused by the flamboyant outfits, the multicoloured hair and the fact that their children wanted to be artists and musicians, when they had worked so hard to learn their trades and toiled away throughout their adult lives.

For working-class kids like Gary and me, university wasn't an option in the 70s. I was expected to leave school when I was 16, and my dad found me work in the print industry, right where he worked in Old Street. It was an apprenticeship – I was going to be a compositor, one of the people who slots together all of the letters for old printed advertisements. For four years, I would learn on the job, and by the time I was 20, I'd be on a good wage.

* * *

Spandau – or Gentry, as we were known then – were starting to take off. We were still playing in pubs, but the crowds were getting bigger and bigger. Our following was growing, and maybe more importantly, our abilities were, too. Gary was really growing as a songwriter, and when Tony sang we could tell that something special was happening. We knew that making it in music would take a lot of hard work and a lot of luck, but we also knew we'd never forgive ourselves if we didn't try.

Gary was pragmatic. "If we're going to make this work, the band needs to come first," he said.

Quickly, I realised I had to choose between the band and the apprenticeship. I needed a job that let me find the time to practise and perform as often as possible, and I couldn't do that with my job at the print factory.

My parents had always known that Gary had a musical gift. He'd started playing the guitar in assembly when he was still at junior school, playing songs he'd written. Music was always his thing, and he was brilliant at it. The apprenticeship my dad had arranged for me in the print trade was a fantastic opportunity for a young boy from Islington with two O levels to his name. This was akin to going to university, so I knew what I was about to ask him was a big deal.

He was sitting in the front room, sipping a cup of tea when I approached his chair.

"Dad," I began, nervously, clasping my hands behind my back. "I need you to do me a favour. Would you write a letter to my boss, asking if I can be released from the apprenticeship?"

Dad was quiet for a little while.

I panicked, trying to fill the silence. "You see, the band has been talking, and I think it's what I want to do. It's what I want to focus on. I don't want to let you down, and I don't want to let anyone in the printworks down. So I think it's best for me to go now, so I can concentrate on the band. I love music. It's what I want to do with my life."

My dad was a kind, gentle man. He'd always been so generous with Gary and me. He wanted us to be happy. Still, I knew that I was asking for something enormous. He had stuck his neck out to get me that job.

Dad smiled and looked a little wistful. I could see the understanding in his eyes. He was a gifted artist, but he never had a chance to develop his talent because he'd been working himself into the ground trying to support us all. He wanted Gary and me to have the chances he was never able to take. He'd done everything he'd been told to do, and always followed the rules – but his working life had been draining and difficult, and it hadn't come with much of a reward.

My dad just looked at me. I recognised the smile in his eyes, a smile that I had seen when Gary had stood for applause in assembly – a smile of excitement and pride. And this time it was meant for me.

He wrote that letter. It said: *Dear Sir, Would you mind if Martin left his job in the apprenticeship because he wants to become a pop star.*

My dad had made a giant leap of faith, and for every gold record or sold-out show Spandau achieved, I would always feel I was paying him back for that letter. Dad believed in Gary and me. He didn't think it was silly, or that we were dreamers. He was proud of his boys, and he felt we had a shot at getting to the top. When it comes to success, luck and talent are both undeniably important. But more than anything, you need someone who loves you, believes in you and can see just how far you could go.

It would have been so much harder to get Spandau started without Mum and Dad's support, but they managed to be our friends, our backers and our biggest fans. Our vision for the band really began in the Blitz, but they never once criticised our crazy costumes or our strange friends.

Once, Dad spotted me, ready to go out, halfway down the stairs. I was wearing a brown monk-like robe and long brown boots. The plan was to look like some sort of nomad.

"Dad," I said, "I'm just going down the pub."

My dad looked at me and quietly said, "Don't forget your keys."

It's one of the sweetest memories I have of Dad – this culture was so new to him, and he was so accepting of it. Still, at the time, I remember being quite frustrated. I was a teenage boy who wanted to be a rebel, and he took it all in his stride, but I loved him so much for it.

My mum was every bit as open-hearted and accepting of her mad sons. She'd never complained when I stuck posters of Bruce Lee and Arsenal all over the bedroom wall, and she didn't mind when my taste in interior design became slightly bizarre.

At the time, you could get the most amazing Edwardian gear very cheaply from charity shops. Now, these pieces would probably be sent to auctions, but in North London, people would dump the contents of entire attics in Oxfam. These jackets were beautifully made, and so stylish, just predating the Peaky Blinders look. If I found one I loved but it didn't fit – after all, people were a bit smaller in those days – I would treat it as a work of art and hang it on my bedroom wall.

It was a big part of the Spandau image and identity. Part of being a New Romantic was all about getting inspired by the visuals of the past. This was what made us a cult band, and what set us apart from punk. It was all about being as flamboyant as possible, and we weren't afraid of excess. The movement was given its name by the *Evening*

Standard, which saw similarities with the Romantic Period in the 18th and 19th centuries.

It's only now that I realise the significance of the past. When I was a 16-year-old kid, this didn't cross my mind – but the Romantic poets thought their age was too modern. They were reacting against the Industrial Revolution, and they wanted to make the ancient new. That was exactly what we were doing. We took that wild, Byronic, dramatic style and combined it with new musical technology. It was a glorious clash of old and new that created something edgy and fresh.

I loved being part of this, and creating a moment that had such a distinctive identity. It felt tribal. When we were dancing in the Blitz, we all belonged together – citizens of a tiny, secret country.

One Tuesday night, I'd been chatting with Steve, and we'd stayed until the bitter end. Steve had lost his keys.

"Don't worry," I said. "You can sleep on my floor. My mum and dad won't mind."

We walked all the way back to Islington, a route we were getting used to. It was just starting to get light, and a couple of shops were just beginning to set up for the day.

"Morning!" chirped Steve, as we walked along, tipping his Robin Hood hat to the local newsagent wrestling with a pile of papers.

The next morning, I woke up feeling the worse for wear. Blearily, I fumbled for my dressing gown. Steve had vanished. Perhaps he'd found his keys and gone home. I made my way upstairs in search of a cup of tea.

"Morning, love!" said Mum, cheerily. "Good night?" She was sitting next to Robin Hood.

Steve, immaculate in his green velvet, was tucking into a giant bowl of Cornflakes while chatting away to Mum. "Your floor is pretty comfy," he beamed. "Shame about the snoring."

Gary and I were so lucky to have parents who welcomed our strange friends. (In Steve's case, quite literally!) It's the best lesson that Mum and Dad ever taught me, and it's the one that I tried the hardest to pass on to my kids when I became a father. Our differences are what make the world fun and exciting. We need to celebrate them. It's so important to welcome people and not judge them. Now, there are no excuses for any kind of prejudice or intolerance, but back then, Mum and Dad were unusual – and their attitude made me realise that open-mindedness is one of the most important things you can teach your kids.

But it wasn't all peace and love back then. There was definitely a lot of competition, rivalry and drama happening behind the scenes – between different bands, between the two art schools, and even between different groups of friends.

One memorable night quickly turned into total chaos. It was in the early days of the Blitz, when the Space Cowboy look was still big. Everyone looked like a futuristic Elvis. Steve had a quiff that must have been about 2ft high. I think he was clearing Boots out of hairspray every Tuesday night.

There was a club just over the road from us, at the other end of Great Queen Street. It was really very similar. It was full of arts students and aspiring pop stars, taking speed and listening to David Bowie. Yet a rivalry between the two clubs had been bubbling below the surface. You felt as though you belonged to one or the other.

Then one night, the other club invaded. It was amazing to behold. There were lots of kids from the Chelsea School of Art, and they all loved the Vivienne Westwood pirate look. Suddenly, I found myself in the middle of an old-fashioned Western saloon brawl, with pirates attacking cowboys, hurling chairs, bottles and anything that wasn't nailed down. Even Barry the Rat was jumping up and throwing things. That poor rat was clinging on for dear life while Barry went for the pirates.

I've always been a lover, not a fighter, so I took the coward's way out. In the dark, I ducked under the flying chairs, sneaked downstairs and locked myself in the toilet. Usually, the bogs in the Blitz weren't a place you wanted to hang out in for any length of time. To be honest, it was difficult to get in at all – like every good club toilet, they were always packed out with people doing their thing. The smell was enough to make your eyes water. I think it had an independent ecosystem. Still, I hunkered down in the dark, breathing through my mouth and waiting for the screaming to stop. I must have been down there for a good 20 minutes before I decided it was safe enough to creep home. I have no regrets. I don't think any bones were broken – but when it came to the furniture, that was another matter.

The Blitz scene was exciting, but it's also the place where we developed our sound. We would get so many ideas from the sheer theatricality and ambition of the crowd. Crucially, we found our ready-made audience in there, too. We were all part of this movement. We were five boys in the club getting up on stage, representing this phenomenon. There was no difference between the audience we envisioned and the audience in the club. We were all one, the same, and the only difference was that we had guitars.

Steve, Rusty and this strange assortment of clubbers did so much to support us and get behind us, and their names had a real cachet. People cared about what they thought. If Steve liked you, people in the music industry wanted to get behind you. The Blitz was attracting plenty of media attention, because of the big, bold personalities on the scene. It wasn't just a club – it was a statement.

The Blitz was Spandau, and Spandau Ballet was the Blitz. It was also exciting, dark and completely hedonistic. But while we played hard in that club, we worked hard, too. In 1979, we were asked to perform at the Blitz Christmas party. In fact, that was the first time we actually performed as Spandau Ballet.

Gary's friend, the writer Robert Elms, had seen the words graffitied on a toilet wall in Berlin, and the name seemed to fit. It sounded glamorous, elegant and a little offbeat, and definitely classier than "The Islington Ballet". We found out that the name belonged to a German band but in those days it was who had the hit first. And after that gig, the hype really started for us.

We'd been growing our cult reputation with secret gigs in strange places. We performed at the Scala cinema in London's King's Cross, long before it was regularly used as a gig venue, and we played a secret showcase on the HMS Belfast moored on the Thames. One early gig I loved took place in Sadler's Wells Theatre in London – it's a venue for ballet, so it was the perfect place for Spandau Ballet to play. Looking back, it's crazy to think about how much was happening, and how we took it all in our stride.

There was a bidding war between record companies who wanted the band. Eventually, we signed with Chrysalis. By November 1980, our first single, 'To Cut A Long Story

Short', had been released, and we made the top five, selling half a million copies. Just a few months ago, I'd been hiding in the Blitz toilets and begging my dad to release me from my printing career. Now, my best mates and I were on *Top Of The Pops*, and getting recognised on the street.

I think the arrogance of youth is a mixed blessing. Now I look back and wish I'd celebrated a bit more and really felt the weight of those early achievements. I wasn't as excited as I should have been – I was an 18-year-old thinking, *But when will we have a number one?* Yet I think it's natural to look to the future when you're young. I think if I'd let myself get overwhelmed by how much had happened to us, and how quickly it had happened, I might have become distracted by fame and started to focus on the wrong things. It helped that I was sharing this experience with my best friends, and that I was surrounded by people who were starting to become very famous.

More and more of our Tuesday-night friends were turning up on *Top of the Pops*: Culture Club, Sade, Animal Nightlife, Ultravox and Haysi Fantayzee. Maybe I took it for granted, but it felt like our time. The Blitz itself only lasted for about a year. But the spirit of the club, and people like Steve, defined the whole era.

5

Martin Meet Shirlie, Shirlie Meet Martin

Shirlie & Martin

Martin

It was a Thursday evening, and my mum had just finished washing up the tea plates. The electric fire fake coals glowed bright orange, and we had settled down on the sofa in front of the TV just in time for Led Zeppelin's 'Whole Lotta Love' to announce that *Top of the Pops* was coming on our screen. As the opening credits faded away, John Peel, as if he was in our living room, stood out against the crowd to announce that, The Human League, Tears for Fears and Eddy Grant would be on the show alongside Duran Duran singing 'Rio' and also a new band called Wham! I didn't know it at the time, but that last sentence of introduction was about to shape the rest of my life.

Gary and I sat there criticising some of the bands and talking through the rights and wrongs of each song... until Duran Duran came on with 'Rio'. It was like a shot through the heart. We both knew it was a great song and on top of that, they looked so good. But competition is a good thing... so they say.

Soon after, John Peel introduced the next new band, Wham! From the opening sounds of the horns playing 'Young Guns' I was transfixed, not just by the energy this band had, or the fun they were having, or even the singer's voice.

But by the girl with the white hair. The girl in the white dress. The girl who was filling up my television screen. My heart literally skipped a beat, my throat went dry and I felt like I was in my own bubble. The girl in white danced and moved around the stage, and at one point she sang straight down the length of the lens and into my living room. It was the strangest, weirdest feeling – we made eye contact. I almost wanted to look away so that she couldn't see me staring at her.

Who was this blonde girl? Who was this incredible-looking thing that had made my stomach turn to knots? Whatever this feeling was, it was beautiful and I loved it. Was it love? Was this love? But it couldn't be, so why did it feel like it? It sure did feel like it, and it was wonderful.

*   *   *

I fell asleep thinking about Shirlie – her face, her hair, her legs. I could barely remember the song, but every time I closed my eyes, I saw her face. (OK, and her legs.)

The great thing about being in the entertainment bubble in the 80s was that it meant I knew I had a real chance of meeting this blonde girl from Wham! Sooner or later, I'd find someone who knew her or I'd bump into her. I had no idea what I'd say, or how I'd cope when I found her, but that was a problem for the future.

A few weeks later, I had my chance.

With a little gentle sleuthing, I'd discovered that the blonde girl from Wham! who had been keeping me awake at night was called Shirlie. After that appearance on *Top of the Pops*, their records were doing really well, so I started going to all sorts of parties on the off-chance that they'd be invited, too. But I wasn't expecting to find her in a theatre the night I and the rest of the band went to see my friend Paul McGann in the premiere of a new musical, *Yakety Yak*.

Yakety Yak featured everything I loved. It was about the gap between the 50s and the 80s, and you had rock 'n' roll, charisma, drama and punk. I was expecting it to be a memorable night. But not in the way it turned out to be.

At the after party, I was standing at the bar with the band. Because it was a premiere, I was dressed up, in a peacock-blue silk jacket. I'd made a real effort with my hair, and even put some make-up on, because that's what we all did. At least I hadn't come dressed as a monk or a Space Cowboy. I must have mentioned Shirlie to a couple of people, trying to sound casual and cool about it.

"Does anyone know that blonde girl from Wham!?" seemed like a reasonable thing to ask. If she heard I'd been going around saying, "I've seen the future love of my life on *Top of the Pops,* can someone introduce me?" I think she would have been scared off and run for the hills!

So there I was, sipping my gin and tonic, doing my best to play it cool when my friend Steve Norman nudged me.

"Hey, isn't that the girl you were asking about?" he said.

I looked over. The theatre bar was dark and dusty, decorated in ancient red velvet and ornate, tarnished brass. The air was thick with smoke and the sound of tipsy laughter. I felt as though I was surrounded by friendly vampires – my bandmates, actors, artists and musicians. The people who come alive at night, when darkness falls. Life's colourful people who make it worth living.

My heart jumped and my mind raced. I was taken aback by just how much prettier she was in real life. I saw that sweet, sexy smile for the first time, as she laughed at something George said. She looked as though she was having more fun than everyone in the room put together.

My heart felt as though it could burst. Was this love, or did I need to call an ambulance?

"Why don't you go over?" asked Steve.

Why didn't I go over? I wanted to, but my body wasn't responding. I had stage fright. All of those years with Anna Scher and being on stage with the band hadn't fazed me. I'd been on TV – I'd shown my *bum* on TV. And yet this was going to be the most important performance of my life.

"OK, yeah, I'll go and meet her," I said to Steve, desperately trying to hide my fright. Was my voice breaking *again*? I sounded like a kettle whistling!

In two seconds – it felt like two years – I was on the other side of the room, beside Shirlie. She was even more gorgeous close up.

"Hello, it's so good to meet you!" I beamed, smiling so hard that my face ached.

"It's nice to meet you, too," she replied, coolly.

She didn't have that sultry, sophisticated attitude I remembered from TV. Instead, she appeared slightly shy and vulnerable, and I was drawn to her even more. The more awkward I felt, the harder I smiled, stumbling through small talk about the show. I had to keep going, as I didn't know when I'd get to see her again. Eventually, I had an idea.

"We're all going on to a wine bar in Islington. It's called Cheers! You should come along."

To my utter shock, she agreed. "Sure, sounds good. We'll see you there."

Honestly, I barely remember how I left the theatre and reached Cheers.

Gary could tell something was up. "Are you OK?" he asked.

I was utterly dazed and confused. "Um, fine," I mumbled. "Just, you know, thinking about the show."

But he knew me too well to be convinced.

At Cheers, I attempted to talk to my mates and seem as normal as possible, but I couldn't stop staring at Shirlie. Would she come over? Could I go over? Would I seem too keen? I *had* to play it cool. If only I could remember what cool meant. Eventually, and desperately, I walked over to her and George. I'd written my number – well, my mum and dad's number – on a paper napkin.

"I'd love to see you again!" I said, trying to soften my smile and look friendly and normal – I had said hello to lots of girls over those last couple of years, but none that had done this to me!

When I was performing with the band, I had so much front and so much bravado. I loved the attention, and I felt as though there was nothing I couldn't do and no one I couldn't speak to. But when I was meeting Shirlie, I felt like a 16-year-old boy who'd never spoken to a girl before. I remember feeling so glad I was wearing make-up, because at least it meant she couldn't see I was red-faced underneath.

She thanked me for the number and put it in her pocket. Was that a good sign or a bad one? Surely all sorts of men were constantly trying to chat her up. Maybe her pockets were full of phone numbers. Should I have asked for her number instead?

I didn't want to seem pushy and I wanted to give her a bit of space. So I headed back to the band, trying to force myself to relax and have another drink with the boys. All I really wanted to do, though, was go straight home and wait by the phone until she called me. It was ironic, really. The show had been all about teenage life in the 50s, those early days of dating, when girls would rush home from high school and hope their crushes would ring them up. I'd spent so long pursued by screaming girls. Now I was the one caught between hope and heartbreak, longing for the phone to ring.

Shirlie didn't ring the next day. Or the day after that, or the day after that. I tried to forget her. I tried to move on. But every time anyone called the house, I was first to the phone, yelling, "I'll get it!"

After three weeks, I had nearly given up hope. Maybe I didn't say the right thing, maybe it was the make-up, maybe I should have paid her more attention.

Then one evening, my mum knocked on my bedroom door, poked her head round and said:

"Martin, didn't you hear the phone ringing? It's for you."

She smiled at me as if she knew I had been waiting for this call all along. "It's Shirlie". She smiled again, and I smiled back.

Shirlie

After that first appearance on *Saturday Superstore*, fate seemed to take over. Life was filled with weird coincidences – some were strange, and others were exciting. Wham! was asked to go on *Top of the Pops*, even though our record wasn't in the official Top 40. I know that George and Andrew had been a bit gutted about that. So was I, to be honest. I knew how badly they wanted it, and I thought their song, "Young Guns", was really good.

We kept coming close and then falling down, and being on *Saturday Superstore* hadn't helped sell as many records as the label hoped. Still, it did one magical thing. The *Top of the Pops* producers had loved our performance, so when one of the other bands cancelled their appearance at the last minute, they had space to fill. It was a very lucky break. When the song was released in October 1982, it went into the charts at number 73. By November, we'd gone up *70 places*. Wham! were in the top three.

Looking back, it feels as though that month had more drama and excitement than most people experience in a lifetime. I was so excited for the boys, who were fulfilling their potential and doing the job they'd dreamt of. I'd always known how talented they were, and now the world was waking up to it, too. Still, our lives were starting to seem a little less fun. We were constantly rehearsing, working and planning for the future. Andrew was still my best friend but we were no longer together in any romantic sense. To be honest, it never felt that we were, really. But as Wham! grew, we grew out of each other.

We were moving in a different league now. On top of their record deal, the boys had signed a publishing deal, which meant they would be earning royalties on the songs they wrote. To celebrate, the publishers had taken us out to the south of France.

"Just bring your passports," we'd been told, before being driven out to the middle of nowhere. Were we being kidnapped? No, we were going in a helicopter.

I'd only ever been on a plane once before, to Torremolinos with Tracey. Our family holidays were trips to Southend and Barry Island. Suddenly, I was sipping my very first glass of champagne, 10,000ft in the air, trying to feel like a pop star. The three of us were a long way from Bushey Meads now.

There was a lot more champagne, and plenty of parties. We were still trying to make our old life fit with our new life, and it wasn't easy. During the day, George, Andrew and I were still doing all of the same things. We'd drive up to Watford, go swimming at the leisure centre and then go up to London for a party or a show.

During the day, if I stayed disguised, everything was fine. My hat and sunglasses acted like an invisibility cloak. We could have fun together without feeling too self-conscious. But everything felt a bit different in London. We'd have a great time if we went out dancing, but we were expected to go to various events and parties and I always felt a bit insecure. It was the 80s, and everyone else looked so glamorous and done-up. I never seemed to be wearing the right clothes, and I hated putting make-up on. I'd always avoid it if I could get away with it.

When George mentioned going to the theatre to see a new play, *Yakety Yak*, I didn't think much of it, as people were always inviting us to plays. We'd just been swimming and my hair was still slightly damp. It was the end of autumn, and it was starting to get colder and darker. I hoped I wouldn't catch a cold. George fancied it and I didn't mind driving, so I bundled myself back into my clothes, some slightly scruffy trousers and a jumper I'd pinched from my sister's wardrobe, and concentrated on keeping warm.

"Maybe I should go back home and get some make-up," I said to George, and then changed my mind. "Oh, you know what, I can't be bothered. Let's just get in the car!"

Obviously, the three of us had no idea that we were in for a life-changing evening. We sang. We laughed. We wound the windows down, because we all still smelled of chlorine. I was feeling completely relaxed, until we reached the theatre and I felt a stab of anxiety.

"George," I hissed. "You didn't tell me it was a premiere. There are all these celebrities here. I thought we were just going to see a play."

"So did I," he whispered back. "Still, look… Spandau are here!"

He nudged me in the ribs, and I nudged him back. Being in love with Martin from afar was all well and good, but being in the same room as him meant I had to play it cool. The trouble was, I wasn't sure George would let me.

We'd nearly bumped into them before, at a party, and I'd hidden from them. The boys in the band were always surrounded by the most beautiful, sophisticated, dressed-up girls. There was absolutely no way I could compete, so I did the most sophisticated thing I could think of and ran away. Martin had been starring in my dreams for so long. When we met, it had to be perfect. That night, I was a long way from perfect, unless Martin had a thing for swimming pools.

My crush on Martin had started in George's bedroom, and then firmly established itself when I saw him on the cover of *Smash Hits* magazine.

"He looks really, really... kind!" I sighed. Even when Martin was surrounded by other pop stars on George's wall, I thought he had a unique aura. An unusual, gentle quality. Logically, I suspected you couldn't be that gorgeous and not have an enormous ego – but when I looked at Martin, there was something indefinable about him that made me feel peaceful and serene. "I think he's probably a really *good* person."

George laughed at me for a long time. "Oh, Shirlie." He sighed, then chuckled. "We always *think* that about really good-looking people. It's what our brain does to trick us into believing we're not that shallow. It's common knowledge we think gorgeous guys have all kinds of special qualities, but they're just lovely to look at."

I rolled my eyes at George's cynicism. He looked at me, sighed again, and said, "OK. Let's see what we can do." He knew I'd seen plenty of pretty boys on the cover of *Smash Hits*, and it wasn't like me to react like this. And he loved a project.

So from that moment, George was on constant Spandau alert on my behalf. I think he knew I needed to meet Martin, just to calm down about Martin. But neither of us was expecting he'd be at the theatre that night. What was I going to *do?* There wasn't time to run home, change and put on layers and layers of make-up. I'd just have to front it out.

By all accounts, *Yakety Yak* was a fantastic show, but I can't remember any of it. All I can recall is sitting in the dark, wondering where Martin was sitting, and trying not to stare. Who was he here with? Another girl? What could she be like? Once the play had ended, I'd decided I was just going to persuade the boys to get back in the car and drive home. I was far too nervous to try to meet Martin.

George had other ideas, though, and enlisted our friend David Austin for help. "Shirlie wants to meet Martin. Why don't you bring him over here!"

I hoped I'd be lucky and perhaps the ground would open up and swallow me before Martin made it across the room. I backed into a little alcove, but it was a pointless hiding place. Suddenly, Martin was right in front of me, smiling at me.

I'd felt embarrassed about not having any make-up on – but Martin was wearing enough for both of us. For a moment, my feelings wavered. Maybe he wasn't who I'd hoped he was. He looked so sophisticated and polished. He was wearing a very expensive, bright-blue silk jacket – and his hair was teased and backcombed into a sort of sculpture. He must have spent longer getting ready that evening than I had during every night of my life put together.

I kept staring at my shoes – these scruffy boxer boots I used to wear with everything. They were fine for dancing in, but much less suitable for being chatted up by a pop star. Martin seemed so glamorous that I felt a bit faint. Even underneath the heavy make-up and hairspray, he was still the best-looking person I'd ever met. Ever *seen.*

I kept waiting for him to get bored and go away. But he kept smiling at me. I couldn't quite believe it. When I found the courage to look up and meet his eyes, I could recognise his kind face. He might have had a pop star's outfit on, but he was sweet and sincere.

"Do you want to come to a wine bar with us after this?" he asked.

"Sure!" I squeaked.

Quite honestly, getting through the play had been such an ordeal, I wasn't sure I could cope with a wine bar. I'd never been to one before, and it seemed *very* Spandau, so sophisticated and adult. You couldn't dance in a wine bar. But George wouldn't let me sneak away.

"Brilliant, let's go!" he grinned, and off we went to Cheers in Islington.

The wine bar was a bit easier than the theatre. For a start, it seemed slightly darker, so I felt less self-conscious about the way I looked. I started to relax, but I wasn't quite ready to go up to Spandau. The women in the group all looked like models. None of them were wearing their sister's jumper, that was for sure. Not for the first time, I felt as though everyone had been given some sort of secret manual for adulthood and I'd been queuing for the loos and missed it. It seemed as though George, Andrew and I were the only people there who were laughing and joking. Everyone else was so serious.

We were thinking about going home when Martin walked up to me. The three of us held our breath.

"I'd really love to see you again," he said to me. "Here's my number. Will you give me a call?"

I couldn't speak. I put the number in my pocket, nodding. George could barely look me in the eyes. I knew we all wanted to jump up and down and start scream-ing, but we had to at least *pretend* to be adults until we'd returned to the car.

On the way home, George pestered me. "So, when are you going to ring him? You're going out with Martin Kemp! You're gonna be a Spandau girl!"

Andrew was just as excited for me – I think he'd forgotten that we used to be boyfriend and girlfriend. "A proper pop star, Shirlie. This is so exciting!"

I was trying to keep calm. "Can you imagine how many girls there must be ringing him up? I can't call him. And he'll always be away on tour, anyway. And we've got to focus on the band."

Even so, I could feel my face getting red and glowing – like that tiny, precious scrap of paper in my pocket. Did he really like me? Did he really want to see me again? There was only one way to find out, but I wasn't sure whether I was bold enough to try it.

I spent three weeks staring at that piece of paper, staring at it as though Martin's phone number could be a secret code. I might never have done anything about it, if George hadn't been brave enough to take the matter out of my hands.

6

The First Date

Shirlie & Martin

Martin

From the moment I'd first laid eyes on Shirlie, I'd been thinking about finding the perfect place to take her out. It was the early 80s, I was a young man, and for the first time in my life I had a bit of money in my pocket. Where could I take her that would impress her? I thought about tiny bistros, grand restaurants, champagne, oysters, dishes being brought out on silver platters. When Shirlie phoned me that first time, I was running through all of these glamorous dinner scenarios – so I was a bit taken aback when she suggested Tuesday night at Camden Palace.

It's now known as the nightclub KOKO, but back in the early 80s, Camden Palace was the place to be seen, and on Tuesday nights it was the place to go. Perhaps it was a leftover from the Blitz legacy. Tuesday night was dancing night. Anyway, after giving it some thought,

I decided it could be the perfect place after all. It was easy to get to, a place we were familiar with, and there would be plenty of opportunities for talking and kissing over cocktails. Admittedly, I was also quite pleased that so many of my mates would be there. Of course I wanted Shirlie all to myself – but what man doesn't want to be seen at the coolest club in London with the most beautiful girl in the world?

When the big night came, the butterflies arrived. I rarely felt nervous before concerts, or even going on *Top of the Pops*, but this was different. I spent ages getting ready, worrying about whether I looked OK. I'd had plenty of magazine covers and photoshoots during which I'd not given my looks a second thought, but this was different, this was special.

I walked up to the Palace, trying to steady my breathing, convinced the whole world could hear my heart beating. Then it sank. As I approached the entrance, I saw her. The most beautiful girl in the world – standing next to her best mate, George.

Don't get me wrong – I really liked George, but I didn't know him very well. The fact he'd turned up with Shirlie made me feel absolutely gutted. Had I made a mistake? Maybe she just wanted to be mates and didn't want to go on a proper date at all.

Luckily, the Palace worked its magic – and George made it clear he was determined to be our matchmaker, as well as a chaperone. Soon, a friendly hello kiss turned into, well, hundreds, maybe thousands, of kisses. We'd try to lose George and sneak off into a corner. Then we'd open our eyes and come up for air, and he'd be there. It was fair enough – he'd driven all that way with Shirlie, and he didn't have anyone else to talk to.

Years later, he'd tease us about it, saying, "I didn't know you two would be snogging all night!" Now, it's one of my favourite memories – not just the thrill of kissing Shirlie, and the magic of our first date, but seeing how much she meant to George and how close their friendship was. I was falling in love with her – and it made me so happy to know she had a friend who knew just how special and loveable she was, to the point of being happy to play gooseberry on that Tuesday.

Shirlie

After I plucked up the courage – well, George plucked up the courage – to ring Martin, I was terrified when Martin suggested, casually, that we go out for dinner. I'd never been on a proper date before. I'd seen the Spandau videos, and I could picture the sort of place a Spandau boy would take you to. Candelabras, thousands of forks, lobsters and oysters... The idea made me feel as though I was going to have a panic attack. That was when I had a brain wave.

"I'm going to be at Camden Palace on Tuesday," I said, attempting to sound relaxed and sophisticated. "Maybe I could meet you there?"

We made a plan and, for a second, I felt relieved. I'd got away with it. Then it occurred to me that I would actually have to go.

"Martin will be there with all of his mates," I gasped, suddenly realising the flaw in my plan. "I can't go on my own!" I turned to George, pleading, "You have to come with me." After all, he'd got me into this mess!

As Tuesday drew nearer, I wasn't sure whether I felt more excited or more terrified. We arrived early. Were we too early? What if Martin didn't turn up? What if he'd gone in and we'd missed him and we accidentally waited outside all night? Then he appeared in front of me. I'd made myself so nervous about meeting this sophisticated, glamorous, gorgeous pop star, worried he might take one look at me and realise he'd made a mistake. But the second his eyes met mine, I knew this was meant to be. I didn't see a handsome pop star looking down at me – but a kind, gentle, tender-hearted man. I knew everything was going to be OK – in fact, better than OK.

All I remember, after that moment, is kissing Martin – and being so caught up in the kissing that I completely forgot to feel self-conscious. George was delighted, then he was amused, then I think he may have become slightly grumpy. After all, it wasn't much fun for him, standing about while we smooched. Still, I think it was worth it for the satisfaction he got from playing Cupid.

Eventually, the lights came on and it was time to go home. Martin promised to call me. George teased me all the way home, but I tried to be rational, calm.

"He's about to go on tour! I bet he goes on loads of dates, with loads of girls. I may never see him again!" I said, as the engine hummed and the city roads turned suburban. But looking back, I think we both knew I was beginning to fall in love.

7

A Nightingale Sang in Berkeley Square

Shirlie & Martin

Martin

Just days after our Camden Palace date, Spandau were due to set out on a month-long European tour. We'd be travelling to Spain, Germany, France, Italy, Portugal and Switzerland – five boys on the ultimate lads-on-tour trip. I'd been looking forward to this tour for months. This was what proper rock stars did! We were going to be out on the road, having fun. But things had changed overnight. I'd met the most amazing girl, and I was so scared of losing her. What if Shirlie met someone while I was away? Her band was becoming really famous. She could be going to all sorts of parties and meeting all kinds of exciting people… What if she got back together with Andrew? I was going crazy thinking about this.

I was torn in two. I knew our tour was a huge opportunity for all of us. We had dreamt of playing these venues and getting paid to travel the world. This was everything we'd been working so hard for. All that time we'd spent in tiny pubs and little back rooms had paid off. Not long ago, I was shifting equipment for the others and watching them from the back of the school hall. And now we were playing stadiums in Spain. I should have felt like the luckiest man on earth. But my happiness was bittersweet. All I could do was hope that Shirlie would wait for me. I was looking forward to getting back to London in a month.

Of course, everything would be different if we were doing it now. I could have been on the phone to Shirlie seconds before the plane took off. I might have been able to speak to her during the journey on FaceTime, if the plane had Wi-Fi. Now, even if you're thousands of miles from your loved ones, you can still talk to them every day. But back then, you had to find a phone – you couldn't take it with you. Talking was expensive. Speaking to someone back home, when you were in a foreign country, could cost thousands of pounds.

I didn't let that stop me, though. I had fallen in love.

Early in the tour, I managed to call Shirlie from Italy. Luckily an operator connected us, so I didn't have to speak to her dad, who answered the phone. That was the part

I'd been dreading. I'd been certain her parents would be suspicious of me – I was worried they'd see me as a flash pop star with loads of girls after him. Mind you, I was worried that was what Shirlie thought of me, too.

"Hiya," I said, grinning down the phone. I'd been dreaming about hearing her voice for days.

"Um, hello," replied Shirlie, coolly.

I started to panic. Was she going off me? She must have got back with Andrew, she must have done! All these thoughts flashed through my mind. We chatted very briefly, with some awkward silences that I tried to fill – I was due at a sound check, and I knew the call probably cost the same as a car.

"I've got to go, but I'll try to ring as soon as I can," I told her.

Years later, I found out that Shirlie's mum, dad and little sister were all standing beside her, listening in – and she was so shocked and surprised to hear from me that she couldn't say too much.

In those days, when you were away from home, you sent postcards to your friends and family – so that was how I spoke to Shirlie when I was away. The phone calls were never quite long enough, and sometimes they made being away from her even harder. Whenever I was desperate to speak to her, I wrote down my thoughts. In a strange way, I felt a little bit like a soldier, writing from the trenches and knowing my correspondence might be checked and censored. Obviously, I had the freedom to write whatever I wanted, but I did so knowing her dad would probably be the one who picked the post up from the mat. Mind you, I'd always get to a point towards the end of the trip when I knew I'd get home before the postcards, so I'd started to save them up to give to Shirlie in person instead. Those ones were always slightly more private than the parent-friendly versions!

Only a few years before I would have been living my best rock star life, waking up hungover with my sunglasses on and hitting the bar again or hitting the pool. Now, I'd head straight for the most touristy shop I could find and stock up on postcards. I was the one in the corner, missing my girl and scribbling away to her. For me, the best thing about hotels wasn't having your own TV or room service. It was the fact that they always provided stationery.

At that point, I had only met Shirlie a couple of times. I swear that the first time Shirlie's street door swung open, I had walked into an argument. It was one of those moments when you catch the end of an argument and people see you and put on their best smiles. Shirlie warned me it would be chaos, and she was right.

I got on with her mum straight away. She had a brilliant sense of humour and she sometimes made me blush. "Shirlie, he's just like Elvis!" she once whispered a bit too loudly. Understandably, her dad was less keen on me. I knew Shirlie was the apple of his eye, and he was suspicious of her pop star boyfriend. Still, I tried my hardest to win him round. He'd been doing some building work and told me that he'd get cold on site, so I splashed out on a thick, padded jacket for him.

"That should keep you warm in the mornings," I said.

I'd spent a bit of money – I wanted to buy him the nicest coat I could afford. The next time I saw him in it, he'd sawn the sleeves off, and padding was falling out of the armholes.

"That's... a bit different," I said, taken aback.

"Yeah, fits much better now." He grinned.

Not long after that, I bought another flash gift, for Shirlie this time – a shiny jeep. When we returned from holiday, it was sporting an uneven coat of matt black paint.

"I fixed your car for you," said her dad, when we tried to come to terms with what had happened to the car.

Still, I felt as though I knew her. If we hadn't both been in bands, maybe I would have tried to play it cool and make myself less available. The fact was, I wasn't available, I was thousands of miles away from her – but being apart just made me want her more. When I'd fallen for her on *Top of the Pops*, she seemed strangely familiar to me, as though I might have known her in a past life. Somehow, the phone calls and postcards made things even more intense than actual dates. When we finally landed on British soil, there was only one thing on my mind.

For my next date with Shirlie, I knew I needed to do something really, really special. My friend Sade was playing a gig at Ronnie Scott's, a jazz club in London's Soho. She had the perfect voice and it was the perfect venue – sexy, intimate and sophisticated. I was desperate to impress Shirlie. If this didn't work, I didn't know what would.

When we met that night, she looked even more beautiful than I remembered. She wore a very short tunic dress with long suede boots, brown as maple leaves – and Shirlie, who had just been to Ibiza, was the same colour as her boots. She was the sexiest thing I'd ever seen in my life. I'm not even sure that I managed to tell her how incredible she looked. I think I just stammered and blinked.

Shirlie was all I could think about for weeks, but my memory hadn't been able to do justice to just how gorgeous she was – or how funny she was.

"Did you miss me?" she grinned, arranging her face and doing a ridiculous imitation of Plug from the Bash Street Kids in the *Beano*. Shirlie couldn't have looked less like Plug, but the voice was uncanny. I couldn't believe she could be so gorgeous and glamorous, but so silly and playful, too.

A Nightingale Sang in Berkeley Square

Soon we were whispering, giggling and flirting – but it felt like time stopped when Sade started singing. Her incredible, soulful, sexy voice was utterly arresting. Sade's performance was seriously special. Still, I couldn't stop thinking about Shirlie's long, tanned legs stretched out under the table.

Silvery smoke swirled around the club, making everything seem soft and seductive. We didn't want the night to end. So when Sade stopped singing, I couldn't bear to let Shirlie go back to Bushey.

"Shall we get a drink somewhere?" I suggested.

The trouble was, there was nowhere to go.

We walked up and down London, up to Soho Square, west towards Piccadilly, past the seedy shop doorways on Brewer Street and over Berkeley Square. We must have been freezing, but the cold didn't seem to matter at all. The moonlight illuminated our path, and dirty, dreary, wintry old London seemed to glitter and shine. It was putting on a show for us.

In Berkeley Square, we heard birdsong, as though an invisible presence was conducting a feathery choir. It was magical. Years later, when we recorded our album together, we came across an old song called 'A Nightingale Sang In Berkeley Square'. It was written just before the Second World War and Vera Lynn made it famous. Yet when we heard it, it seemed to evoke that magical night in the early 80s. Singing it with Shirlie brought back so many memories and it made me fall in love with her all over again.

It was far too late for Shirlie to get back to Bushey, and I think we both knew we didn't want to go back to Islington together. That night was so special because we were finally alone. I hadn't minded having Steve Strange sitting at the breakfast table, but this was different. Still, we'd been walking for hours and nothing was open. What could we do?

I had an idea. "Shirlie, do you think…?" I said nervously.

Shirlie spoke at the same time as me. "Martin, I was thinking… maybe we should find a hotel?"

Of course we should find a hotel! I'd been longing to ask, but was worried that Shirlie wouldn't want to spend the night with me. Unfortunately, we'd started to walk east, away from The Ritz – but I think I was too young and intimidated to try to check into The Ritz after midnight anyway. We walked and talked, looking for somewhere small, discreet and cosy – I didn't want to take Shirlie anywhere sordid, but I had to admit our options were limited. At that time, some hotels were still a bit suspicious of unmarried couples, and women used to transfer their rings to their left hands during check in, to look respectable. A pair of lovesick teenagers with no luggage, wandering around in the early hours of the morning, could have been a bit of a dodgy prospect.

Still, we managed to find a little place in Holborn. It was small, and slightly grubby, but it would have to do. We checked in, and the manager didn't give us a second glance. We walked into our room, holding hands, a little bit nervous, but sure of each other. Of course, I'd wanted to take Shirlie to a place that was just as special as she was. But she made it special. Shirlie lit up the room. We may have been under a candlewick bedspread, with rock-hard pillows and a creaking mattress – but we were with each other and it was perfect.

The next morning, I couldn't believe I was beside her. I was so happy. This was everything I'd been dreaming of and hoping for.

"Martin, I think I've got conjunctivitis." Shirlie sat up, eyes sealed shut. "I can't see. Can you take me to the bathroom?" At least we had an ensuite!

Once again, I took Shirlie by the hand. My heart melted. I felt more strongly attracted to her than ever. Shirlie had seemed so tough, composed and sure of herself. Now, I could feel her vulnerability and softness. I got to be the one helping her and protecting her.

Together, using the scratchy loo roll in the hotel bathroom, we cleaned her up so she could just about manage to see. I was experiencing a new, exciting emotion. For most of my life, I'd felt like a kid. I was Gary's baby brother, the shy boy my mum used to worry about, the quieter one who was ready to follow the leader. Now I felt protective. It was a privilege, too. I had the impression Shirlie didn't show this side of herself to many people. I was hooked.

The trouble was that in a few weeks we were going off on tour again. It wasn't just about Spandau, either. After all, Shirlie had been away filming a music video in Ibiza. She was going to be off travelling the world, too. I didn't know whether we would be able to make this work, but I was determined to try. After all, being away from her would hurt like hell.

Shirlie

When I was a little girl I constantly asked my mum, "How do you know when you want to marry someone?" And my mum would always answer with, "Hmm, you just know." And now I was beginning to find out. I'd found Martin irresistible from the moment I'd first laid eyes on him. And that was the problem, really. In my heart, I could feel his kindness and his goodness. He seemed pure, sweet and straightforward. And I knew I was falling just as my mum had said.

But my brain had other ideas. "Really, Shirlie?" it would sneer at me. "Why would this heart-throb, this world-famous pop star, pick you? He has millions and millions of other girls after him. What makes you think you're special enough for him?"

Now, I know my brain is capable of coming up with all sorts of negative nonsense, and that I don't need to listen to it – but back then, I didn't know how to question my inner critic. And my brain had a point. I'd seen the screaming girls – *I* was a screaming girl. Why would a young man want to fall in love with someone and commit when he had the world at his feet? Martin had seemed so confident, too, chatting me up and giving me his number. How did I know he wasn't out doing that every night? George's words echoed in my head: "You don't know that he's kind. He's just good-looking!"

Mind you, Martin *had* made a big effort with me, and he'd gone out of his way to give me his number. Presumably, he wouldn't have bothered if he didn't think I was worth bothering with. And now I had a foot – a toe – in his world. I was in a band, too. My life was exciting as well.

In Camden Palace, I wanted to kiss Martin all night. Not even poor old George could stop me – every so often we made a half-hearted effort to include him in the conversation, but kissing Martin was just too addictive. Also, I knew he was going on tour. Honestly, I wasn't sure that I'd ever see him again.

"He could easily meet someone else," I said to George. "He's going away for ages."

George didn't say anything, but I could tell what he was thinking. If Martin *did* break my heart and meet someone else, George would burn all of his Spandau posters.

While Martin was on tour, I whiled away the days, trying my hardest to focus on having fun with George and Andrew. Still, every so often I couldn't help but imagine what Martin was up to, and *who* he might be up to something with. Was he kissing beautiful French girls in berets, or sipping sangria with sexy Spanish women?

One day, I was upstairs in my room, listening to music, when the phone rang. After a few seconds, I heard my dad bellowing up the stairs.

"Uno momento!" he yelled. "Shirlie! Shirlie, it's for you! Phone call from Italy!"

Italy? Who on earth did I know in Italy? I don't think we'd ever had an international phone call in the house before – in fact, I think the furthest south anyone had ever rung us from was Brighton. It must be a mistake. Or could I be in trouble?

"Um, hello?" I said, hesitantly, gripping the receiver as though it could jump out of my hand.

"Hello sexy!" Martin said, which made me blush even more because the whole family was standing beside me listening to every word. Even though he was thousands of miles away, and the phone was crackly, he sounded exactly the same.

We didn't speak for too long. My mum, dad and little sister who were stood around the phone knew who it was – I'd told them a bit about seeing Martin, and they'd seen him on *Top of the Pops*. A pop star, calling from Italy! I felt very shy. It was only the second time we'd spoken on the phone, and my family were making me extremely self-conscious.

I was desperate to put the phone down so I could hug this secret to myself and think about Martin somewhere quiet. *He must really like me!* He didn't have to phone, but clearly he wasn't amusing himself with a coach-load of girls from Continental Europe. He'd phoned me, in the middle of the day, from a foreign country. Dad would get upset when Mum phoned Gran in the middle of the day, because the rates were more expensive then. Goodness knows what this must have cost Martin.

Over the next few weeks, I looked forward to the calls and the postcards. By the time he came back from tour, I felt as though I knew him. I didn't even mind getting conjunctivitis after our magical Berkeley Square night. After all, Martin had fallen for me after seeing me with no make-up on. We were getting serious. If he couldn't cope with a crusty eye, he wasn't the man for me. I could hardly be with someone and pretend that I was never, ever ill. If I'd have known what our future held, I would have laughed at the idea that conjunctivitis was something to worry about.

Even though the Spandau boys weren't especially welcoming to girlfriends in the group, the girlfriends were kindness itself. I really hit it off with Steve Norman's girlfriend, Gail, and we decided to share a flat. We found a tiny place together in Crouch End and made it as cosy as we could. I had a tiny room with a single bed and bought my first bed linen – a very grown-up purchase. It was a floral set from Marks & Spencer, with little pink roses embroidered on white cotton. I guess it was early shabby chic. It was very feminine and appealed to my sense of the aesthetic.

Martin was delighted when I moved in with Gail, and used to stay over every night. I was so happy – he could have been out, doing anything he wanted, but he wanted to be with me, under my M&S sheets. The trouble was that Martin was a handsome boy – tall and broad-shouldered. Fitting him into it was tricky, and it was almost impossible to find room for both of us. Every morning, I woke up wedged into the wall. I didn't get much sleep then, partly for obvious reasons and partly because of the single bed situation. Still,

I'd always choose being squashed and sleepless over having the bed to myself when Martin was away.

One night, I was drifting off to sleep, smooshed against the wall, with Martin's arms wrapped around me. *I feel so safe with him here,* I thought to myself. In my last waking moments, Martin whispered my name into my hair.

"Shirlie," he said, softly, "I love you."

I will remember that moment forever. It was as if fireworks were exploding inside my body. I was loved! Martin loved me! Even my mum had never said those words to me out loud before, and I knew she loved me. I could feel Martin's love surrounding me, protecting me, as soft and warm as his skin. But in my sleepy state, I wasn't quite ready to say it back.

I'd been trying so hard not to let myself love him, just in case everything went wrong. Still, I knew I couldn't fight it and soon I'd be ready to tell him how I felt. But for now, I'd pretend to be asleep. I could wait until morning and see if the lovely dream had been real. There was nowhere I'd rather be than beside my love in the little single bed. But when you're in a pop group, you never get to stay in the same place for very long. A new adventure was on the cards – a trip that would change me forever...

8

Wham! in China

Shirlie

Imagine a world in which you have to listen to the music you love in secret.

My earliest memories are musical. After Martin, our children and animals, music is probably the great love of my life. No matter how tough, sad or painful parts of my life have felt, music has always been there for me, comforting me. And the people I'm closest to feel exactly the same way. Music has helped me to make new friends and connect with the people I love. I believe that everyone has a right to listen to music.

So looking back, it seems really weird that Wham! were sent to play a strange concert in a part of the world where pop music was forbidden.

In 1985, China was still processing the aftermath of the cultural revolution. Slowly, life there was changing and the

Chinese people were being allowed a little more freedom. But the country was mysterious, and as a westerner, I couldn't imagine what life was like under communist rule. There was still very little information coming out of the country. It was difficult for people to get in and out, and there was lots of secrecy and silence. So when Wham! were chosen to be the first western band to play in the country, it was a big deal.

Wham!'s manager, Simon Napier Bell, had spent 18 months trying to convince Chinese officials that the concert would be a good idea. Queen and the Rolling Stones were also being considered. Looking back, we were an interesting choice because we were relatively new. We weren't established rockers – we were kids, ready to dress up and dance, and we had a balance of boys and girls on stage. When I think about what life was like for a young music fan in China, I realise we must have seemed almost futuristic to the kids at the concert.

It's bittersweet. I've read accounts from Chinese Wham! fans, who have talked about how much the gig meant to them and how their memories of it are very precious. But all of my memories are very, very painful. I saw people and animals being treated in a way that broke my heart. I spent every second of the trip feeling frightened, missing Martin and being desperate to get home. And the journey out of China ended up being the biggest disaster of all.

As the trip drew nearer, we were on the lookout for a new girl. Dee was the opposite of Amanda. She was utterly focused and extremely ambitious. I loved working with her, and we had such a great time making the 'Club Tropicana' video, but she was the first to realise that her ambitions would take her outside Wham! Dee has a stunning singing voice, and she simply didn't get to sing that much when she was dancing onstage with George, Andrew and me. So after the band had its first hits, we were without "another girl" again.

When Dee left we needed a new girl, so Simon Napier Bell suggested a girl called Pepsi. Just by the sound of her name, I knew we would get on. She sounded fun. I decided I'd get to know her, so I suggested going to pick her up rather than her meeting us at George's house. I thought it would give us a chance to bond.

Even though I was a seasoned dancer by then and going on *Top of the Pops* had become as normal as getting the bus, I still felt secretly insecure. I was so used to putting myself down. At the time, part of me believed I was only in that world because of my friends, and that I'd been lucky. I didn't feel beautiful, or special, I was still scrappy and punky. This girl was chosen by the record company. She'd be fantastically glamorous, statuesque and curvaceous. *All boobs and bum*, I thought glumly, while contemplating my straight-up-and-down figure.

We arranged that I would pick her up from Finsbury Park. I navigated the nightmare system around the station, waiting for someone I hoped would match the band's sense of humour and fun. And then I saw Pepsi. I knew it was her, partly because I'd been given a very vague description, but mostly because she was doing that thing where you squint quizzically at car windows, looking for your lift. She was gorgeous, but tomboy gorgeous. I'd been expecting false lashes and heels, not jeans and a jumper.

She tapped on my window. "Shirlie?"

At first, the drive was quiet as we tried to make small talk. Pepsi and I were both trying to work out whether the other one was aloof or just nervous. Then, as an icebreaker, she asked if she could put a tape on.

"I just recorded this," she said, smiling. I think she wanted me to know what she could do.

As soon as Pepsi's incredible voice filled my little car, I gasped.

"Oh my God!" I murmured. "You sound just like Shirley Bassey!" Shirley Bassey was one of my all-time favourite singers.

Pepsi beamed so happily that I could feel the warmth of her smile on my face, like sunshine. We started talking and couldn't stop. By the time we reached Radlett, she was my new best friend.

Much later, Pepsi told me that she felt a bit anxious at Finsbury Park Tube Station. She had big dreams and ambitions and she wasn't sure why she had to go and see "these white kids who rapped". But as Wham! became more famous, Pepsi and I became each other's allies.

It was becoming apparent that we were backing singers and dancers, and that the boys – George especially – were on a different trajectory. I don't think anyone made a conscious decision to push us away or separate us. Looking back, I think it was one of those things that can happen when there's a combination of record company people and management all having opinions about what everyone should go and do. Pepsi's friendship has been a lifelong gift. I think the fact that she could eventually see a life for herself away from Wham! made it much easier for me to understand that the boys and I were growing up – and growing in separate directions.

Leading up to our Chinese trip, I started getting a sense that something didn't feel right. I'd spent a couple of years travelling the world with Wham! I'd been everywhere from America to Japan, and while I didn't enjoy being away from home, I was always able to get on with it. But this time I felt a great deal of anxiety.

"I don't think we should go on this trip," I confided in Martin. "I'm really not sure about it, something doesn't feel right."

Martin was his usual, positive self. "Shirlie, this is a huge opportunity. You're going to somewhere that almost no one gets to visit, and you're going as part of the biggest band in the world. I wish it was me and Spandau! I'm really proud of you and the guys. You should go for it."

Not long ago, I would have confided in George. More than anything, I wanted us to have one of our late-night car chats, where he'd sit beside me in the passenger seat and help me talk through my fears. Usually, I was the pragmatic one and he was the emotional one, so I would have loved to get his take on the trip and what was going on. The trouble was that even within the band we were drifting apart.

Wham! had become megastars in such a short space of time. We'd been teenagers, having so much fun dancing on George's white carpet – then we'd blinked and suddenly become the faces on the posters we used to gaze at. George's talent was immense. Andrew, Pepsi and I all knew that it was bigger than all of us combined, and it was an inevitable future.

There was another platform – as big as we were as Wham! – waiting for George to step onto. You just knew it was coming and that there was so much more ahead for him. But I longed for that friendship, and for things to stay so intimate and cosy, a place where we both used to feel safe. We were each other's agony aunts, best friends and everything in-between. The world adored the boys as a duo, and the two boys didn't need anyone around them anymore. The more successful they became, the less they needed us around. But to be honest, Pepsi and I were beginning to get bored as well. We were just backing dancers but we knew we too could do more.

Our hobby, our passion project, and our friendship had become this strange machine. We wanted George's talent to have as much room as possible to flourish. But this meant that fun had become work, and we were all starting to feel sad, strained and exhausted. Deep down, I think I knew the China trip was the end of the force that had brought us all together. Wham! weren't bringing pop to the eyes and ears of the people who needed it the most. We were political pawns, being used to spread a message and tell the world that everything in China was OK, when the opposite was true.

Pepsi had become one of my very best friends, and I don't know what I would have done without her on that trip. We were already very close, but I think that was this is what bonded us for life. We flew to Hong Kong, which was a British colony at the time. It was intense, full of heat, light and noise. The humidity was like nothing I'd ever experienced. From the moment we stepped out of the airport, we were drenched in sweat. Years later, when I started going through the menopause, I realised that certain parts felt very familiar – it was just like being back in Hong Kong.

Even though we were far from home, Hong Kong looked recognisably western. To tell the truth, I was a little bit disappointed. At the time, I didn't completely understand that Hong Kong was a British territory and not "real" China. I'd been expecting to see lots of men looking like Martin's old hero, Bruce Lee. Being on tour means you spend a lot of time waiting around and looking for ways to stay busy. For Pepsi and me, that usually meant a trip to the shops. George and Andrew used to tease me and call me "Shirlie Shopper", because I could always find something to buy. I met up with Pepsi in our hotel lobby and we visited the luxury shops, but everything was beyond our budget. After all, we didn't really need designer finery, we wanted clothes we could move in.

We hadn't expected Hong Kong to be so grand. We were surrounded by opulence and wealth. But when we came out of one extremely fancy store, we nearly walked into a man who was sitting on the pavement outside. My eyes struggled to process what was in front of me. It looked as though his leg was covered in green fuzzy stuff and I couldn't quite make sense of what I was seeing.

"Oh my God," whispered Pepsi. "His poor leg."

Suddenly, I realised it was rotting. My head swam. We were surrounded by people spending thousands on luxury clothes. Why wasn't anyone doing anything about this man and his terrible health problems?

We both panicked, feeling very young and very scared. We had a little bit of cash on us and chucked it in his cup, before running back to the hotel. At reception, I tried to ask the staff to send an ambulance over to help the man. After all, he'd looked like he was dying.

The man at reception looked as though he was trying not to laugh. "That was just a beggar, don't worry. We have a lot of those."

It didn't make any sense to me. In this place, I could see so much luxury and money. Why couldn't they help people in need?

Still, it was when we flew to Beijing that the real trouble began.

Usually, when we were on tour, strangers would stare or crowd around me every time I took my baseball hat off. This was especially likely to happen in Asia, and I'd experienced it in Hong Kong. My short, white hair was so unusual then that it attracted plenty of attention. As I knew Beijing was going to be very different, I'd prepared myself to be stared at. It wasn't necessarily because we were part of Wham! – in fact, I didn't think the people of Beijing would necessarily know our music well enough to recognise us. There was no *Top of the Pops* here. But I thought that the fact we all looked so western, and so different, would generate a bit of curiosity. I didn't always enjoy the attention, but Beijing was so much worse.

No one would look at us, at all. There were no friendly smiles or waves. People almost seemed to be avoiding us. Now, I know there were so many rules about the way Chinese people had to behave that they were terrified of interacting with us in any way. But at the time, it made me sad. Everyone seemed so unwelcoming and unfriendly. It seemed like proof that we never should have come.

Hong Kong had been so shiny and glamorous, so the drabness and sadness of Beijing shocked me. I'd hoped that at least we'd be able to stay in a nice hotel and decompress before performing. At this point, I'd started to realise that Wham! was changing, because I was being kept away from George and Andrew. They'd been picked up at the airport in limousines and taken to a luxury hotel, safe from screaming fans. The rest of us were bundled onto an ancient coach and taken to a different hotel – one that seemed more like a boarding house that was last decorated during the Great Depression. The beds were harder than the floors. When I opened the curtains, the room seemed to get darker. Stern notices on the doors warned us that we had to be in bed, with the lights off, by 11 o'clock at night.

If someone had told me on the night I'd met Andrew that in five years we'd be best mates, in one of the world's most successful groups and touring China together, I'd have had a total "pinch me" moment. This should have been one of the most exciting points of my career, but I was utterly miserable. The hotel was making Pepsi and me deeply anxious, and I wanted to find George and Andrew and ask if we could move to wherever they were staying. Of course, these days, your friends are only ever a text message or a WhatsApp away. But in those days, the only way I could get hold of my two best friends was through a long line of publicists, tour managers and security guards.

That was when it hit me that I wasn't a best friend any more. I was an employee. I missed Martin so much that I ached. We were made to go on an official tour of the temples of Peking. I lit handfuls of incense sticks and prayed, praying for Martin, marriage and children. Anything that meant I'd never have to go on tour again.

In the film *Wham! in China: Foreign Skies,* there's a two-second clip of me standing in a wet market, clapping my hands over my eyes. Simon Napier Bell had arranged to have our trip made into a film – after all, it was supposed to be of great historical and cultural significance. This meant we couldn't relax after our long journey, and get ready for a show, in the way we would on a normal tour. We were taken out to see the sights. That two-second clip doesn't show how it felt to be trapped in a real-life horror movie.

Beijing was a true assault on the senses. Because China was very strict about pest control, everything smelt of musty, dusty chemicals. Towards the end of the trip, I learnt that the government had killed all of the birds, focusing on sparrows, believing them to be rodents. This meant there had been a three-year famine in China. Birds eat the insects that attack the crops. Without birds, there's no harvest. And sparrows eat more moths than anything else.

It was as if I was stuck in a very old wardrobe, as the scent of mothballs followed me everywhere I went. That smell mingled with the stench of the wet market, which reeked of blood, death and decay. It was dark and crammed full of different stalls, and at first I couldn't tell what anything was. I peered into the grey and gasped, feeling a sharp pinch on my arm.

"Shirls, no, look away, don't look," whispered Pepsi, just as I made sense of the horrific image in front of me.

A man was skinning a live cat. The image was so horrific that my brain took an eternity to process what my eyes had seen. I screamed. I turned to run, but it was impossible to get out, every turn I took bringing me face to face with more horror. I craned my neck to look up, thinking that was the best way to avoid what was at eye level. But I saw a washing line of dead dogs, all looking as though they'd been boiled alive.

Loving animals has always been at the very core of who I am. At the time, I'd braced myself for a culture shock, as I knew Chinese people lived very differently from me. But this cruelty broke my heart. I thought of every single animal I'd loved, and imagined them beside the animals that were bleeding and dying in front of me. I simply couldn't process the pain and violence around me. This wasn't happening in some back street, it wasn't tucked away, hidden out of sight. This was being presented to me as a scene from everyday life in China. There was nothing I could do to put this moment away, to compartmentalise it and make it seem normal. I still have nightmares about it, and I support charities that rescue animals from China.

The wet market took my appetite away, which was no bad thing – because the band catering in China was unlike anything else we'd ever experienced. Usually, before a concert, you have a rider (the part of the contract that includes the artist's food and drink requirements). Singing and dancing on stage requires an enormous amount of energy, and it's vital to eat well before a show. It's rarely anything fancy, but you need food to keep you going and give you an energy boost, such as sandwiches, fresh fruit, maybe some chocolate. We had no idea what to expect when we reached the Worker's Gymnasium before the performance.

"Where do we go for dinner?" I asked one of the crew.

"Here it is," he said, gesturing to the chequered parquet floor.

I looked down and counted seven metal bowls – they looked like a cross between a dog's dish and a Victorian chamber pot. I didn't recognise any of the food I could see below me. We were expecting noodles, and maybe some vegetables, but everything looked grey and under-cooked. After the wet market, I couldn't manage to force anything down. For the rest of the trip, I lived off strawberry milkshakes.

The concert was very, very strange. Just before we came on, a group of backing dancers took to the stage. Looking back, I realise it was bizarre to send a dance troupe out to entertain an audience in a country where dancing is forbidden. I've tried to imagine how strange and shocking it must have seemed to the people in the audience. Still, I'm so grateful to those breakdancers. They didn't just warm up the crowd, they got them used to the idea of people dancing on stage in skimpy outfits.

The crowd was huge. 12,000 people had come to see us – but they were like no crowd I'd ever seen before.

Usually at a concert, you feed off the energy of the people watching you. It's the biggest buzz you can experience as a performer. You can see thousands of people who have dressed up for a night of fun, and they're dancing along with you and singing as loudly as they can. There's truly nothing like it, and it makes you feel completely connected to every single fan.

In Beijing, the crowd felt almost funereal at first. After the Cultural Revolution, people were only permitted to wear dull, sanctioned colours, so everyone was in muted blue, green and grey outfits. No one was allowed to dance or sing. It seemed as though no one was even smiling. Pepsi and I bounced across the stage in our 'Wham! Rap' get-up, tiny leather bodices and matching hats. Suddenly, I felt horribly self-conscious.

I'd always had a complicated relationship with my looks and my body, and always felt as though I wasn't pretty enough to be a pop star. The funny thing is that when you *are* a pop star, that melts away. You're too busy to worry about what you look like, or who's looking at you. When you're performing on *Top of the Pops*, everyone else around you is in loads of make-up and skimpy outfits, so you get used to your own boobs and bum very quickly – you have other things to concentrate on. But on stage in Beijing, it hit me that I was being stared at by thousands

Top left: Christmas 1966, 4-year-old me with my dad who loved to dress me in little fur coats. He always called me Snagglepuss. I was painfully shy and wouldn't leave his side. **Top right:** Christmas at my house – my parents went for it. My dad was so tall he had the ceiling covered in no time.

Below: Donkey derby at Butlins Skegness. I won the derby but wanted to swap the free holiday for the donkey. My sister Nicola is hugging the donkey. She also wanted to keep it. My dad is pretty proud of me and so am I!

Top left: My school photo, wearing my Brutus shirt, aged only 11 – but it was the start of looking cool, so I thought. **Top right:** At my parents' house and on my way out to the Blitz… the mirror never looked so good. **Bottom left:** Me on holiday. **Bottom right:** Best friends – I always felt safe in his arms.

Top: Andrew and me standing outside my house with Rocky, our German shepherd. It was the norm to park your car on the front lawn.

Bottom: When George could go out, and no one cared. Us sitting on Brighton beach.

Top left: Filming the 'Highly Strung' video in Hong Kong. **Top right:** Journeys to Glory: another tour bus, but we were number 1 with 'True!' **Bottom:** Another stadium and another night on stage with Spandau.

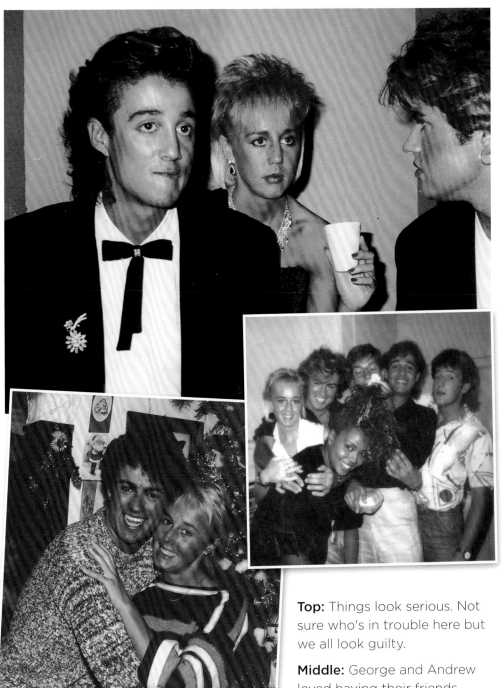

Top: Things look serious. Not sure who's in trouble here but we all look guilty.

Middle: George and Andrew loved having their friends around.

Left: Christmas at my mum and dad's: George and I steal another cuddle.

Left: On the set of 'The Freeze' video, wearing my PX jacket and big 80s designer trousers by Simon Withers.

Bottom: Sitting in the garden with Frank and Eileen, Martin's parents.

Top: Pepsi and I backstage.

Right: We love to dance, dancing to Wham! rap.

Bottom: The boys looking sporty in Fila – Pepsi and I looking wicked in leather.

Our very first holiday together, which was the first time we had actually been on our own. Porus, Greece.

of people, and most of them had never seen a woman who was dressed as I was, moving like I was.

As always, I looked across the stage at George for energy and reassurance, but I could tell he was struggling to find his mojo. We were all being as professional as possible, and trying our very hardest, but the situation was so strange that capturing the Wham! magic was a real struggle. Then, out of the corner of my eye, I saw something that triggered the same feelings of pain and panic as the wet market. Security guards, or they may have been armed policemen, were attacking a young fan with a truncheon. It was brutal and shocking. Even if the fan had been behaving badly, I don't think anything could have justified that level of violence. And this wasn't someone being drunk and disorderly, or someone who was making the concert unpleasant for anyone else. This was just someone who wanted to sing along to the chorus or tap their feet to the beat. After that, I couldn't concentrate on our performance at all. What I had seen was haunting me.

Unbelievably though, the worst was yet to come.

On the day we were due to leave, I was walking down the hotel corridor when I heard raised, familiar English voices. I followed the sound and noticed an open door – one of the musicians in the band was trying to help another band member who was refusing to leave his room.

"He thinks he's been possessed by the devil," the guy explained to me. "He's been drinking his own piss, too."

Oh, God, what was this country doing to us? I'd recently seen *The Exorcist* and been terrified by it. I didn't want to spend time with someone who believed he'd been in the grip of demonic possession.

"Who's that? Shirlie? Tell her to come in!" said the possessed man. "I need to see her."

From the doorway, I could tell the curtains were drawn. Even though there was bright sunlight outside, the room looked eerie.

"Sorry, got to pack! We need to get to the airport!" I cried, legging it. I had to get back to Pepsi, and I wouldn't let her leave my side.

We made it to the airport and boarded the plane for Hong Kong. George and Andrew had already flown there, and I assumed their plane was much nicer than our one. The seats weren't covered – you could see where they'd been nailed in. Instead of overhead locker compartments, there was netting, the sort you'd get on a coach. Our bags were just piled in. Pepsi took the window seat and I sat beside her.

"I'm exhausted." She yawned, curling up as best she could and resting her head on the corner, ready for sleep.

The seat beside me remained empty until we were about to take off. Then... *Oh no!* I noticed someone was making a beeline for me – that demonic band member. To this day, I've no idea why he was so fixated on me. Perhaps it was my white T-shirt and jeans and my white blonde hair – maybe he wanted to seek out an angel to release the devil. But he immediately started talking nonsense.

"Shall we play football?" he asked, beaming.

All I wanted to do was keep him calm. I was terrified I would make him angry and then he'd fly off the handle. Who knew what he was capable of doing?

"Ah, football. Maybe when we land. In fact… that's a shame, I've forgotten to bring the football," I garbled, improvising wildly.

He seemed to take that in his stride for a little while. But once we were in the air, he took off his mirrored shades and started growling at his own reflection.

"Pepsi… *Pepsi!*" I said, poking her, talking out of the side of my mouth to avoid attracting the guy's attention.

"Shirlie, shhhh! Sleeping!" Pepsi replied, snuggling into her corner.

The band guy reached into a bag at his feet and pulled out an object. Even before I saw it, I knew this was going to be bad. It was a Swiss Army Knife. As soon as I saw the blade gleaming in the light, I thought, *I'm dead.* He was going to kill me and there was nothing I could do about it.

Pepsi still wouldn't wake up. As carefully as I could, I reached behind me and waved. George's mum and dad, and the band's publicist, Connie, were all sitting behind me. I just needed one of them to see me and raise the alarm. But no one seemed to notice. Then the guy started to stab himself in the stomach. At that point, our security guards, a couple of ex-SAS men, noticed what was going on. That's when everything in my memory goes blurry.

My whole body went limp and heavy, so when Pepsi suddenly woke up and jumped into the seats behind her, she couldn't drag me with her. I noticed scarlet splotches all over my clean, cream T-shirt. Again, I was back in a horror movie, covered in someone else's blood.

The pilot was told the plane was being hijacked. Because of the situation in China, everyone was especially sensitive to potential attacks, so he put the plane into a nosedive, planning a crash landing. We were upside down and everything in the overhead nets thudded to the floor, sounding like a drumbeat punctuating the screams of the passengers. Most people didn't know what my seatmate was doing, so when the plane started to plummet, they assumed we were all going to die in a plane crash. *I* thought I was going to die in a plane crash. It felt as though we were falling out of the sky. Maybe this guy really *was* possessed by the devil, and the devil had taken control of the plane.

Somehow, I'd found my way to Connie's lap. She was murmuring a Buddhist chant, "Nam Myoho Renge Kyo," over and over. I felt a strange mix of emotions. I was terrified, but numb and oddly peaceful. All I could think about was my mum hearing about the plane crash on the news. I was so sad and scared for her. But I knew that Connie's lap was the best place I could possibly be. If I had to die somewhere, I could die there. Her chanting was so serene, so soothing, during a time of complete panic.

Miraculously, we managed to land. I'm not even sure where we were – presumably somewhere else in China. The second we touched the tarmac, airport security rushed on the plane to sedate the guy in the band and take him to hospital. Later, I learnt he was a practising Catholic and the recent death of his father had caused him to have a breakdown. He got better eventually, and went on to tour with other bands, but we didn't stay in touch. I think we both had our own issues to worry about.

Everyone who'd been on the flight remained in a state of shock and panic. Somehow, I managed to call my mum. Long-distance calls were so expensive and complicated that I couldn't stay on the line for long enough to explain what had happened. All I could say was, "Mum, don't worry, there was an accident on the plane, and you may hear about it on the news, but I'm fine." If one of my kids did that to me now, I'd be climbing the walls with worry and panic!

Even now, Martin says he still struggles to get his head around everything that happened to me on that trip. It will stay with me forever, and it's made me into the person I am today. In some ways, it made me more tender and in touch with my vulnerability, and in others, it toughened me up.

I quickly realised I didn't have a place in Wham! any more, and there was no point being sad about it. I needed to make peace with the direction the band was going in and start making a new place for myself in the world, with new friends. But going to China also made me so sure of my feelings for Martin. I'd felt so sad and lost without him. Missing him so much had made me realise I couldn't play it cool any more. I'd been in love with him for a long time, and now I knew just how deep my feelings were. He wasn't just my boyfriend, he was my future. I wanted to be right by his side.

It wouldn't be easy, I realised. He was integral to Spandau, and they were soaring. He had a real role in his band, and he would keep touring and travelling for a while. But I was starting to understand something I'd always known, somewhere inside me. Ultimately, I didn't want to be a pop star forever. It was a means to an end, and that end, I hoped, would be having a loving husband, a family and a beautiful home. It didn't matter what I did next, as long as I kept my goal in mind. I really didn't care about being famous. Although I knew I was so lucky and privileged to have seen the world, I was hoping the next part of my life would just be about being beside the people I loved.

9

A Baby, a Bride and "the Wheelbarrow"

Shirlie

When I was growing up in the 1970s, it was drummed into me that getting pregnant was the worst thing that could possibly happen to me. Sex education didn't really happen in the classroom. Everything we knew came from whispers, rumours, gossip and stories of what happened to big brothers and sisters. Deep down, I think I believed that if I wasn't using birth control, I could probably get pregnant just by looking at a boy for too long.

My lovely mum was a cautionary tale. She'd had five of us, and she was unhappily married to my dad. I knew she adored her kids and wouldn't give us up for anything. But she was living through us. I couldn't imagine living a life like hers. I longed for freedom. Yet, in my early 20s, once I met Martin, something shifted. Baby fever hit!

A Baby, a Bride and "the Wheelbarrow"

I'd always felt so full of love and longed to have someone to express those loving feelings. My mum was, in lots of ways, the first love of my life. Dogs and horses gave me the feeling of being able to love unconditionally, and then I had Martin. Love was all around me. But when I started thinking about having a baby, I felt a pure, unignorable yearning. It was more than a feeling or an emotion – it was physical. My longing took over every single cell in my body. Having a baby was all I could think about.

I think it really started when Tony Hadley had his first baby, Tom, with his wife Leonie. When I met Tom, I was utterly overwhelmed. I couldn't get over the fact that Tony and Leonie had managed to make a tiny person. This baby was so beautiful. Soft and warm, with such tiny toes and sweet little hands. I'd always thought babies were cute and adorable, but this was something else. It felt as if I was a wise man witnessing a miracle birth in a stable. Babies became my religion, and suddenly I wanted one more than I'd ever wanted anything in the world.

When it came to my career, and even my relationship with Martin, I'd taken things in my stride. With Wham!, and later with Pepsi and Shirlie, I'd been able to live in the moment. I knew I was lucky to have a job that let me dance, get creative, have fun and see the world – but it had never really stirred up any profound passions inside me. With Martin, I'd found unconditional love. I had so much faith that our relationship was bigger than anything else, so I knew we could overcome whatever hit us. Even though I missed him like crazy when he was away, I felt secure in his love. But my love for the longed-for baby I dreamt of holding in my arms felt like a particular kind of unrequited yearning.

Not long after the Hadleys started their family, though, I received some devastating news.

Ever since I was 15, I'd suffered from completely debilitating period pains. No one knew what to do with me or how to fix it. My mum sometimes had mild cramps, and she'd warned me that I might reach a certain point in the month and need some paracetamol and a hot water bottle. She was as frightened as I was when my period was marked by a spell of fainting, vomiting and diarrhoea.

At the time, women's healthcare wasn't taken seriously, and our local GP wasn't sympathetic. Mum was really worried, but she'd take me to the surgery to be told, "You'll just have to get used to it, most women do," when I would be doubled over in pain, struggling to stay conscious. Years later, I found out that my dad's mum had the same terrible troubles, and she used to feel sick and pass out without understanding why. It was comforting to learn that it hadn't come from nowhere, and that I was descended from women who had the same problems as I did. I struggled, but I couldn't imagine going through all that in the 1920s. At least I had modern painkillers and sanitary products.

Sometimes, during Wham! tours, my period pain would get so bad that I'd pass out in the loo, and poor Pepsi would have to go and find me. Once, during a rehearsal in America, I was in so much pain that she rang for the paramedics.

"It's just my period," I mumbled, dazed, while they checked my vital signs and asked me if I knew the date and who the president was.

"No ma'am. This isn't your period, this is much more serious."

The panicking tour manager was hopping agitatedly next to the ambulance while I was placed inside it on a stretcher. "Shirlie, will you still be able to do the show tonight?" he asked, while I grimaced, feeling a wave of pain break against every single one of my internal organs.

"I don't knowwwwww," I murmured, passing out again.

I *did* do the show, but they had to inject me with a lot of pethidine.

In my early 20s, when I was starting to earn more money, I learnt about private healthcare. After seeing a specialist following my traumatic trip to China, I realised that if you're lucky enough to be able to shop around for a doctor, you may find one who could help. And after years of being fobbed off by my GP, Shirlie Shopper was ready to pound the pavements and look.

I ended up at the Portland Hospital, having a consultation with a beautiful doctor named Ursula. Her surname was Lloyd, not Andress, but she could have been a Bond girl. She was a stunning brunette with flowing hair and enormous brown eyes, petite but powerful, with one of the calmest, kindest auras I've ever encountered. Ursula arranged for me to have a series of tests and then sat down with me to explain the results.

"Shirlie, it looks as though what you have is severe endometriosis. This means that extra womb tissue is growing where it shouldn't be, in your ovaries and fallopian tubes. This is what has been causing you such an enormous amount of pain for so long."

Ursula spoke beautifully, and her words were music to my ears. I wanted to cry – but from sheer relief. Usually, if I'd gone into hospital and been told that I had a medical problem, I would have felt terrified. Yet this made me feel as though I'd been given a gift. I had my sanity back.

For over five years, I'd been doing battle with my body. Every single month, I'd dreaded my period, knowing I'd be out of action and out of control for days. The worst part was that I'd hear my old GP's voice in my head and worry that he was only saying what everyone else was thinking. "Why is she making such a fuss about nothing? Most women just get on with it, why can't she?"

Even though I knew the pain was real – bad enough to make me faint and throw up – there was a tiny part of me that had always questioned this and wondered whether everything was really as awful as it seemed. Finally, my horrible periods made sense. I had proof that nothing was as it should be. Science was on my side.

But the diagnosis of endometriosis came with the world's worst PS. Ursula's eyes seemed to soften as she spoke slowly and very gently. I knew she was trying very hard to find the right words so she could say something difficult.

"Shirlie, the thing about endometriosis is that it can cause problems with your fertility."

I saw the seriousness in her eyes before I was able to make sense of her words. Inf, infer… what? What did that word mean? It came to me in slow motion. Infertility. I might not be able to have a baby. My longed-for baby.

The room started to swim before my eyes. Was this a bad dream? Everything felt too hot, too loud and too close. My soft cotton T-shirt started to irritate my skin. This couldn't be right. Surely my dream couldn't end before it started? I don't think I realised just how badly I longed for a baby until the possibility was taken away from me. I'd known so little about my body, I didn't even consider that I might not be able to have a child. Surely, that was just what women *did?* All those years spent worrying about getting pregnant when I wasn't ready – and I'd wasted them.

Kind Dr Ursula could see just how badly I was taking the news. "Shirlie, don't worry," she said to me. "At this stage, we're able to help, and the endometriosis could cause problems. But it doesn't mean you won't have children. What I will tell you is this. I'm not sure what your current situation is, but if you're in a relationship with someone you want to have children with, don't wait for too long. Don't put it off."

As if I'd put it off…

I returned to Muswell Hill as quickly as I could, running through the front door of our apartment.

"Martin! MARTIN! We need to have a baby! Now!"

OK, those may not have been my exact words, but that's how much panic I had in my heart. As far as I was concerned, we had no time to lose. Ursula's diagnosis had crystallised my baby fever, and my course of action was clear. Honestly, and I'm ashamed of how selfish this sounds, my longing for a baby was so intense I'd almost forgotten that Martin needed to be a part of the process. I was in my early 20s, and I'd already had a great career and seen the world. I felt completely ready to be a mum. Surely Martin would just realise this was a brilliant idea and follow my lead?

Martin didn't match my mood straight away. I'd half been expecting him to pick me up, twirl me around the room and say, "Let's do it! If she's a girl, we'll call her Martina." Usually, in our relationship, I came up with the plans, and he'd say, "That sounds brilliant!"

We work so well together because I love to organise and he's so laid back. Admittedly, a baby would take a lot of organising, but I didn't think he'd take much persuasion. Instead, he looked a bit shell-shocked and then slumped on the sofa, patting the space beside him to get me to join him.

"OK, Shirl, this is a big one. I think we need to have a good talk about it. Realistically, I'm not sure this is the right time. I'm away so much, with the band, and what about Pepsi and Shirlie? I'd love to think about this in the future, but I'm not sure I'm ready to be a dad just yet."

I was reeling. With the benefit of hindsight, I understand. Martin was in his early 20s, too. His career was blowing up, Spandau were at the very peak of their fame and he already had big responsibilities – to his other band members, the crew, the management and more. Spandau weren't just a band, they were a business. Martin had always been very concerned about the people who worked with him, and he took their jobs as seriously as his own. He didn't want to do anything to jeopardise their future, and he knew that having a baby would make it really hard to focus on work. For once, he was being much more practical and pragmatic than me.

Taking a deep breath, I tried to explain everything Ursula had told me. I told him that now I knew what my condition was, we might not be able to wait. I wasn't on the pill – it messed with my hormones too much – so it would just be a case of trying and then waiting to see what happened.

"It may take a while," I finished. "So perhaps it makes sense to start now and, maybe, by the time it actually happens, we'll be ready? And if Tony and Leonie can make it work, I'm sure we'll manage."

I could tell Martin wasn't completely convinced, but the cogs in his brain were starting to whirr into action.

"OK, let's try it and see what happens," he said. "I love you."

He kissed me, and I felt a little buzz of excitement. Soon, we'd have a baby!

A month came and went, and so did my period. I'd started my treatment and that eased some of the pain – but there was no pain greater than the first moment when I realised I wasn't pregnant. Even though Ursula had warned me that the endometriosis meant I wasn't especially fertile, I was shocked.

Deep down, I think I was still a schoolgirl who believed I'd get pregnant the moment I stopped trying not to be. I felt as though my body had let me down. I couldn't tell if I wanted to weep because my hormones were out of control, or whether it was simply the crushing disappointment of not getting what I'd always longed for. Still, onwards and upwards... I simply had to keep calm, stay patient and try again. At least trying was a lot of fun!

Another month came and went. And another one, and another one. Why wasn't it working? What could we be doing wrong? My moods changed. I had moments of feeling like an utter failure. Sometimes I felt furious, and sometimes I felt completely baffled. I tried mysterious fertility drugs. But I had to bin them after they started to trigger menopause symptoms and I found myself collapsing in a restaurant with boiling hot flushes. On stage, I'd dance for hours every night without breaking a sweat. Suddenly, I was feeling so ill from these drugs that I was pressing my face to the flatware, dripping and trying to cool down.

My closest friends and family knew what was going on, but I didn't want to burden them with our struggles.

I've always loved being a problem-solver, and I'm the person who does her research and applies logic first. I was reading everything I could get my hands on and trying every method I could think of. That's not to say we didn't get some unsolicited advice along the way.

Once, we were at my mum's house, having our tea, when she loudly whispered to Martin, "Have you and Shirlie tried 'the wheelbarrow'? That ought to do the trick." Martin turned bright red – he may have had a hot flush at this point.

Life was starting to get difficult at work, too. As soon as I realised I was ready to be a mum, I'd entered a kind of fantasy land. Mentally, I'd completely checked out of Pepsi and Shirlie. Our management would call us about plans for the new album, or tell us that they wanted us to go to Japan, and I didn't feel any excitement – I was just anxious and slightly bored. I'd already been to Japan. I wanted to be at home, not on stage.

Pepsi knew something was up. She was – and is – one of my closest friends. Honestly, I think our friendship has remained so strong because we complement each other. We have matching values, but very different priorities, so we've always been able to support each other without competing. From the moment I met Pepsi, I knew she had an amazing musical gift, along with the dedication and ambition to back it up. And she knew that my ambitions didn't lie in that area.

She'd chosen to be a pop star and worked incredibly hard because she was on a particular path. I worked as hard as I could because I didn't want to let anybody down – but I'd ended up in her world by accident, and I wasn't particularly worried about staying there.

She was much more independent than me and didn't want the same things as I did. I still remember being completely astonished when she bought her first flat.

"But how can you live there, all by yourself?" I wailed. I couldn't even stay by myself when Martin toured for six weeks. I'd move out of our apartment and move back in with my mum.

"I love my own company," she replied, grinning.

Pepsi's kindness and generosity got me through that difficult period. I would daydream about being a mother, closing my eyes during meetings or looking out of the window, pretending I was in a beautiful house, cuddling my beautiful future baby, and that "Pepsi & Shirlie" didn't exist. Pepsi was the one of us who really stayed alert, asked the right questions and kept our careers going.

Even though I was deep in the grip of baby fever, I realise I was incredibly lucky to have a job to go to. I think that period of my life would have been even harder if I'd been at home, worrying, obsessing and waiting for Martin to come home and do "the wheelbarrow". Pepsi completely understood that all I really wanted was to be with Martin and have a family, and she didn't put any pressure on me to prioritise our band. I still think about how lucky I was to work with someone so wise, compassionate and understanding. I'm sure this is why we're still so close today. She appreciated our differences, and she didn't have to want what I wanted to know how I felt and to help me get through it.

When you're desperate to get pregnant, your eyes see the world through a baby filter. From the outside, I think my life must have looked exciting and enviable. I was a young pop star, riding high in the charts, travelling all over Europe, America and Asia, going to parties, wearing whatever I wanted and living with one of the most handsome, fanciable and famous men in the world. But whenever I saw a woman walking down the street with a pram, I felt like rushing over and asking if we could switch places.

Babies were absolutely everywhere, in cafes, in parks and at the shops. I'd have days when I felt crushed – it seemed so painful and unfair. Rationally, I knew it wasn't true, but it felt as though every woman in the world had a baby but me. If I hadn't been diagnosed with endometriosis, I don't think I would have felt so jealous. I think I would have simply looked forward to the moment when I did get pregnant. But every baby I saw made me feel as though the biological clock was chiming to indicate another hour had passed. Was I running out of time?

It didn't help that Princess Diana was pregnant with William, and every newspaper, magazine and TV show was analysing her outfits and appearances. At the time, it didn't occur to me that she could possibly have any problems or difficulties. I just remember her loose Laura Ashley dresses and her shy smile, and thinking she looked like the happiest, most serene woman I'd ever seen. I didn't want to dance on stage in tight, white little outfits. I wanted a smock dress and a bump to go with it.

Still, at least Martin was getting plenty of time to get used to the idea. As the months passed, his fears started to dissolve and he was becoming as keen as I was. I think things were changing within Spandau and all of the boys were starting to grow up. Even though I'd always thought they were so sophisticated and adult, when they were together they seemed too young, and too caught up in the idea of being rock stars, to think about settling down and having a family. Yet something was starting to shift. Tony had his baby, and the boys were all becoming men, establishing lives, families and identities beyond the band. In some ways, I think this was quite stressful for Martin, but I also think he liked finding dreams and ambitions outside of music, too.

Whenever our relationship has faced a major change or transition, I've been the one pushing it forward, living in the future – and Martin is the one who has to sit with the new idea for a bit and catch up with me. But when he arrives, he's fully on board. Yet, when I knew he felt ready for fatherhood, it didn't make life any easier. I think I had an old-fashioned, romantic notion that if we both wanted it enough, it would happen, but we still struggled.

After a couple of years, I started to look into adoption. I was devastated by the idea that I couldn't have a child of my own, but I had so much love inside me that I longed to do something with it. To me, it made sense – it would have been wonderful to give a child another chance and raise them in a safe, cosy home with loving parents in a nurturing atmosphere. But the adoption idea was over before it started.

"I'm sorry, but you and your partner aren't married, you don't have steady jobs and you're away often. You simply aren't suitable candidates," explained the lady from the agency, in brisk, clipped tones.

We were speaking on the phone, but I could picture her in a dull, grey office, typing furiously, striking a big cross through our file. Dashing our hopes without giving us a chance to prove ourselves. Breaking our hearts with a red pen.

A Baby, a Bride and "the Wheelbarrow"

Having a baby always mattered much more to me than getting married – but I was starting to think about marriage, too. Martin never, ever made me feel insecure, and a day wouldn't go by where he didn't tell me how much he loved me. He was always deeply generous with time, too. It wasn't about the presents, as being with each other was simply enough. We spent our money on phone calls, flights and hotels just to be with each other. If he was on tour in one country and I was on the other side of the world, we would find a country and meet in the middle, praying we had the same days off.

It was hard at times, and sometimes it felt like we were in isolation. We had a job to do but we also needed each other. So I never felt as though I needed him to prove the way he felt for me. But not being married to him was hard. I wanted to be his wife – partly because I was fed up with my very old-fashioned grandmother complaining about her granddaughter "living in sin". If I could give her a great-grandchild, I wanted to make sure that she loved and accepted them as part of the family.

Within Spandau, there was still a sexist 70s culture where girlfriends weren't taken seriously – even when I'd been on the scene for a few years. In fact, most of the band had very long-term girlfriends, but we were still treated with suspicion, as though we might just be the new face of the week. I knew I'd have much more respect from the band as Martin's wife or the mother of his child. It would affect my standing in other ways, too. Martin was a pin-up, and although I tried my hardest to ignore any made-up speculation about our relationship, I thought that getting married might mean it was taken more seriously in the press. Even in Wham!, and then in Pepsi and Shirlie, I thought it could make a difference. We were expected to drop everything to go on tour or do magazine shoots or TV appearances. If I married Martin, maybe I would be seen as more of a grown-up woman with a family, not just a girl who could be ordered around by record company executives.

As always, I wasn't shy about telling Martin what I wanted. "You keep telling me how much you love me. Well, why don't we get married?"

It wasn't that I'd fantasised about our wedding day – or any wedding day, to be honest. The idea of walking down the aisle in a giant dress was a nightmare, not a dream come true. I could picture my dad beside me, effing and blinding, taking exception to the guests, my female relatives swooning over Martin, George and Andrew laughing at the naff decorations, maybe cutting in with Pepsi during my first dance… urghh, no thank you! It was a disaster waiting to happen! I'd have been happy to quietly sneak off to a registry office one lunchtime and just get it done. I didn't want a wedding, I just wanted a marriage. What we had already felt like marriage, but I needed the world to treat me as Mrs Martin Kemp.

Martin was a little shocked. He's much more of a romantic than I am. I think he'd imagined he would put together a beautiful proposal one day, in the distant future, when the time felt right. (It might have looked like a big budget Spandau video – perhaps he would have hired a wind machine!) But Martin had never cared about convention or doing what was expected of him. His parents were very happily married, unlike mine. Maybe that was the only real difference between us. He knew that if two people love each other, their relationship is so strong that it doesn't need to be made official. But because I'd grown up and seen my parents living together unhappily, and my dad bullying my mum, I understood how rare it was to be in a happy, loving relationship – and I wanted to lock it down.

"Shirlie, it's just a bit of paper," Martin would say. "Neither of us wants a big wedding, we're going to have a family one day, we already live together. What's the point? I love you with all my heart. I couldn't possibly love you any more! We don't need to get married to prove that to anyone."

I realised I'd have to take matters into my own hands.

When we'd been together for about three years, Spandau spent a year in Ireland. Steve Norman, the saxophonist, had injured his knee during a performance, so the band couldn't tour. They ended up in Dublin, working on a new album together. Martin and I hated that time. Because of my commitments to my band, I couldn't come to Dublin with him – so I'd fly in on a Thursday and come home on a Sunday night. Even though we were used to spending time apart, those flights home used to break me. I'd be sticking my head in a magazine, hiding my tears, already counting down the hours until the following Thursday.

I was starting to wonder how much longer I could go on for. With Martin, I understood what I was letting myself in for when I met him. We were both in the same situation, working in the music industry, working to uncertain schedules, and being away all the time. One day, in Dublin, we were ambling down Grafton Street, part of the famous shopping district. I think it was a busy Saturday, and we were holding hands, giggling and gazing into shop windows, enjoying the luxury of having the other one all to ourselves and having nothing to do. There was a tiny vintage jeweller on the corner, which had always been one of our favourite spots for window shopping. I love jewellery with a history and a story, and I used to spend a lot of time wondering who had worn the glittering necklaces and earrings on display, and what their lives were like.

When we were looking at the pretty pieces, a display of engagement rings caught my eye.

"Are you gonna buy me one of those, then?" I said. The words just popped out. We'd been talking about marriage for ages, but I had no idea that I was going to propose to Martin that morning – or what his reaction would be.

"I suppose I'd better. Come on!" he grinned, taking me by the hand.

If the engagement is official once the ring is on your finger, then we left the shop engaged. Once he was on board with the idea, generous Martin wanted to buy me the biggest ring in the shop. Or possibly all the rings. But even though I loved looking at the beautiful jewellery, I didn't feel I needed to wear a giant diamond. If Martin had proposed with a Haribo gummy ring, I would have said yes.

That night, Martin went down on one knee and asked me for my hand – so he had his more traditional proposal in there, too. Then we had Steve and Gail over for champagne to toast our news. It was a really joyful day. I still wasn't thinking about planning the wedding, but it felt as though we were one step closer to having a family – and to building our future. The only traditional, old-fashioned part I cared about was taking Martin's name and giving that name to our baby. It's a choice that everyone feels differently about, and not everyone agrees that it's something women should do. But I suppose I'd never had any choice about the name I'd been born with. I'd inherited it from my dad and I wasn't that attached to it.

Being with Martin was a choice – the best one I'd ever made, and I'd choose him again every single day. I was choosing to make a life with him, and trying to make a baby with him. Sharing his name was a way of telling the world that we were a real team. Yet my body still hadn't understood the message. We kept trying, and trying, and trying again. The months turned to years. I was starting to give up hope and believed the endometriosis had won. Then, towards the end of 1988, we went on holiday.

For years, Pepsi had been telling me about the beautiful island of St Lucia, where her family were from. I used to dream of it. Clear blue waters, beaches where the sand felt like icing sugar, warm weather and golden sunsets. It sounded like utter paradise. An image was starting to form in my mind. Me and Martin, alone, away from all of the noise and hubbub of our normal lives, getting married – just the two of us.

A Baby, a Bride and "the Wheelbarrow"

I started to do my research. Lots of resorts in St Lucia offered weddings. Of course, everything was very different 30 years ago. Now, you'd organise things years in advance, with a wedding planner, an elaborate reception and a lot of fuss. Back then, you could just fly out and get married if you fancied it. So that's what we did.

In Watford, I found a white minidress from a little boutique. To be honest, I didn't even think of it as my "wedding" dress – it was an "in case I get married on holiday" dress. It was short, off the shoulder and made out of the same spongy material as an old-fashioned swimsuit. I bought a white bow for my hair. I rolled it all up and shoved it into my suitcase – I was used to going on tour and packing light, so I was good at finding clothes made from materials that didn't crease.

We flew out in November and spent a few days lying in the sun, resting, relaxing and recuperating from work. After about a week, I popped down to the hotel reception and asked, "Can you do weddings?" It was all very casual. I might as well have been asking for a late check-out or an extra egg at breakfast.

"Hello ma'am," the receptionist said. "Yes, we do. The next day we have available is 14 November. Does that suit you?"

14 November. 14 November. *Something* was happening on that day. What could it be? Suddenly, it came to me. I'd been trying to conceive by tracking my basal temperature, to work out when we had the best chance of getting pregnant. 14 November was my ovulation day.

"The 14th would be perfect!" I beamed. "Thanks very much!"

Of course, it didn't mean anything, necessarily. I'd tried to conceive on ovulation days before and nothing had happened. Still, I felt a little tingle. Something about that date gave me a very good feeling indeed.

The big day arrived. To be honest, it didn't seem like a big day. I wasn't anxious or overwhelmed. I didn't feel like a nervous new bride, worried about the trip down the aisle and the beginning of my future. I was in paradise with the love of my life. We knew in our hearts exactly how we felt about each other. It was time to make it official and share it with the rest of the world. For the sake of tradition, Martin and I got ready separately. I put on my new dress and then made my way to the clifftop where the ceremony was meant to take place.

I'd been planning to walk to the ceremony and gather my thoughts while enjoying the soft sea breeze. But as I walked along the beach and caught sight of the area in the distance, I started to panic. The hotel had set up the space, and it was everything I'd hoped for – quiet, remote and secluded, on a clifftop overlooking the sea. I could just see the flutter of a soft, white cotton gazebo. It looked stunning. The problem was that I hadn't worked out how I was going to get up to the top of the cliff. Climbing would take a long time, and I'd be late for my own wedding. Also, I'll admit that I'd been imagining Martin's face and the way he'd look at me when he saw me in my outfit. In my fantasy, I hadn't been covered in dust and pebbles, holding my shoes.

Luckily, I caught sight of a jeep driving along the road beside me. It was an emergency wedding car! The driver kindly stopped for me and offered me a lift. I didn't arrive at my wedding in a Rolls Royce or a gleaming white limo. Instead, I was standing up on the back of a battered jeep, surrounded by empty petrol cans and spare tyres. Yet I wouldn't have had it any other way.

The ceremony was perfect. Just Martin and me, with our officiant and a couple of people from the hotel who had kindly offered to be witnesses. It was a very simple, traditional ceremony, but after she pronounced us married, the officiant said something that has stayed with me forever. Touching our clasped hands, she beamed at us and said, "I bless any children you have."

At that moment I thought of my grandmother, and the way she'd felt about us as an unmarried couple. I'd resigned myself to living with her disapproval. Of course, her attitude had always made me feel sad, but it hadn't ever been enough to change my mind. We'd been trying for a baby for years at this point. Still, when I heard the officiant's words, I could almost feel my grandmother's feelings dissolving. Maybe our babies didn't need to come into the world because of wheatgrass smoothies, or temperature charts, or even "the wheelbarrow"! Maybe they'd just needed a blessing.

10

The Blessing Comes True

Shirlie

We didn't know it at the time, but Harley was conceived on our wedding night, 14 November 1988, as the soft wind blew the curtains, to the sound of Mica Paris's 'You Are My One Temptation'. As soon as we arrived home from our trip, the celebrations started. We'd had a wedding and a honeymoon, and now our friends were desperate to toast us.

It was such a joyful time that, for once, I'd stopped thinking about pregnancy and my body. I'd spent so many years trying, planning, dreaming and despairing. It was wonderful to focus on something else and let my baby fever fade into the background. I had a husband – I was a wife! And it felt as though everyone we knew wanted to give us a wedding reception. So when I had to leave a party early because I was feeling ill, I assumed I was tired and I'd had a little too much to drink. The hangover lasted for the whole of the next day. And the next day. This was weird. I'd only had a couple of gin and tonics. What was going on?

I did what I always did when I was feeling poorly and went to see my mum.

"It's really strange," I told her. "Do you think I've picked up some kind of bug? I'm hot, I'm nauseous, I'm a little dizzy – but no one else seems to have it. Martin is fine. You'd think I'd have caught it from someone."

When Mum looked at me, I almost knew what she was going to say before the words came out of her mouth. My heart leapt, even as another wave of nausea rose up through my body.

"Do you think," she said, slowly, "that you could be pregnant?"

My poor mum didn't see me for dust. I rushed back to the flat and Martin, stopping at a chemist on the way.

"Martin," I said carefully. "I think—"

"I know!" he interrupted, looking as though he couldn't contain himself. "I was starting to wonder! Do you think...?"

Martin has always been the smiliest person I know, but his grin was so enormous it could have broken his jaw in half. He reminded me of a little boy on Christmas Eve. We were both so excited and so scared that we couldn't quite say the words. We'd been disappointed so many times and I didn't want to get our hopes up. But this felt different.

We went to the bathroom together and I did the test. We waited, and waited, and waited. I think it took two minutes but it seemed like two hours. The second line appeared. We were having a baby.

Martin wrapped his arms around me, holding me tightly, as we both welled up and whispered to each other.

"I can't believe it! I can't believe it!" I kept murmuring, holding the pregnancy test in wonder, staring at the lines in the little window as though this was the lost Ark of the Covenant, tears rolling down our faces.

"Oh, Shirlie! Our baby! Our family!" said Martin, dreamily.

In that moment, all of my worries evaporated. I'd been scared about whether he'd ever really be ready for this, but he was every bit as excited as I was. I was experiencing more joy than I'd ever felt in my life before, and he doubled it. We spent hours up in that bathroom, unable to contain our happiness. It was as though we'd won the lottery. No, it was *better* than winning the lottery.

For the next few months, we treated the pregnancy test as though it was our baby. We kept it in the bathroom cabinet for ages, and every day we'd take it out and gaze at it in wonder. Telling our friends was wonderful, because they'd known how badly we'd longed for this moment. When my best friend Gail came round, she was barely through the front door before I'd dragged her inside and said I had something important to tell her. I waited for her to scream and hug me but, instead, she smiled. Then she slowly lifted up her jumper.

"Oh, Shirlie, I'm so, so happy," she said, looking almost relieved, "because I'm pregnant, too! I didn't know *how* I was going to tell you. I'm three months along. We can be mummies together!"

The timing was perfect. Getting pregnant was the best thing that ever happened to me, but being pregnant alongside my best friend was a joy. It was such a glorious experience to share.

I was lucky, because I loved being pregnant so much. I think my uncontained enthusiasm helped, but it was as if the universe was trying to pay me back a bit after years of crippling period pain. Gail came over and I made healthy salads and smoothies for us. My body grew huge, and I adored it. When I'd been younger, I'd wasted so much time worrying about my body and wanting to be slimmer. Now, I felt enormous – literally great with child. But as far as I was concerned, it was the bigger, the better. My bust went from a size 28 to a 42! I felt like an Earth Mother, bursting with fertility.

During my pregnancy, I was very active and still performing as part of Pepsi and Shirlie. Looking back, I was quite arrogant and very naïve. When I asked Mum about childbirth, she was quite vague.

"Oh, it's not too bad," she said, airily. "You just popped out, really!"

Because I was hypermobile, and dancing on stage even at the start of my third trimester, I didn't think I needed to bother with any birthing classes. I'd imagined going into labour and wowing the doctors and nurses. Surely everything about motherhood was going to be completely instinctive – and natural. I'd just lift my leg, point my toes into the air and gently, gracefully, push my baby out of my body.

Obviously it didn't quite go as planned.

After my experience in China, I'd become interested in Buddhism and started to explore different kinds of alternative medicine and healing. Most hospitals seemed so sterile, and my experience with the beautiful Doctor Ursula had really opened my eyes to the idea that it was worth choosing a doctor who was right for you. You didn't just have to go to your local GP and do what they told you. I was so excited to find a hospital called The Garden, because I hated hospitals and this sounded like a magical experience like a part in Shakespeare's *A Midsummer Night's Dream*.

I longed to bring my baby into the world as naturally as possible. I think The Garden was so relaxed that Harley really took her time – once my contractions started, it took her 48 hours to make an appearance. It was a magical August night and, as Martin was driving home from the hospital, he noticed the sky was filled with a huge, golden harvest moon. It was a present from the universe, a sign from somewhere, marking the birth of our beautiful little girl. That's why Moon is her middle name.

11

My New Identities:
Dad and Reggie Kray

Martin

When I was bitten by the acting bug, I knew it was going to be one of the greatest loves of my life. Still, during my 20s, acting was the one that got away. Being in the band gave me the chance to perform – and Spandau were very lucky to be around during the era of the music video.

The MTV cable channel was launched in America in the summer of 1981, and record companies quickly realised that video was an investment. If they spent a bit of money on a production that looked really good, that money was multiplied by record sales as the video was shown all over the world. Music videos became three-minute mini movies, getting more and more elaborate with bigger and more extravagant plots.

My experience as a child actor haunted me. When acting was good, I felt total flow. I loved being in the zone, with the sense of focus and the chance to be completely absorbed in my work. When acting was bad – well, I had to take my clothes off and felt horribly self-conscious about the whole thing. Also, my acting career had started organically. I'd got very lucky with Anna Scher, and she'd given me the room to develop a skill without pushing me into it.

The opportunities just kept turning up. Towards the end of the 80s, we knew the band was probably reaching the end of the road. Gary was keen to quit and do something else altogether. The music scene was changing, and we had to make way for a different style of pop, as dance and DJ culture started to take over. Our record sales were beginning to drop. I'd had to beg Gary to make our album *Heart Like A Sky*.

"We really need to make one more record before we give this up," I pleaded, more out of insecurity about the future than actually wanting to carry on.

Deep down, I didn't want to make any more music, but I was scared of a future that didn't have the band in it. And what about the others? We all had partners, and some of the boys had young families. I'd grown up in Spandau, which meant I hadn't really grown up at all. Ever since I was 17, I'd had a record company managing my life. Now I was approaching my 30s – what could life possibly look like without a structure that came from tour schedules and recording sessions? I was in a state of arrested development and panicking when opportunity knocked.

Our old friends Dominic Anciano and Ray Burgess had an exciting project. We'd worked with them a few times over the years, as they'd ended up directing some of our videos. They had the backing to make a feature film, securing the rights to the story of the twin gangsters, Ronnie and Reggie Kray, and they wanted me and Gary to play the lead roles. We were brothers, we were Londoners and, even though most people didn't know about it, we had acting experience.

Filming started when Harley was on her way and, at first, it was easy to leave Shirlie. She was surrounded by her friends and family, and was blooming. She adored being pregnant. I felt as though my life was completely coming together. My career was taking off in an exciting new direction, and I was about to become a father. I couldn't have been happier, and I was fully focused on the future. When you work in entertainment, you always feel a bit insecure about your work. No matter how well things are going, you know you won't always be working and everything could disappear tomorrow. This brilliant new job meant I'd be providing for my growing family.

Still, not everything was easy. It was very hard for the other members of Spandau to come to terms with the fact that Gary and I were moving on. We avoided mentioning *The Krays*, or the future. If only they knew Gary had wanted it over months ago, but I'd kept it going.

At one of our last gigs, we reached the theatre and noticed every single seat had a flyer advertising the film, with my and Gary's faces on it. I felt so guilty and very awkward. I knew that if I wasn't doing this job, I'd be feeling lost and very jealous of anyone who was coming out of the band with a plan.

Towards the end of filming, Harley was born and Shirlie struggled with post-natal depression. Harley was a gorgeous baby, and I was so proud of my two girls, but I think that the reality of motherhood hit Shirlie quite hard. She's so loving and nurturing, and we both believed that as new parents we'd instinctively know what to do. It was a shock to realise that we felt like children ourselves, fumbling around in the dark and trying to get used to our new reality. I was lucky. I could go off into an exciting new world every day and pretend for a living. It was hard work, but it was also what I loved and was really fun. Shirlie didn't get to have any time off.

The premiere of *The Krays* was so exciting. It was a moment that I'd been waiting for. Ever since I was a kid I'd dreamt about being an old-fashioned movie star, like James Cagney, Marlon Brando and Elvis. And this was my moment. Gary and I had our names all over the posters, the flashbulbs were popping and everyone was dressed up clapping as I walked arm in arm with Shirlie into the Leicester Square Odeon.

It felt different from the rush of a Spandau concert. Deep down, I'd always felt a little bit insecure about my role in the band. At the beginning, I was happy to be the one on the posters – I felt as though that was my job. But the others were such talented singers and musicians. When Tony sang, he got to display his true talent. He was out at the front, giving so much soul and meaning to all of those beautiful songs that Gary had written. Steve's saxophone set us apart too, and I was in awe of John's drumming.

I wasn't envious of their talents. I was just glad to be in a band with people who could play like they did. Still, I wished I was a better musician. It was nice that people liked the way I looked, but it didn't have anything to do with who I was, or what I was capable of. On a good day, it was a joy to hear a song on the radio, or get a good chart result, and have four friends to share it with. On a bad day, I sometimes struggled to feel as though any of that success really belonged to me. The hit song 'True', which was all bass synth, was as it happens the only song I didn't play a bass guitar to, and became our biggest hit... so I had to mime along on the TV.

But I could be completely proud of *The Krays*. I knew I'd done a good job – and although I really hoped Shirlie and my mum and dad liked it, I didn't need anyone to praise me. I felt secure. I was so happy to be at the premiere, though, that I'd forgotten to warn Shirlie about what was coming up.

She knew her husband was playing a violent gangster who was believed to have murdered people. She was braced for parts of the film to be shocking. But neither of us was prepared for the most shocking part of all. My love scene with my co-star, Kate Hardie, who played Reggie's wife, Frances.

There is *nothing* romantic about filming a love scene. This wasn't even a rude one. Reggie proposes to Frances and presents her with a beautiful brooch before they kiss. It's set in a rose garden and it's very tender. Soft music plays in the background. Filming with Kate was awkward though, with the two of us trying to make each other laugh to ease the tension.

"Shall I lean my head to the right or the left?" asked Kate. "I don't want you to hurt your nose on my face!"

"I don't mind," I replied. "As long as you haven't been eating onions, my nose will be fine!"

The trouble is that if a film is any good, it's *convincing.*

So when poor Shirlie saw the final scene, she wasn't watching a pair of actors trying to do one of the more embarrassing parts of their jobs as quickly and efficiently as possible. She saw her husband, and the father of her newborn baby, whispering tender, loving words to a film star. I've thought about it, and I know that if the situation were reversed I'd hate to watch Shirlie acting in a love scene. But because the finished product looked so different from what I remembered, it simply hadn't occurred to me that watching me was going to be difficult.

"You were really, really good," said Shirlie, afterwards. "I think this is the start of big things for you, Mr Movie Star. But I wish I'd brought a cushion to hide behind. I don't think I can bear to see you kissing anyone else, ever again."

It was one thing for Shirlie to see me covered in fake blood, engaged in a shoot-out. I suppose it's obvious that it's not real. But on-screen romance was hard to watch, and the work I was getting offered in the early 90s involved plenty of on-screen kissing – and more.

The success of *The Krays* meant that Gary and I were in line for lots of exciting opportunities, and we had the chance to audition for film roles in Los Angeles. In the early 90s, after the massive success of films such as *Basic Instinct*, every movie script sent to me seemed to feature a big sex scene. I suppose it was a way for an independent film to make a splash without having to feature expensive special effects.

I *hated* filming those scenes. Obviously, there's nothing sexy about them. If you're very lucky, you get to make them with someone who knows how awkward they are, who you can have a laugh with between takes. But even when I managed to get past the difficulty of filming, and feeling strange and self-conscious, it was really hard to put that work into the world knowing it would make Shirlie very unhappy if she saw it.

Still, Shirlie was always pretty pragmatic. But I knew deep down it was killing her.

We were both torn. She desperately wanted me to be at home with her and Harley – but she knew I loved to work, and that I couldn't wait to land my next film role.

I missed her like crazy when I was away, but I was also happier than I'd ever been. I'd spent my 20s being swept away by life's tides. I always felt grateful to end up where I'd landed, but it felt as though fate was in charge of my final destination. Now, I was choosing where I wanted to go. I was working to establish myself in an industry I truly loved, and I had my beautiful, brilliant wife and my gorgeous daughter beside me. Life couldn't have been better.

But we had even more good luck to come.

After Harley was born, Shirlie and I knew that we wanted another baby. Still, because Harley took years of trying, we didn't think it was going to be easy. We promised ourselves that we wouldn't get too hung up about it.

"If it happens, it happens," we said to each other.

It was a really busy time. I was going to America and, when Harley was really tiny, Shirlie was still making music as a member of Pepsi and Shirlie. Harley was a very sweet-natured, happy baby, but she kept us very occupied, too. We didn't really give ourselves time to think too far into the future. We just wanted to enjoy being a family, and to keep little Harley out of mischief.

I've always thought that Harley's birth must have helped Shirlie's endometriosis, clearing out all of the tissue and growth that had been making it so hard for her to conceive, because it felt as though we'd blinked for a minute and suddenly Roman was on his way. We had no idea what to expect, but he made it clear that he was a showman, even before he'd come out into the world.

When Shirlie was just over eight months pregnant and in the last throes of her pregnancy, I was offered a film role in Los Angeles. We had to make some difficult decisions.

I'd be away for a while and, if I left without her, I would miss the birth. There are rules about when you're allowed to fly to America during a pregnancy, and Shirlie was well past the cut-off point. They don't want the baby to be born on the plane and, more importantly, they don't want the baby to leave the country with an American passport. What were we going to do? We decided to risk it. We'd be staying with Gary, and George was out there, too. We'd be surrounded by friends and family, so we figured we might as well go out together. After all, the baby wasn't due for another two weeks.

Little did we know that baby Roman wanted to give us a sneak preview of what was to come when we were at passport control.

If you've ever been to America, you'll know just how strange and stressful that immigration queue can be. You might get off the plane feeling relaxed at the prospect of a fortnight's holiday. You're looking forward to a day at Disneyland, thinking about the enormous breakfasts ahead of you, and wondering if you should have brought a slightly bigger pair of shorts. Then, as you edge towards the front of the line, you start to feel as though you're starring in *The Shawshank Redemption*. The customs officials seem so serious and stern, able to see into your soul. They make you feel like a criminal even if you can't remember what it is you're meant to have done. The minute you cross that red line you feel guilty of something.

And this time we *were* guilty, and I could see it was written across Shirlie's face. We were smuggling our unborn child across the border under a pile of coats.

Poor Shirlie had a huge winter coat, a cardigan and a sweater swaddled against her bump to disguise it. She was uncomfortably hot. Not trusting myself to speak, I squeezed her hand when we were both called up to the booths. Luckily, the counters were set at chest height, so the bump was concealed – but Shirlie's face was so flushed she looked like a neon sign. I saw a droplet of sweat gather on her forehead and roll down to her chin, like a crystal falling off a chandelier. *It's OK, breathe, we'll be out of here soon,* I thought, hoping she could read my mind.

For a second, she turned white, then neon again. She let out the tiniest sigh. She looked like she was in a lot of pain.

Oh no… I'd seen her do this before.

Shirlie was doing everything she could to stay conscious while the official checked her passport. Luckily, he was so engrossed in the forms that he didn't look up and see what was right in front of him – a heavily pregnant British woman who appeared to be going into labour. Still, he seemed to be taking absolutely ages. Was he reading passport forms or Ikea flat-pack instructions in 17 different languages? It was just taking forever.

Shirlie was amazing. She was so brave and just managed to stay conscious until we were out on the other side. We fell into each other's arms, a collision of coats and cardigans.

"Martin," Shirlie said, hoarsely, "I think we should probably go to a…" She broke off, wincing. Another contraction had arrived and I wasn't waiting for any more. I grabbed the coats.

We took a taxi to Cedars Sinai – famous for patients such as Frank Sinatra, Elizabeth Taylor… and our second child.

Well, having caused maximum drama, Roman wasn't ready to come out just yet. Shirlie had been going through Braxton Hicks contractions, which sometimes happen during the later stages of pregnancy as your body prepares for birth. They feel exactly like the real thing, but it was really Roman announcing himself as a coming attraction. He had a message for us, and it was "Stay tuned!" The doctors were able to reassure us that everything was healthy and normal, so we left the hospital and headed for Gary's house. At least Shirlie would have some time to relax before Roman arrived.

10 days later, the day came. Unlike his big sister, Roman's arrival was very quick. I think Harley felt very cosy in the womb and was reluctant to leave – but Roman

couldn't wait to get out and greet us. He came out with his right arm raised up against his head, in a sort of power salute, part rock star, part Superman.

The Los Angeles birth experience was a strange one, too. Harley's hippy birth at The Garden had been a little on the woo side for me, but it was joyful, nurturing and gentle. I wanted to film the birth so my baby could see the moment they joined the world, but no nurse would be filmed holding Roman, just in case we caught them doing something wrong and found a reason to sue them. Culturally, the experiences were completely different. Still, nothing could bring us down. Our little family was complete, and we were high on joy. From that moment on, the four of us were a little gang.

Over the years, Shirlie and I have received plenty of feedback on our parenting – and not always from our kids. We were both very aware of what we loved about growing up, and what we struggled with. I wanted Harley and Roman to be as close as Gary and I, but I also wanted to encourage them to embrace their own individual identities and paths. There's no doubt that having a big brother like Gary is what set me on my path. His talent, drive and dedication inspired me. But while I never felt as though I was in his shadow, he was the one who made an effort, and I never really pushed myself. Following in his footsteps meant I was going somewhere exciting – and it wasn't until I was well into my 30s that I felt I was really breaking out on my own. I wanted Harley and Roman to support each other and have plenty of common ground, but we wanted to make sure they both had the room to go and do their own thing.

I think it was especially important to Shirlie that our kids grew up in an environment of unconditional love. Her house had been chaotic, filled with noise, squabbling siblings and parents. She wanted Harley and Roman to live in a home that was filled with love and peace, where there was space to move and everyone could hear themselves think. Early on, we both realised that the four of us needed to be a squad. We were all best friends. And instinctively, we knew that we couldn't ask our children to respect us unless we showed respect for them as well.

We never had a naughty step, or time-outs or bribes. We always tried to be as honest and straightforward as possible, and never used the phrase "Because I say so!" We just wanted to be consistent and to make sure there was room for discussions and debates rather than arguments. When Harley and Roman started school, some of their friends' parents said they weren't sure about our methods, and they thought the children might be growing up too fast. The thing is that we had to do things a little bit differently, because we weren't a normal family – or rather, we were often in situations that normal families don't face.

*　*　*

Harley is one of the funniest people I know – in fact, the only person who is as funny as Shirlie. When we're all together, the two of them make me laugh until tears are running down my face and I'm begging for mercy. It's like having Peter Cook and Dudley Moore in your kitchen, riffing off each other. Harley has an aptitude for music, but she also has a real talent for accents.

Harley's always said she wants to be the one behind the camera, not in front of it. But she's beginning to edge towards the limelight and is starting to share her beautiful voice with the world. Her latest single 'Space' has just entered the country charts at number one. Yet she's always just wanted to get her head down and graft. She hated school and didn't want to go to university, so we decided to invest the money we would have spent on her course fees on building a photographic studio for her. She was earning money from taking photographs within a year of leaving school. We're lucky in that I've been able to introduce her to some of the best photographers in the business – but she's proved herself time and time again.

Roman also had an unconventional academic path. He's been entertaining people since before he could talk, and it was obvious to everyone that he was destined to be in entertainment. Harley can be uncomfortable about attracting attention, but Roman does it with ease. It's fascinating to watch, because he's not needy with it – just very relaxed in the spotlight. I think that's why we ended up choosing the parenting style we picked. If we'd been parents who believed children should be seen and not heard, we would have suppressed so much of Roman's personality. I think one of the reasons that he's such a natural broadcaster is because he's never had to fight for attention – he's always known that he'll be listened to!

I'd much rather my kids are on the loud side, because the alternative could have been tragic. When Roman was about two and a half, we'd gone on holiday to the south of France with George, Kenny and a load of friends. It was a baking hot day and everyone was lazing around the infinity pool. The view was stunning, the kids were playing happily and I felt completely relaxed.

The awful thing about being a parent is that you can pride yourself on how well everything is going – and it only takes half a second for you to stop paying attention and then something terrible happens. We know that children need careful supervision around water, but I wasn't worried about Roman. There were 10 of us around the pool, in George's house in St Tropez, keeping an eye and an ear out, and he was playing with Harley, who was very mature around water. It was a scorching day, clear blue skies with a scent of jasmine in the air drifting over from the beautiful garden. But just as I allowed myself to nod off, I suddenly found myself sitting bolt upright. I hadn't heard a sound or seen a splash, but when I looked at the pool I realised Roman was under the water, not moving.

I *flew* into the water and dived in to get him. He hadn't been there for more than a couple of seconds, but it was long enough to terrify me. I scooped him out – his eyes were open, looking up at me from under the water, but he was frozen – amazingly, he was fine. He'd been fascinated by the water flowing over the edge of the infinity pool and, as he leaned over to stare at it, he'd fallen in and the jets on the side had pushed him under.

Roman was giggling about his underwater adventure, but I was devastated. For the next couple of days, I found myself crying almost constantly. I couldn't stop thinking about what could have happened and the consequences if I'd been too late. For me, parenting had been filled with joy and was so much about being in the moment, that the incident took me by surprise and brought home to me just how vulnerable my children were.

I felt vulnerable, too. Every day, in a different way, you realise your life isn't simple and straightforward any more. No matter how exciting and rewarding my life was before I became a dad, this was something else. I was in a different realm. Being Harley and Roman's father has brought me joy on a level that I didn't know it was possible to experience. But seeing them hurt or in trouble has brought me more pain than it was possible to feel. Still, I would never change a thing. Becoming a dad is the greatest and most rewarding role I've ever taken on.

12

"They Need to Operate"

Shirlie

Martin's near-death experience started on the Los Angeles freeway.

We'd been living in LA for the last few years, enjoying the easy living that comes with California. Multi-lane traffic, beautiful people driving their beautiful cars at 90 miles an hour, the sunlight gleaming off the bumpers, and The Beach Boys on the radio. The great and the good of Hollywood was all here buzzing, and concentrating on major deals.

Zooming around with Martin was very different from crawling around Hampstead at four miles an hour. We loved driving along the Pacific Coast highway with the sea on the left and the Hollywood hills on the right. California really felt like home. I put my arm across the back of his neck as he was driving. It's something that I did a lot.

"Shirlie, just rub back of my head for me," he'd beg as he often would – and I was always happy to do it.

Martin had never looked healthier or more handsome. He was glowing and tanned, he loved going to the gym, and was really looking after himself, in accordance with California culture. Every time he went to an audition, he was competing for parts with the most gorgeous people on the planet – people who lived on their looks, who would choose wheatgrass over whisky every time.

I reached over to rub his head, and that's when I noticed it felt strange and out of shape. I wasn't sure I recognised it. Still, I was more curious than anxious.

Maybe he'd overexerted himself at the gym, or maybe he just needed to adjust the car seat.

"I think you should see someone – I think you have a bump on your head," I said. "It's probably nothing, but get it checked out."

It wasn't a soft tissue lump – it was his skull, as if it had changed shape. Martin told me he'd take care of it and went to see a doctor.

"They said it was nothing," he said, laughing. "You worry too much!"

Sometimes I wonder whether Martin ever went to the doctor, or if he just wrote it off as another one of Shirlie's flights of fancy. He knew that ever since I'd come back from China, I'd become a semi-professional worrier. I blew things out of proportion and he calmed me down. But even I stopped worrying about the lump.

Still, a couple of months later, the lump was still there. I asked myself if it had grown, but it was hard to tell. We'd come back to Highgate for Christmas. We'd planned to stay in London for a little while to spend time with the family. Frank and Eileen, his mum and dad, came to stay on Christmas Day, and it was such a happy occasion.

Being at home in frosty England in December felt a little bit magical, after all of that California sunshine. Harley and Roman were breathless with excitement about Santa's visit and having the chance to spend time with their grandma and grandpa. I'd cooked dinner in our cosy kitchen, and everything had gone strangely smoothly. The turkey was juicy, the roast potatoes were crispy – even the sprouts were tasty. As twilight turned slowly to night, I looked at the people I loved most in the light of the Christmas tree and felt very, very lucky. At that moment, I loved my life and everyone in it. Things hadn't always been easy, but I'd reached that perfect moment, and I felt incredibly grateful.

Shortly after Christmas, Martin flew out to film *The Outer Limits* in Canada and noticed that the lump was growing out of control. As soon as he returned to London, he made an appointment with his GP, who referred him for a scan. The GP thought it could be a calcium growth and, to be honest, I *still* wasn't too worried. Martin seemed so fit and healthy. I was sure it couldn't be anything too serious and that the doctors would quickly sort it out.

It was a typical grey wintry day when Martin went to hospital. The novelty of being back in London was starting to wear off. I was trying to get Harley off to school while trying to persuade baby Roman that not everything was for eating or climbing on. I was on my feet constantly. When the phone rang, I snatched it up, assuming it was Martin calling to say that everything was fine, but I was half-thinking, *That'd better not be another double-glazing salesman.*

It was Martin, and he sounded very, very far away. He was completely spaced out, almost drunk on fear. "I have a brain tumour," he said. "They need to operate."

My body went into shock. I didn't scream or cry. I just felt numb. Like a marionette, having my strings pulled by the universe. But I somehow found my shoes, bundled Roman into a car seat and drove off. I still don't know how I made it to the hospital safely – or without getting a speeding fine.

Martin's consultant explained what he'd found, but we were both too shocked to take anything in. Hysterically, I begged to take Martin back to California to get a second opinion. The doctor must have made a mistake. How could my handsome, healthy husband possibly have a brain tumour? No other doctor had spotted it.

"I really don't want to get on a plane, I want to stay here," said Martin. Maybe it was the lights in the consultant's office, but his tan seemed to have vanished since he left the house that morning.

We drove home in silence. His operation had been scheduled for the following Monday. I couldn't bring myself to tell him just how scared I was. He'd always been the one to comfort me, reassure me and tell me that everything was going to be OK. But this time he couldn't. And in that moment, he certainly didn't have the words to tell me how terrified and vulnerable he felt.

I'd like to say we spent the weekend enjoying Martin's last window of freedom, but we were still deep in shock and barely speaking to each other. Thank goodness for Harley and Roman. We managed to cobble together some version of normality for them. Daddy had hurt his head, but he was going to hospital and they were going to make him better. Kids are brilliant at keeping you in the moment, too, and stopping you from brooding. Every time Harley wanted to show us a picture, or Roman stood up and sang a song, we could forget what was happening for a little bit.

On the Sunday, my friend came over and shaved Martin's head in preparation for the surgery. Martin was still the beautiful man I'd fallen in love with, but his shaved head broke my heart. I kept thinking about the moment I'd met him in the theatre, all those years ago, and how much he looked like a poster come to life. His hair wasn't just part of his good looks. It had been an expression of his creativity, and it had defined his image. I wondered how much it bothered him. I suspected he didn't want to seem vain, as he faced such serious surgery, but he was losing an important part of his identity. It must have hurt.

By five o'clock on Monday, I must have paced every inch of tile on our tiny kitchen floor at least a thousand times. I couldn't eat, concentrate or sit still. I just walked around and waited, longing for the phone call, hoping for news that everything had gone well and Martin was going to be OK. The kind consultant had assured us that he would perform the operation to the very best of his abilities but also warned us, "This is an extremely complicated procedure, and I can't make any promises." Finally, the phone rang. Martin was conscious. The operation had taken much longer than expected, but they had been able to remove a tumour the size of a grapefruit.

I drove back to the hospital with Frank and Eileen, still dazed. As soon as I saw Martin, I broke down. The tears came so hard, and I couldn't breathe properly. Gently, Eileen led me to the corridor to help me get my breath back.

I felt a warm hand on my shoulder. "Oh, love, are you OK?" a voice said. "Can I get you a drink of water?"

It took me a moment to realise my comforter had been standing next to the bed beside Martin's, the mother of a teenage son who had also gone through some major surgery. My heart swelled in that moment. I couldn't quite believe that someone who was going through the same sort of pain as me, visiting a loved one in hospital, was able to be so kind and so selfless. That moment gave me hope. No matter what I was going through, or how difficult it was, I was never going to be on my own. Another burst of hope shot through me when I felt another hand in mine. Martin's. He was exhausted from the surgery and couldn't speak, but he was able to give me a reassuring squeeze.

To some extent, everyone's life is filled with tragedy and drama. When I was younger, I used to look at other people and wonder how they knew how to live. As a little girl, everyone else seemed to know what they were doing, and seemed to have easier, happier lives than mine. Then, when I became an accidental pop star, I felt confused and panicky. Life was great fun, but lots of it seemed to be completely beyond my control. If the universe had any kind of plan for me, it was never going to let me in on the secret – or even give me a clue. Life was mad, scary and chaotic, and just when everything felt happy and calm, the rug would be pulled from under my feet. There were points when I would have swapped lives with anyone in the world for the sake of a little stability.

Now, I realise that any stability we have is imaginary. Anyone I've ever envied, even briefly, has almost certainly muddled their way through their fair share of tragedy and drama. Also, when we go through something scary, painful and shocking, we tend to rationalise it. We want to believe that we always knew everything would work out. The alternative is much scarier. We don't want to look back and admit that we were confused and terrified, and that our happy ending is down to luck.

Yet I never want to forget the way I felt after Martin's operation. It would be easier to tell myself that deep down I knew he'd get better and life would go back to normal. But the truth is that I *didn't* know. I was desperately scared. Since he was ill, I've lost count of the number of people who've been through major surgery and asked me for advice and comfort. They've been scared, too. We tell each other it's important to "stay strong".

We put an enormous amount of pressure on ourselves to hide our feelings, to keep things together and to make sure our friends and families don't feel burdened by our pain. But I know that I felt desperately vulnerable and uncertain at that time – and remembering this is what helps me to appreciate every day we now have together. It also reminds me to offer comfort and support to people who need it, and to understand that they may not feel able to ask for it.

Martin's illness changed our lives forever, in huge ways and in tiny ways. I'm not sure I'll ever be able to describe the tumours as a gift or feel grateful for them. But I'll always be grateful for the way it brought me closer to people, opened up my sense of compassion and taught me that, together, there's nothing we can't survive.

13

The Luck of the Draw

Martin

Do you believe in fate? I'm honestly not sure I do. There are some things in my life that seem as though they were meant to happen. I know there are some people I was definitely supposed to meet. But more than anything, I think I believe in luck.

I was lucky when I bumped into Shirlie at the theatre. Lucky when Gary and his mates asked me to join the band. Lucky that Dominic Anciano and Ray Burgess bought the rights to *The Krays*, after making all of our Spandau videos. But strangely the luckiest thing that has ever happened to me was going through the experience of having a brain tumour.

OK, technically it was the experience of having *two* brain tumours.

When Shirlie first discovered the strange, bumpy groove on my head, I didn't panic. In fact, I was too calm.

"I reckon that's always been there, I just never knew." I laughed. "Maybe your skull changes shape a bit as you get into your 20s!" Because it *was* my skull we could feel. If the growth had been soft, I think we'd both have panicked, but the bumpy bit was clearly solid bone.

It was an exciting time. I was between London and LA, flying out for work and staying for a few weeks. The work was starting to get more regular and more exciting. I was getting decent roles on big TV shows, and I was thrilled when I was offered a job on the *Outer Limits* reboot, filming in Canada.

The Outer Limits had been a big sci-fi show in the 60s. It was a little like *The Twilight Zone,* but a bit darker and weirder, with more of a focus on the science of the supernatural. The remake was a big deal, and everyone wanted to be considered for a part. I was delighted when I was given a great role with a brilliant storyline. I was a scientist who'd discovered the secret of eternal life, only in my experimenting, I'd made a mistake – even though I'd never die, I'd age at an accelerated rate.

Towards the end of filming, my life took a terrifying turn. Truth became stranger than fiction.

I was getting ready for my final scene – my character had gone to hospital, having reached the age of 200. Sitting in the make-up trailer, I went through my lines.

Make-up trailers are such noisy places. You have five or six make-up artists, a gang of chatty actors and the radio turned up as loud as it'll go, so that people can hear it over the roar of the hairdryers. You can barely hear yourself think. Yet, when I put on my bald wig, everyone went very, very quiet. You could have heard a pin drop.

I stared into the mirror. I could feel my head heat up under the bald cap and a bead of sweat came running down the side of my nose. I knew I was in trouble there and then. That lump Shirlie said she could feel as she stroked the back of my neck had grown. I had never seen it like this. It looked huge. I could see the make-up artist trying not to look and acting as if she hadn't noticed. I just wanted to get this last scene over with so I could call Shirlie.

My concentration was on the floor during that last scene. I couldn't remember any of my lines, but I scrambled my way through it with a few extra grunts and puffs. What on earth could be wrong with me? Something terrifying was happening to my body. I'd thought I was in the best shape of my life. I was in the gym all the time, I wasn't drinking alcohol, and I'd been living on salads and taking extra vitamins. I thought I was as healthy as it was possible for a human to be. But my head said otherwise.

As soon as filming was over, I flew home and made a doctor's appointment for as soon as possible. I was referred for an MRI scan, and I knew that something was wrong when the doctor rang me at the gym.

"I'm really not supposed to tell you this over the phone, but we need you to come in for a consultation as soon as possible," he said. "We found a lump."

I was confused. A lump of what? The word "tumour" hadn't entered my head – even though, unbeknown to me, there *was* a giant tumour inside it. A lump sounded embarrassing but non-threatening. Something we could deal with.

"OK, what do we do next?" I asked.

The doctor was doing his best to be reassuring, but I could tell from his tone that this was serious. "I'm going to refer you to a consultant, and we'll go from there," he said. "The best thing we can do is move quickly on this one."

Shirlie rang me immediately – the doctor had tried the house first. "How are you feeling?" she asked.

It was a strange question, because physically I felt great. Never better. But mentally, I was badly shaken up. Still slightly jet-lagged, having spent an eight-hour flight doing anything I could to distract myself from my own fears. Just hours ago, I'd been a happy, successful actor working on a big set, looking forward to the future. Now, I was back in London and possibly seriously ill with an unknown condition. I couldn't work out what had happened, or how it had happened to me.

The next couple of days just passed in a blur. Was this it? Was there any coming back from this, a massive lump on my skull growing with every breath? I felt like I had a creature attached to me that wouldn't let go, his claws digging in further with every minute that passed. My mind was all over the place.

Shirlie took charge and organised my first appointment with the consultant, Dr Alan Crockard. I was too stunned to feel nervous and, walking into Dr Crockard's office, I felt reassured. It was an old-fashioned room with a high ceiling, bright and clean, with heavy, dark furniture. Dr Crockard sat down opposite us at his gleaming, wooden desk. It was somehow solid and reassuring. You could imagine Gregory Peck sitting at that desk in an old-fashioned film, delivering justice. This was a man we could trust. Surely he wasn't about to give us bad news?

"Mr and Mrs Kemp, thank you for coming in so quickly. Now, I have your scan, if you'd like to take a look." Dr Crockard gestured towards what appeared to be a piece of modern art.

All I could see was huge, floating blobs of black, white and grey, illuminated by a light box. Shirlie and I just stayed silent and looked at the X-ray. I could feel the blood drain from my face.

Dr Crockard continued, "So, that very large grey area at the top there – that's a tumour. And there's a much smaller tumour just here, under the brain – about the size of an almond."

It was the first time anyone had used the word "tumour" – and not just one, but two. From that moment, I felt as though I was trapped in a bubble that was rapidly filling up with water, though I was still aware of Shirlie and the doctor.

Shirlie had started crying. Usually, her tears broke my heart and I'd take her in my arms and hold her until she was OK. But I couldn't move. I couldn't feel or respond to anything that was going on in that room. I didn't have the space to process it. Shock is a very strange experience because it blocks out every emotion and response. I wasn't sad or angry or scared – just utterly numb, as if the devil had put his hand in my mouth and ripped my breath from out of me.

Dr Crockard explained that he believed he could help me, but that I would require a major operation. He would open my head up and cut out the large tumour. He wouldn't be able to reach the smaller tumour at the same time, but said, "We'll monitor it. We have a little time before we need to worry about that."

He smiled at us, and I knew he was being kind and reassuring, but I almost wanted to laugh at his choice of words. *He* may not be worried about the second tumour yet. But even in my state of shock I could see it was sitting right in the middle of my head. You don't have to be a doctor to know you're in trouble. Was that the little fella that was going to kill me?! I felt sick.

The operation would be scheduled for the following Monday – as quickly as possible. I took Shirlie's hand and we walked out in silence. We couldn't find the words to tell each other how we were feeling – or to comfort each other. But I think we managed to communicate just by being together. Neither of us wanted to burden the other one by breaking down. I wanted to tell her just how much I loved her, but I couldn't speak or begin to understand the full implications of the conversation we'd just had. Was I going to die?

My mum and dad were staying with us, and I knew that the news would devastate them. Mum, like me, had always been a weeper. She cried when she was sad – and when she was happy – and I knew that what I needed to say would hit her hard. Between us, though, Shirlie and I got the news out.

"And Dr Crockard says he thinks Martin has a really good chance with the operation – he seems to know his stuff," said Shirlie, desperate to find something positive to say that would stop Mum's tears.

Dad did what all men from North London do during times of crisis. He said, "Martin, put your coat on – we're going to the pub."

I never usually drank with my dad, but after three pints of Guinness with him, I was starting to feel philosophical, if not optimistic. We never spoke about what was going to happen over the coming months, but I'd never felt so connected to him. It was strange, as I had a feeling that I was letting him down.

That weekend, Shirlie's friend Claire, a hairdresser, came over to shave my head before the operation. She ended up just giving me a short crop. My head looked so strange and lumpy that she felt embarrassed to see me so exposed.

I told her not to worry. "Honestly, I couldn't care less! I'm just worried about staying alive at this point," I said, almost cheerfully.

During my recovery, *everyone* was obsessed with my hair and asked me whether I missed it. Now, I realise this was a way for people to focus on something minor. Talking about tumours is scary, and people worry that they are going to say the wrong thing or learn something they would rather not know.

Going through a serious illness knocks everyone's confidence and, over time, it would get harder to deal with the changes to my face and body. For the next couple of years, I wouldn't feel like myself, or look like myself. I wouldn't be able to recognise my face when I looked in the mirror. But that was a minor detail. All I wanted was to get rid of the tumour and to be able to look after Shirlie, Harley and Roman.

On the day of the surgery, Shirlie stayed with me until the last possible second. I'll never forget seeing her face getting smaller and smaller as I was wheeled away from her to the operating theatre. She was trying to smile, but I could see the tears glistening on her cheeks under the flickering hospital-hallway lighting. Her lips were moving – she was mouthing, "I love you." Would I ever see her again? Was this it?

I'd gone into the hospital as "Martin Kemp: celebrity". As I'd checked in at reception, a nurse had recognised me and asked for my autograph. It seemed like a final flare from my old life. Less than a week ago, I'd been making TV shows and I was used to being recognised – and was always happy to smile and sign. But in that moment, it was as though she'd mistaken me for someone else. The man I thought I was – "past me".

Even saying "I'm here for neurosurgery" seemed strange. I'd come here for *brain surgery*. I kept shocking myself with that information. When I was a dreamy schoolkid who hated paying attention in class, the other kids would tease me. "Oi, Kempy, are you stupid or something? You need brain surgery!" Well, they'd finally had their way. I did need brain surgery, and I was about to get some.

It's such a bizarre scenario that it's impossible not to think of jokes and odd memories, even when medical professionals are minutes away from cutting your head open. This was a nightmare, yet I felt strangely calm in a funny sort of way. Absolutely everything had been stripped away and taken out of my hands. I didn't need to be anyone or do anything. I was totally vulnerable, lying there in my thin cotton hospital gown. But I was surrounded by people who knew how to take care of me.

Once the general anaesthetic was injected, I felt myself surrender. "Say hello to my brain," I joked to the surgeon. Thoughts floated lazily to the surface. *What would happen when I woke up? Would I wake up?* Everything was beyond my control, so I let myself drift into the black.

The next thing I remember was the noise. The Intensive Care Unit was the busiest, noisiest place I'd ever experienced. In the band, I'd been mobbed in the middle of streets all around the world, but this was something else. Machines beeped, wailed and grunted, and the sounds made an unbearable, clashing cacophony that seemed to hurt my head. I also appeared to be plugged in to every single shrieking machine. The wires and tubes looped and undulated around me like spaghetti. Panicking, I looked around for someone who might be able to help.

"Help me," I pleaded with the nurse I found. "I have to get out of here. It's too loud! Please unplug me."

The nurse whispered, "Don't worry Martin, you have to rest, so just try to relax."

I tried to wriggle out of the bed and discovered I was unable to move my left leg. I'd lost the use of it entirely. Luckily the nurse came back before I fell out.

All I wanted was to see Shirlie. I closed my eyes, trying to picture her face, longing for her. But I couldn't see her. I could envisage her hair, and her eyes, but as soon as I started to imagine her other features, the details swam in front of me and multiplied, changing into a combination of every face I'd ever seen. I couldn't focus on one image or one memory. Looking around the ICU, trying to work out where I was and who I was, I discovered I couldn't see out of my left eye either. What had they done to me?

Shirlie came in with my mum and dad. I had no sense of time – she may have arrived five minutes after I'd woken up, or after five hours.

"Oh, Martin! They said it's gone as well as they hoped," she said. Her eyes were shining, and she was smiling very hard.

I barely knew what was going on or what was happening to me — I'd just about managed to remember I'd been ill and that I'd just had a big operation — but I could tell Shirlie was trying very hard to be brave and to stay positive. My mum, bless her, wasn't doing so well — she was crying her eyes out. I longed to say, "I love you," but I wasn't able to talk — so I took Shirlie's hand and squeezed it as hard as I could and wrinkled my nose up as if to say *Look, it's still me!*

I spent the first three weeks in hospital under observation. How did I get through it? I became an opium addict. Because of the nature of my operation, I couldn't have regular painkillers — I needed something much, much stronger, to disrupt pain signals without disturbing the parts of my brain that the doctors needed to keep an eye on. I knew I was allowed a limited amount of opium every day, so I'd save it up. I'd wait until the last minute, trying to endure as much pain as possible, so I could trip and hallucinate.

I was so scared, and so bored, and tripping on painkillers was the only way for me to escape from the reality of the situation. The kind nurses had to inject the drugs into my leg — it started to look like a pincushion after a few days — but I didn't care at all. Just a couple of weeks ago, I'd been so image-conscious, wanting to look as good as possible for the sake of my career. Now, I was a pasty, swollen wreck, constantly flashing my bum for a fix.

I had some memorable hallucinations. In real life, the director Mike Leigh was filming in the courtyard outside my room. I was constantly hearing calls of "Action!" and "Cut!" It didn't take very much opium to make me believe that I was back at work, doing something on a film set. Another time, I spent some bizarre but very happy hours as a tiny ant, exploring, of all things, the Wimbledon Women's trophy. In my mind, I was crawling along, investigating the gleaming golden corridors, small enough to inspect every engraved, embossed detail.

Shirlie, my brother, mum and dad were frequent visitors, but after a while, I had to ask Shirlie to monitor my guest list.

"I know it's very hard for people to see me like this," I explained, haltingly, gesturing to my pale body and swollen head, which was still cut open. I looked like something from a horror film. In fact, I made my ageing mad scientist character on *The Outer Limits* look like Brad Pitt. "But I really need people to be positive when they come to see me. It's lovely to have company, but it's not much fun to be surrounded by people crying all the time."

Obviously Shirlie couldn't do much about my mum and dad, and of course I understood how upsetting it was for them to see their younger son at death's door. But Shirlie kept some semblance of normality going. When she came to see me, she made me feel as though I was at home. We'd chat, watch rubbish telly and eat Bounty bars. I didn't have much of an appetite and Bountys were all I could keep down. She was probably responsible for at least 90% of the bars sold south of the Watford Gap.

One day, Gary came in for a visit and watched me as I picked up a Bounty from my huge bag, tearing through the wrapper to get to the chocolate.

"You want to be careful with those," he teased me. "You're going to get fat."

I couldn't stop laughing. There I was, barely able to walk – bald, puffy and praying that one day my brain would work again – and my brother was winding me up about my weight. He'd been in Hollywood for too long! I still eat Bountys, and the taste of coconut takes me straight back to that period of time in hospital. But it's a memory of a good experience. It tastes of luck – it reminds me of just how fortunate I am to have my family, my work and my health.

After three weeks, I was allowed to go home for a rest. The doctors needed to make a special metal plate. This would be fitted over my brain in place of my skull, which was heavily damaged. While the plate was being made, I could be back with my family on Hampstead Lane.

During that time, I felt OK. Being at home was a brilliant cure. I didn't even miss my opium highs. It was so wonderful to be back with Harley and Roman that I wasn't looking for a distraction from pain or boredom. We had to let Harley know what was going on. Obviously we didn't present her with a load of hospital scans and confusing medical terminology, but we couldn't pretend that the situation didn't exist. And because we were straightforward with her, Harley wasn't fazed by it.

"I'll look after you, Daddy," she'd say, sometimes just stroking my lumpy head when I was lying on the sofa. I looked like a complete wreck. Harley's sweet nature and generosity and loving heart is pure Shirlie.

As my brain started to recover, my sight had returned and my left leg was beginning to come round. Because the top of my head was open, I was able to hear all of the fluid around my brain moving. It was a little bit like the sound of the sea, or the noise you think you hear when you put a shell to your ear. Every time I turned my head, I'd hear a "woosh". It wasn't unpleasant, just a little strange. I'd been desperate to get back to "normal" — even though there was no more normal, really — and begged Shirlie to take me out to Highgate Woods, so we could walk our Doberman, Emma.

Spring was just arriving and, even though it was a little chilly, the sun was making a cautious appearance. The trees were glistening pale gold in the light, and crocuses were starting to push their heads out from under the earth. I was admiring nature and thinking about how much I was enjoying the fresh air among the trees, when I realised a thick wooden log was spinning towards me. Another woman, walking a big dog, had tossed him a stick – but this stick was the size of an entire branch. I had a bandage from my operation, but my vulnerable, chopped-up brain was completely open to the elements. The giant stick hit me straight on the front of my head and it nearly took me out entirely. I felt like my head was the centre of the universe.

I wasn't too worried about the next operation. Getting the giant tumour out had been the hard part. Fitting the plate would be fairly straightforward – yes, it was still "brain surgery", but it was slightly less dramatic brain surgery. Little did I know that the real problems were just beginning.

It took the doctors nearly three weeks to make the plate. By the time it was ready, my post-operation brain had changed too rapidly and the plate wasn't really fit for purpose. The brain fluid had become used to having more space, and when the plate went on, nothing would drain properly – everything would gather and collect in the wrong place. This meant I was in excruciating pain.

My brain wasn't floating on a cushion of fluid. It was hitting the bottom of my skull, and the pain was worse than every single hangover I've ever had in my life, put together. I used to picture Thor, the Norse god of war and thunder, pounding his almighty hammer inside my head. The pain was so great that I wasn't able to sit up.

"We're going to try to raise the bed, inch by inch," explained one of the doctors. "As soon as you're able to sit up, your fluids will begin to balance, and your brain will start to fully recover."

But I just couldn't do it. The pain was too intense. The weeks blurred, and soon I was back on the opium and barely conscious. I had another four operations to drain the collecting fluid, but nothing quite worked. The bathroom was out of bounds – I had to have a catheter because I couldn't even go to the toilet by myself.

One day, Shirlie came in to see me, and it hit me that I must be completely unrecognisable to her. My exposed head was beating and pulsing, and everything was pale and swollen. She'd fallen for the boy on the cover of *Smash Hits*, and now she was married to a Talosian from *Star Trek* – a freaky alien with a huge, terrifying brain.

But Shirlie never seemed to mind. She never once mentioned that she was finding this new life difficult to cope with. Still, when I was conscious enough to think about it, I hated feeling as though I'd let everyone down. I'd wanted to provide an amazing life for the people I loved the most – but we were struggling. When I was in hospital, I was removed from a lot of the day-to-day practical problems that Shirlie had to deal with, about money, the house and looking after Harley and Roman. She never came to me with these worries and anxieties, but I hated knowing that she must be struggling and I couldn't do anything to help. I had to start getting better. I had to sit up. But the pain was impossible to bear.

One evening, I saw something strange on TV. I was in my private room and I watched TV all day long. It didn't matter how boring or obscure a programme was, I could find something fascinating about it. I've always loved TV, and I've never loved it more than I did when I was trying to get through those days in hospital, hour by hour. Flicking through the channels, I caught the start of a documentary about fire-walkers – people who are able to walk steadily across hot coals while feeling no pain. Traditionally, in Northern Greek villages, this happens every May as a tribute to St Constantine and St Helen. Various cultures have been practising fire-walking for thousands of years. While scientists have many theories about the way the heat is transferred, and how it's possible to do it without getting badly burned, it's thought that there's a meditative element to fire-walking. It's all in your brain. The people I watched in a documentary didn't just ignore the pain caused by the heat of the coals. They didn't feel it at all, because they were able to send their brain elsewhere, and they refused to let any pain register.

I thought about my opium trips and hallucinations. To some extent, I'd been able to manipulate my brain. When I was hallucinating, I had some control over what I was seeing and where I thought I was. It must be a case of mind over matter. If people had been walking over hot coals for thousands of years, surely I could sit up? Where would I like to be if I wasn't in hospital? How would I like to feel? I thought about Greek islands, and then holidays, pools and sunshine. I thought about being somewhere hot and sunny with Shirlie. Relaxing, I imagined feeling the sun on my back, cool, clear water lapping my toes. The sound of my beautiful wife's laugh, hearing her sounding happy. Eating a cold, sweet, creamy strawberry ice cream. I focused on every single sense, the sounds I would hear, the way my skin would feel in the heat and the taste of the ice cream. I was far, far away... and, suddenly, I was sitting up!

Amazingly, the pain in my head stopped instantly. It was astonishing. For weeks, I'd been in constant agony. This excruciating pain had become part of the background noise of being alive – or, rather, barely alive. Thor had stopped thumping his hammer. All was calm, all was quiet and I breathed a massive sigh of relief.

If it hadn't been for Shirlie, Harley and Roman, I don't think I could have managed to sit up. The pain had been so great that, in some ways, I felt ready to die. As the hours passed, I had a lot of time to evaluate my life and think about my experiences. I'd only just turned 33, and I knew I'd had a brilliant time. In three decades, I'd crammed in so much more luck, success and fun than most people manage by the time they've reached old age. Maybe I'd been through all my luck. If that was the case, I had nothing to complain about. If it had just been me, I don't think I would have been able to find the energy to try to get better and the stamina to make it through. There were times, I think, when I would have been ready to give up and accept my fate.

But I couldn't leave my family behind. I had to live for them. It didn't matter how difficult or painful my recovery became – I knew that if I didn't try my hardest to get out of the hospital, I'd be leaving five-year-old Harley and two-year-old Roman without a dad. It would break their hearts, and that thought broke mine. I wanted to be around to watch them growing up.

I knew that we could have some incredible times ahead of us. I wanted to help Harley learn to ride a bike and to read Roman more bedtime stories. I thought about my dad, and how he'd created a home for me, growing up. I needed him when I was three, and I still needed him when I was 33. And Harley and Roman were going to need me for years to come.

Most of all, I had to get better for Shirlie. I'd been so lucky to have this wonderful woman in my life. I'd spent over a decade with her beside me. I'd been lonely in luxury hotels, on tour, calling late at night and hoping she'd pick up the phone. I'd been blissfully happy, snuggled up to her in her single bed, in her first tiny flat. Finally, we'd reached a point where I'd been able to give her the life she longed for.

We had our gorgeous home and our beautiful family. I had been going away to do the work I loved, but we could be in LA together – I wasn't spending half the year on tour, flying around Asia. Shirlie had been endlessly patient and generous. She was the love of my life, and we'd both worked so hard to make it work. If we'd survived albums, tours and feature films, we had to survive this. I had to recover.

As soon as I sat up, I called for a nurse to let Shirlie know. Mike Lee was still filming outside, so poor Shirlie got stuck on the way to my room, waiting for various crew members and camera operators to let her through.

"You'll have to wait while we get set up," one grumpy cameraman told her.

But Shirlie was firm. "It's my husband, you don't understand. I've been waiting for weeks for him to get better. I'm not waiting any longer!" she said, sharpening her elbows and ignoring the cameraman. Shirlie was used to my work making demands and getting in the way of our time together – but that wasn't going to happen any more on her watch!

Soon after that, I was able to go home again. I was excited to be back with the kids, but it was becoming clear that even though I was on the mend, I was a long way from normal. I'd developed a kind of spatial dyslexia, and I couldn't tell the difference between left and right or up and down. I'd set off to go to the kitchen, and then find myself confused at the foot of the stairs. I was sleeping badly and having panic attacks – and I knew I still had a ticking time bomb at the bottom of my brain. Not only had I been through all of this, not knowing whether I'd ever fully recover – I knew it was only a matter of time before we had to do something about the second tumour. How would we reach it? Would it kill me? Had I been through all of this for nothing?

I tried to focus on the positives. Instinctively, I knew that was the only way to get better. Everything that was going wrong with my body was a result of the impact of the surgery on my brain. So I had to make my brain believe that my body would recover. I wanted to believe I was slowly getting stronger and that, one day, I'd be back to my old self again.

I'd already been through so much, and the fact that I'd made it through the first round of surgery meant I'd defied the odds. But it wasn't easy. I'd have a bad day, then a bad week, where the fog just wouldn't lift. Looking back, I think I was severely depressed. I'm sure that removing the tumour must have had some impact on my brain's ability to produce serotonin – the hormone that affects your happiness and wellbeing, as well as your ability to remember things. But my practical circumstances were getting me down, too.

I don't think I realised how much my job was part of my identity until it was taken away from me. Success and fame had been fun, but I wasn't missing parties and premieres. I missed having a purpose. I've always loved working. Even when I was briefly at the printworks, it meant so much to me to fit within a structure, to have something to do, and to know that I was a cog helping the other wheels turn. It's what I loved the most about being in a band – we all needed each other to function and I had to show up when I was expected to, because other people were depending on me. In some ways, that's even truer for acting. Every time I've been on a set, I've realised I need to be on time and do my best, not just for the director or the other people in the cast, but for the lighting crew, the sound technicians, the hair and make-up people and the person in charge of the tea.

Being that ill made me feel incredibly lonely. Every single day, I felt so lucky and grateful for Shirlie, Harley and Roman – but that luck was tinged with my own sense of failure. I wasn't contributing anything. I wasn't the father or the husband I wanted to be.

One of the hardest things we had to face together was the uncertainty of the situation. I was in no state to think about work – and I had a second tumour lying in wait. I wasn't out of the woods, by any means. Shirlie and I had to make some tough decisions about how the family could go on without me.

"Shirlie," I said in a soft voice, "I've been really worried about the house." I confided in her. "I know that if I'm not here, we won't be able to keep up with the mortgage. In fact, realistically, I'm not sure how much longer we can keep up with the mortgage regardless."

Shirlie took my hand and held it tight. "It's been on my mind, too. I think we should sell up and look for something much smaller."

I squeezed my eyes shut, trying not to cry. I think I'd hoped we'd manage to find a magic way of saving our home.

I'd imagined being here for years to come, Christmases with Harley, Roman and our parents, summer barbecues in the garden, taking the kids' pictures before school dances – even bringing in a disco floor for teenage parties.

"Is there any way we can stay?" I asked.

"No, I don't think so." I could hear Shirlie's voice breaking, as though she was choking back her own tears, but then she sounded practical again. "We'll find somewhere just as wonderful and make all sorts of new memories. You know I love a project. And I think it's much better to get this done now than…"

She didn't need to finish the sentence. I knew what she meant. It was better to get everything in order while I was still here. The alternative – waiting until the worst happened, and then struggling through, was unimaginable.

We found a little house in Muswell Hill. Spookily enough, it was right around the corner from the first place we'd shared together, which was a little bittersweet. It was a part of London that felt like ours, and we felt as though we were coming home. Still, it was hard not to remember the way I'd felt back in the 80s, as a pop star with a beautiful girlfriend and no health worries beyond hangovers and jet-lag. It forced me to make myself a promise. *If I get over this*, I thought, *I'm never going to take a day of my life for granted, ever again. If I recover, I'm never going to forget it.*

Luckily, we quickly made friends with our new next-door neighbours, Kath and Rob. Well, Shirlie did – I wasn't up to being very sociable. For Shirlie, I think it was a real relief to have new friends who took her at face value. They didn't know or care about our work, or my illness. Shirlie was just the friendly girl next door with two sweet little kids.

When you're going through hard times, it's great to have supportive friends, and in that respect we were really lucky. We were surrounded by people who wanted to help. But the thing people don't talk about is that you really need friends who are able to show up in a different way. I didn't want people to come and see me and talk about my tumour and how I was feeling and how worried I must be. Shirlie didn't want to have a thousand conversations a day that started with someone saying, "How's Martin?" and tilting their head sympathetically. When life becomes sad and strange, you need people who'll make you feel normal, and talk nonsense about *EastEnders* and the weather and if the bin men are going to pick up the recycling on a bank holiday week.

Still, keeping things normal was hard. Not long after we moved in, I had a bad night. Shirlie woke up to the sound of a loud bang. I'd fallen out the bed and I was on the floor, shaking. At the time, neither of us knew I was having an epileptic fit.

It must have been terrifying for Shirlie – yet, when I picture the scene and imagine myself as an onlooker, I have to laugh. I'd been sleeping naked. At 6ft tall, and a good three-and-half stone overweight from steroids, the thump on the floorboards alone must have been pretty shocking. Panicking, Shirlie rang the neighbours as soon as she'd called an ambulance. As I came round – naked, and not understanding what had happened – I realised I wasn't alone in my bedroom. It was filled with police, paramedics and firefighters – and even my neighbours.

As I lay in the ambulance, I was slipping in and out of consciousness and I had moments of lucidity – but, at one point, I left my body completely. I felt myself slip out of myself. From the ceiling of the ambulance, I could look down at my battered, bruised body and wonder what was going to happen. I stayed up there for a good 20 seconds, before I realised I had to get back into my own brain. To this day, I'm not sure if it was just another hallucination or whether it was a genuine near-death experience. I've always thought that I came close to leaving that evening, but decided to stick around.

At the hospital, I was diagnosed with epilepsy. I didn't realise before, but I'd been having something called a Jacksonian seizure – an epileptic fit that's localised within one particular point in your body. Previously, the doctor had thought I was having panic attacks.

"It explains the tingling you've had in your leg," he told me. "The fits have been travelling up your body, and this one reached your brain, which led to a grand mal seizure – where you lose consciousness and experience violent muscle contractions."

Luckily, the doctor was able to prescribe some medication that would regulate the seizures. It was a relief to know exactly what was wrong and to hear that something could be done to fix it. I take medication to this day – the epilepsy, and some mild dyslexia, are the only real leftovers from my illness. Now, I feel incredibly lucky to live with such minor conditions. I almost feel embarrassed to have got away with it. I nearly died – and all I have to do now is remember to take my medication and allow for the fact that it takes me a little longer than I'd like to learn my lines.

But back then, it felt scary and frustrating. I was glad the doctor could give me a prescription that would help, but the epilepsy seemed to be a sign that things were getting worse, not better. My life felt like *Groundhog Day*. Every morning, I'd wake up, look around and feel as though I'd been hit by a truck. Just when I felt as though I was getting over the shock, and coming to terms with my new life, something would come along to trip me up again. For 18 months, I muddled along, trying to hope, feeling overwhelmed by despair and learning how to live again. Then, it was time to tackle the ticking time bomb: the second tumour. Could we get to it before it exploded?

14

My 90s
New-Age Quest

Shirlie

You know your life has taken a turn for the worse when you find yourself standing outside an indoor tent in Alexandra Palace, watching a demonstration in the middle of the day and crying. But Martin's illness took me to some pretty strange places.

Once the shock had worn off, I became convinced that I must have done something to bring our troubles into being. At the time, I didn't realise I was going through a kind of grief. And once I'd stopped feeling totally shocked by what was happening to Martin, I started looking for answers.

Back then, I couldn't accept the idea that his illness was down to nothing but bad luck. I became convinced that I must have done something wrong. I started searching for spiritual answers, travelling down alternative paths to set it right.

After the disastrous trip to China, I'd become interested in Buddhism, but struggled to connect with the Buddhist community in London. It was the *Ab Fab* era and exploring your spirituality had become very trendy. I'd met one woman who told me, "Chanting is great! I chanted for four hours, and then I got this huge work contract for tons of money!" The other new Buddhists only seemed to want wealth and success, and I felt completely alienated. Still, certain ideas, like karma, stayed with me. Was Martin's tumour a result of karma? What had I done to bring this sickness into our lives?

I'd never been much of a reader, but after Kath helped me get Martin to the hospital, she lent me a copy of Louise Hay's book *You Can Heal Your Life*. It's a classic self-help book and contained lots of new-age philosophical and spiritual ideas I'd never encountered before. She suggested that most illnesses and ailments are manifested by our state of mind – and if we can change the way we think, we can start to heal ourselves.

This was what I'd been desperate to hear. Dr Crockard, and the doctors and nurses who'd looked after Martin, had been wonderful, but even after a major operation like brain surgery, it's not possible for most hospitals to offer much in the way of aftercare. It's their job to deal directly with the problem, but when it came to the emotional and mental impact on Martin and our family, we were very much alone. All I wanted was for someone to come along and comfort me, take care of me and tell me what to do. I'd felt so isolated, and Louise Hay's voice – via Kath – arrived when I needed it most.

Ever since I was little, I'd struggled with my throat and glands, developing flu-like symptoms if I was especially stressed or anxious. As soon as Martin became ill, I started feeling ill, too. It was to be expected. I was sleeping badly, worrying constantly, trying to look after Martin, the house and the kids – I was exhausted. But according to Louise Hay's book, there was another reason for the fact that I was perpetually suffering with a sore throat. It was connected with my secret, silent fears. If your throat hurts, it's because you're unable to open up and talk about what's scaring you. Obviously, that's not something you can treat with Lemsip!

In her book, Louise suggested I repeat an affirmation every day. I had to hold my throat while saying, out loud, "All is well." All was very much *not* well, but I gave it a go and found it strangely soothing. Bizarrely enough, my swollen glands became a lot better – and I haven't really had any problems with them since.

Louise's words helped me to make sense of my endometriosis, too. Period pains were supposed to be a result of denying your femininity. I remembered how much I hated and resented my periods when they started. They meant I couldn't spend time with my dad, at the stables, riding horses and looking after them. Periods got in the way, and I didn't want them – and I didn't want to grow up. Perhaps that was why they made me feel so awful – I'd barely been able to accept that I had to have them.

Obviously, I was desperate to know whether Louise had any ideas or advice about brain tumours. Her book revealed that any problems in the brain could be connected with suppression of the ego. I thought about Martin, his work and his role in the band, and realised this made a lot of sense.

Martin was an incredibly good-looking man, but I'd always wondered whether it bothered him that he received so much attention for his looks and not for his talent. As the bass player, he'd kind of been on the sidelines in Spandau – he didn't get to sing or write the songs. When *The Krays* was a huge success, I'd started to realise how much it meant to him to have a creative outlet that he felt completely connected with. Reading Louise Hay's book made me realise how much our bodies can be affected by our subconscious thoughts. Martin had never spoken to me about these feelings, but I was so desperate to find answers that I wanted to look for anything that could be buried beneath the surface.

Martin has never been a jealous or competitive person, or an attention-seeker. But reading this book did make me wonder about how much room he'd made for his own goals and ambitions. He'd always been so relaxed and easy-going and, from the outside, it looked as though success just came to him. He'd been offered so many amazing opportunities – but I wondered whether he'd ever really allowed himself to acknowledge his ego, or to push himself beyond the chances that came his way. I thought about what he'd told me about his teen years, and his early passion for acting, his love of Elvis Presley… Was he in trouble because he'd not let his ego fully express itself?

The old Martin would have thought this idea was a load of old nonsense. But the tumour meant he felt just as vulnerable and anxious as me. I read about a healing fair taking place at Ally Pally.

"I really think you should come along with me, as there may be someone who could help us there," I pleaded, waiting for Martin to laugh.

Instead, he looked serious and nodded. "If you think it's a good idea, let's check it out," he said.

Of course, it was great that he wanted to come along. I didn't want to force him. But the fact that he was so willing to try something so far outside his comfort zone was a little worrying. His illness was changing him.

The fair had drawn a very mixed crowd. There were plenty of people who looked like us, in jeans, T-shirts and baseball caps. I think I found this a little bit reassuring, and a little bit disappointing. I suppose I'd hoped for figurative and literal bells and whistles. Still, once we were inside, I found myself drawn to a big reiki demonstration in one of the exhibition spaces.

At the time, I didn't know very much about reiki. Now, I know it's one of the most disputed alternative therapies – and I wouldn't recommend it to anyone instead of traditional medicine. But, at the time, I was drawn to anything that promised healing. Four young people – three boys and a girl – were giving demonstrations, and I became convinced that they would be able to treat Martin. I was so vulnerable, and so desperate, that I wanted to believe these strangers could fix him.

"Please go and ask them if you can have a session," I begged Martin.

He agreed. At the time, his mobility had improved significantly, but he still looked utterly beaten up, grey, strange and swollen. Once, he would have been far too proud to have put himself on display in that condition in front of a crowd of people. He should have been performing on the big stage, in the centre of the venue – not getting reiki in a little pop-up tent. Still, I watched, hoping for a miracle.

The girl and one of the boys took a foot each, and the others laid their hands on Martin's head or stomach. They looked very focused and serene. Nothing happened, yet soon tears were streaming down my face. I was dumbstruck by the kindness and generosity of these people. They didn't know me or Martin. They were under no obligation to help us. But out of the goodness of their hearts, they were giving up their time to help people in need.

I was in such a state that I truly believed in miracles and magic. I half expected Martin to leap up in the air and shout, "Ta da! I'm completely cured!" Obviously, that didn't happen. Instead, he thanked the practitioners and got down from the exhibition – but I picked up plenty of reiki leaflets on my way out.

"I'm going to learn how to do this," I told Martin. "Maybe I can make you better."

Soon, I'd become completely obsessed with spirituality and alternative treatments. I didn't have a sceptical bone in my body. Anything was worth a try. At the fair, I'd also picked up a leaflet for Feng Shui.

"It says here that we can reorganise our living spaces to improve our lives. It's all about energy flow," I explained to Martin. Even though he was becoming a little bit more open-minded, he rolled his eyes.

Kath was more understanding. "I didn't give you these before, because I wasn't sure they would be your thing," she said, presenting me with piles of Feng Shui books. "Still, now I know you're interested, maybe these will help."

I went from interested to obsessed. It made so much sense to me. I'd always been fascinated by houses, spaces and rooms and had extreme responses to the way people's homes were laid out, sensing positive and negative energy. Over the years, I'd been doing some Feng Shui instinctively, organising our homes to create energy flow. Still, I learnt that some things were in the "wrong" place. Had I given Martin a brain tumour by putting a dustbin in the "health" corner?

Years before Marie Kondo became famous for it, I was practising her principles, getting rid of piles of books, clothes and pieces of art. Now, I wish I hadn't been quite so extreme – but we desperately needed money, so selling some of our stuff ended up being quite productive. Feng Shui certainly didn't cure Martin, but it gave me something practical to focus on when my emotions were overwhelming me.

My New-Age experiments had a range of results. When I'd been feeling under the weather, a friend had recommended that I try getting a colonic. I suppose it wasn't that different from Feng Shui in a way. Get rid of the old, toxic stuff to make room for the new. Someone was recommended to me and I went to her house, in a beautiful mews in Little Venice. Her therapy room was in the garage. When she closed the door, I noticed weird pipes, filled with suspicious brown liquid, running all around the walls. I had a slightly strange vibe and panicked. I wasn't sure what was going to happen to me that day, and I hadn't given anyone her address…

The lady was very chatty, explaining that her husband and her son were both successful composers and wrote songs for huge pop stars like Elton John.

"Oh, I used to be in the music business," I said – before realising that if her family members were in music, too, they might recognise me. Oh, *please* don't let them see me with a pipe up my bottom. But it was too late!

"Mum! The estate agents are here," said a man's voice, bursting into the room, just after the therapist had inserted the tube.

I was facing the wall, staring at the brown pipes, so he couldn't see my blushes. So much for patient privacy. The incident reminded me of a horrible experience I'd had with a gynaecologist once, when she asked if three young male student doctors could watch my examination.

Of course I did, to which she replied, "A girl like you shouldn't be shy, dancing on stage every night and what have you." Firstly, being on stage, dancing to pop songs in front of a paying audience is *completely* different from being on your back in a hospital gown. Secondly, just what kind of a dancer did she think I was?

Still, the colonic experience didn't put me off, and I found myself going deeper and deeper into the journey. Someone recommended rebirthing therapy. Soon after, I was in Pimlico, lying down and practising breathing techniques while a very sweet, delicate lady called Diana Roberts took me back to my conception. I was supposed to have a session for every month that I was in the womb.

In the last session, she asked me, "Why did you choose your parents?"

I was confused. "I didn't choose my parents," I replied, not wanting to add, out loud, "If I could have chosen my parents, I might have picked different ones." Not because they weren't good parents, but they just weren't good together.

I thought of my dad, sometimes loving but sometimes very angry, always bullying my mum and flying off the handle. I then thought about my mum, who I adored, but who sometimes frustrated me by being too gentle, a victim of her own circumstances.

The therapist pushed me again. "We all choose our parents. I need to think about why you chose yours."

I focused on my breath. The room was dark and warm, I guess to replicate the experience of being in the womb. I was wrapped in soft, heavy blankets. Instead of thinking my old thoughts, I tried to tap into my subconscious and let the answer drift out of me.

"I chose my dad because he's big and strong, and I knew he would always protect me," I heard myself say. "And my mum because she's gentle and so full of love. I know she will always love me unconditionally."

The therapist placed a hand on my shoulder. "Now thank them for what they have done."

It may seem weird that I found comfort there, with everything that was happening to me. Martin was still ill, and we were both trying not to think about the fact that he had a second brain tumour and it could kill him. We were beyond broke. After we'd sold our beautiful home in Highgate and moved to Muswell Hill, I'd found out that I'd gone bankrupt. I'd answered the door, with baby Roman on my hip, to a pair of suited men from the tax office, who told me that Pepsi & Shirlie Ltd were broke and we had to shut up shop.

In the 90s, interest rates were rocketing and lots of friends were losing their homes and could no longer afford their mortgages. Pepsi had her beautiful little apartment, just for her, and she had to return the keys to the bank. Everything that could go wrong had gone wrong. My life felt like a cosmic joke. And in the middle of it all, this sweet, spiritual, elderly woman was telling me that I'd chosen my parents and I had to thank them! A few years earlier, I might have stormed out of the room. But in that moment, it made sense. I wasn't sure I completely believed it, but it made me feel as though I had some control over my life and how it would play out. I was able to make good choices for myself, and for my family.

I found the rebirthing course so soothing that when the therapist suggested I learn how to do it with a shaman, I leapt at the chance. This course was back at that mecca of alternative learning, Alexandra Palace. When I started seeking spiritual salvation, I'd no idea that it would mean spending *quite* so much time around Wood Green.

By this point, I'd spent so much time reading and learning about the spiritual world that I felt quite optimistic and hopeful. So many books were piled up around my side of the bed like a knee-high fortress that Roman used to be able to hide behind them. I'd moved far away from my old life, and I was throwing myself into learning about healing. More than anything, I wanted to make Martin better – but I was really desperately searching for any kind of equilibrium. Even the doctors didn't really seem to know what caused brain tumours, but by doing this work, I could maybe try to reverse my run of bad luck. After all, Pepsi & Shirlie was officially over. Even the Inland Revenue had declared it. Now, I was Shirlie the Shaman-to-be.

The trouble was that Shirlie the Popstar was proving difficult to escape. Arriving at the meeting space, I tried to slip away into the corner so I could quietly settle myself and see what was going on. Even with my head down and my hat on, I attracted some unwanted attention. Across the room, I saw a woman's eyes light up. I recognised that expression – I was very familiar with it. This was a hardcore Wham! fan.

I loved our fans, and I knew I owed them a great deal. But I was feeling so vulnerable and so exhausted that I wasn't ready to cope with the inevitable set of questions. "What's George *really* like?" would be the first one. It was impossible to answer without confusing and disappointing anyone. What could I say? "Sometimes we have very lengthy chats about the state of the world and the secrets of the universe – and sometimes we just sit on the sofa and watch *EastEnders*!" Even worse, she'd want to know what was happening with Pepsi and Shirlie, and what I was going to do next. I didn't want to talk about being broke, struggling to keep the roof over our heads, and the fact that my husband was probably dying so going on tour was the furthest thing from my mind. Singing along to my Alanis Morissette CD at the top of my lungs was the closest I came to being in the music industry these days.

Gathering my thoughts, I worked out a plan. I couldn't be Shirlie here – I was… Sarah! So when the time came for us to sit in a circle and talk about what had brought us to shaman school, my answer was ready.

"I'm, Shirl… Sarah, and I'm here because my hus… I mean, I don't know really. I just want to learn more about healing and helping people."

Most of the people in the circle smiled politely. It was a middle-class crew, mostly teachers, lawyers and osteopaths, people who had read about alternative therapy in the Sunday supplements – they were all embracing the New-Age 90s. Even the shaman leading the course looked neat, brushed and buttoned. To my disappointment, he wasn't wearing fantastical, swirling robes or a dramatic headdress. With his tidy blue cashmere v-neck jumper, chinos and thick-framed glasses, he resembled the comedian Jerry Lewis.

Still, the Wham! fan didn't buy that I was Sarah. She was persistent. "Look, are you *sure* you're not Shirlie?" she asked.

I didn't trust myself to speak. I simply shook my head.

The session started. The osteopath was the first to try the therapy. He entered the circle and curled up into the foetal position. Suddenly, he started to rock back and forth. He was shaking with pain. Jerry-Lewis-the-shaman drew himself up to his full height and started chanting. Even the ironed creases on his chinos seemed to be undulating. It sounded like a kind of spiritual beat-boxing – he was making clicking, rhythmic noises with his tongue, while ululating, creating a sort of wordless opera. Forget Ally Pally, he could have been performing to packed houses at the Coliseum.

The osteopath started to scream, "Get them out! Get them out!"

After rebirthing, I'd been expecting everyone to speak sweetly in hushed tones. This was getting scary. What was going on? I started looking around for hidden cameras.

Jerry Lewis briefly stopped his song. "This man was shot with arrows in a past life," he explained. "I need to remove them."

I couldn't quite believe what I was seeing and, out of the corner of my eye, I knew that Wham!'s Number 1 fan was eyeballing me, staring in my direction. How could I go into the circle and relive my past life, when I was spending all of my energy keeping her nose out of my present one? For the next few hours, I was Sarah. What kind of past life had Sarah had? Maybe I could pretend that I'd been shot with arrows, too.

It was a traumatic session. All of these people were struggling in so many different ways. One young woman was summoned to the circle and shared that she'd been sexually abused when she was three years old. Even though I was feeling tense and terrified, it brought home an important truth. Every single person there was going through pain and difficulty, and they were looking for answers, just like me. Martin's illness had made me feel so lonely, scared and isolated. As far as I knew, no one else was there because the love of their life was slowly dying from brain tumours – but everyone had their own tragedy that had led them to the shaman. They all felt they had nowhere else to turn.

My spiritual journey took me in some unexpected directions. Over the years, I've become a little less naïve. When Martin was at his sickest, I was ready to put all of my trust in blind faith and magic – even though Martin himself would sometimes laugh at me. Now, I realise it's worth taking these alternatives with a pinch of salt, but I'm still so grateful for those experiences, and for the people I met when I was exploring other ways of healing.

It's an unregulated world that attracts desperately vulnerable people and, because of this, there are a few practices and organisations that will exploit those who are desperately in need of help. But I was lucky. Nearly everyone I encountered treated me with total kindness and gentleness. Even though I still couldn't say I definitely believe in shamanic work – although I'm definitely not a total cynic – the practitioners healed me with their compassion, warmth and patience.

I had a truly incredible experience with a lady named Caitlin Matthews, a writer and practitioner of shamanic lore. A friend of a friend had suggested I try a session with her, so I drove to her house in the middle of nowhere in Oxfordshire. I arrived at her address and had that familiar feeling of trepidation. Caitlin lived in a tiny, remote village, and I felt as though I was on the edge of a forest.

Years later, when I saw the film *Lord of the Rings,* I felt a shiver of familiarity. The dense trees, the velvety green moss and the feeling of mystery all recalled the place where Caitlin lived. She even had a Hobbit house. It was beautiful but dark, with low ceilings and every wall crammed with books. Caitlin and her husband were experts in ancient folklore and considered to be some of the wisest people in their field.

"Shirlie, come on through!" she said, fixing me with her gaze. She had the deepest blue eyes. Piercing, but somehow hypnotic – like a pair of pools, so calm and beautiful that I couldn't stop myself from diving straight in.

Caitlin led me to her garden shed. I had no idea what lay ahead, but I was pretty sure we wouldn't be interrupted by any estate agents. I felt as though my nerves were about to get the better of me, though. I was miles from home. What was she going to do?

"Shirlie, lie down here for me," Caitlin said, beckoning me to the floor and then covering me with a heavy wool Navajo blanket. That was when I remembered why I was there. Diane Roberts, the friend who recommended Caitlin, had described her as "a midwife for the soul". This appealed to me deeply.

I'd been feeling so lost and so desperate. At this point, Martin's second tumour had been zapped, but his recovery was agonisingly slow. I was worn out from taking care of my husband and my two little children. My friends and family were all rallying round, but I felt entirely burnt out. I'd lost myself. Shirlie, the girl who loved to dance, sing and make jokes and do characters – she'd disappeared. I had no way to express myself creatively. The word I kept coming back to was homesick. I *longed* for home – not for our old Highgate house, but for that feeling of returning to a place of safety and nourishment, a place where I could truly belong.

Caitlin asked me to put on a pair of headphones. I could hear a drumming beat through them. It sounded like a heartbeat, getting faster and faster. Like the Alexandra Palace

Left: In Sydney, 1985.

Bottom: Wham! in China: I lived off strawberry milkshakes after the horrors of what I saw in the wet markets.

Top left: Our wedding in St Lucia, 14th November 1988. **Top right:** Cutting the wedding cake. **Bottom:** People-watching in St Tropez in Cafe Senequier.

Top: Baby Harley Moon is born. It was a gift from the universe. **Bottom left:** Pepsi and me recording our album – it's not easy juggling work and babies. **Bottom right:** January 1993 and our baby boy is born in LA.

Top: LA 1993: my family feels complete.

Bottom: *The Krays* premiere. A big night for the whole family.

Left: Martin recovering. Time is precious and there is nowhere else I'd rather be than with my children.

Bottom: Family holiday in LA, sitting on Santa Monica beach, California 1999.

Top right: Roman always has a lot to say and could entertain everyone. **Left:** Roman with his uncle Gary.

Bottom: New Year's Eve party in 1999 at Gerry Haliwell's house, with Martin's parents.

Top: 'Last Christmas' video shoot. George stepping into frame just as Pepsi and I are getting to know our supposed boyfriends!

Left: Back in St Lucia to renew our wedding vows in 2013, celebrating our 25th anniversary.

Us: then and now.

shaman, Caitlin started to sing the most beautiful, operatic melody. As she was standing over me, singing, I shut my eyes and drifted into a trance. I was flying – no, *floating*. I saw myself as a Native American girl, floating over a riverbank.

Focusing on the image, I realised I was floating past my village and they were weeping for me, mourning me. Suddenly, the ground turned to gold and I was drifting over a desert, hovering over a pale turquoise sky. Soon, I started to feel very warm, soft and peaceful – I'd collided with a cowboy. It was Martin! I felt his presence before I saw his face and reached out for him. A feeling of deep happiness tingled in my toes and crept over my whole body.

After a little while, Caitlin blew on the top of my head very gently. "Shirlie, I'm so sorry," she said, looking downcast. "I couldn't bring your soul back."

"What on earth do you mean?" I cried. Under the blanket, I shivered. This sounded like bad news.

"For now, I've left her with the goddess of the Upperworld. She was very, very frightened and she didn't want to come. I've left her with a little rabbit to look after, and I've asked if she'll come back with me next time, after protecting the rabbit for me. The goddess of the Upperworld rules creativity and visual beauty – she's very colourful and a wonderful storyteller. So if you come back in two weeks, we can try again."

I was excited to be riding this spiritual journey but then had a reality check – was I just reliving *Alice in Wonderland*? Yet I was so enamoured by the story she told me, I could have sat with her for hours. I didn't care if it was the truth or not, as she had a magical way of telling her story. It didn't matter that I'd driven for miles to see her, as it was one of the most moving experiences of my life. For the first time, I'd met someone who confirmed a lot of things that I felt and who made sense of my chaos.

Of course I agreed to come back in a fortnight. In fact, I couldn't wait to go back.

As strange as it sounds, I'd dressed up especially to meet the goddess of the Upperworld and put on my favourite turquoise jewellery to look as colourful as possible. The ritual began again. I didn't see my cowboy, but when Caitlin woke me, she was smiling and her eyes were shining with tears.

"Oh, Shirlie." She beamed. "I've brought her back to you. She didn't want to come with me, but we managed to get her back." Caitlin explained that when people have been through any trauma – typically, sexual abuse – they often lose the creative part of their soul, sending it away to protect it. I'd never been sexually abused, but I remembered being ill with meningitis and the terror and trauma of my trip to the hospital. "That must be why she went away," explained Caitlin.

Lots of people may think this story is ridiculous, but when I went home, I felt so full of peace and light. As I said to Caitlin, even if her story was completely made up, it was beautiful. She spoke so movingly that just listening to her was therapeutic. She reaffirmed that I was a creative person with a very visual mind.

A few days later, I found myself being invited out for a girlie night with my friend. We walked together to the most beautiful colourful house I'd ever seen. It was like a doll's house, covered in silks, chandeliers and trinkets. Her whole home twinkled in an otherworldly way. As she walked in, wearing her turquoise silk dress, looking straight at me, I froze. I was with the goddess of the Upperworld. Of course, it could all have been a coincidence – but who knows?

Three good friends have seen Caitlin and been reunited with their souls. They all achieved this on their first go, which shows you don't usually need a repeat visit. It's brought them all love and luck and they've been able to move forward during periods of struggle.

I'm so glad I spent the 90s learning, questioning and exploring. While my spiritual adventures didn't necessarily give me all the answers, they forced me to ask myself some big questions, and they opened up my heart and mind.

Working with the shaman didn't make Martin better or

give me the powers to heal him. But it made me stronger, kinder and so much more empathetic. Now I realise that Martin didn't get ill because I'd done something wrong. But I'll never stop being grateful for his recovery, and to the people who helped me look for love and peace during the darkest, most painful days. I became gentler and wiser, and I'll never judge anyone who travels down an alternative path to seek help. I often wonder about the people I met during those classes and courses, and I hope they find what they're looking for. I'm so glad I did. And even though it's against the rules of Feng Shui, I'm still hanging onto some those self-help books. You never know when you may need them again.

15

"The Little Fella"

Martin

We're all supposed to hate labels. They're limiting. We all want to believe we're unique, complex and hard to define. But when you love what you do, and you're living in the public eye, it's hard to get too upset about labels. For the first part of my adult life, I had fun with them. I didn't mind at all when my photo was in the papers, captioned "Martin Kemp: pop star". I felt really proud after *The Krays* did so well and I was off in America. For a little while, I was "Martin Kemp: actor". But I hated being "Martin Kemp: brain tumour".

Every time my name was mentioned or my picture was printed, those were the words that came up. They had nothing to do with any talent I had, or anything I'd worked so hard to create. That troublesome, pale-grey shadowy lump was defining me – and I hated it. I understood why the papers were doing it. My brain tumour made me unusual. Shirlie and I were going through an experience that most people would count among their greatest fears. The first tumour hadn't actually killed me, but it had stolen our life as we knew it. Fixing my brain had ravaged the rest of my body. In some ways, I *was* more of a "brain tumour" than a bassist or an actor. When filming ends, you come home from tours – but my brain tumour was there 24/7. You don't get time off from it.

The first tumour had been enormous, but its position had made it relatively easy to cut out. The second one, an evil almond, was stuck under my brain, right out of reach. The surgeon, Professor Crockard, called it "the little fella", which made it sound almost friendly, like a little character. I could picture it, a tiny, old man, sitting under a blanket, complaining that his tea was cold and there was nothing good on the telly. Still, at night, when I couldn't sleep, I knew that old man was planning something sinister. If he started growing, it was game over for me. But getting him out – *if* the professor could work out a way of getting him out – meant I had to go back to square one.

I was still far from recovered from the first surgery. To resolve the problems I'd had with my fluid, I'd been given a course of steroids to balance the levels. The steroids made me feel absolutely awful – heavy, tired and slow. I was three stone overweight, and the inside of my mouth was rotting away. The one upside of the experience was that I could spend so much time at home with Harley and Roman – but it's difficult to be a dad with a broken brain. All I wanted to do was chase them around the garden or get on my hands and knees and pretend to be a lion, a bear or an aeroplane. But after a few minutes of any game, I'd have to crawl back to the sofa to recover.

*   *   *

After a major illness, you have to take each day at a time – to be honest, every hour at a time. You're forced to be patient. You have to take it easy, which is really tough when you don't even know whether you're going to survive. I was trying so hard to be grateful for where I was. Between them, Professor Crockard, Shirlie, Harley, Roman and all of our friends had saved me. I knew that I was lucky to be alive. But the reality was really frightening. What kind of life could I have when I knew my legs, eyes and memory would keep letting me down? I didn't think life could ever get back to normal. I'd not had time to recover, and I knew that yet more brain surgery was around the corner. Everything was going to get worse before it could get better – if it ever got better.

Every few months, Professor Crockard would scan my brain to see how well it was mending after the removal of the first tumour, and to check in on the second. He was anxious about growth, and he knew that if the little fella got any bigger, we had to act quickly. About 18 months after the first operation, we were sitting in his office, looking at the latest scan.

"Martin, unfortunately these measurements indicate the second tumour is starting to grow at an accelerated rate." Professor Crockard pointed at an image on his computer screen, with two little white x's indicating the edges of the tumour. It looked like an evil emoji, a dead cartoon character.

I felt numb. The colour had drained out of my world. Everything seemed as dark and grey as that image on the screen. I felt profoundly depressed. Not sad, angry or even anxious. It was as though a deep fog had come into the office and enveloped me alone.

Professor Crockard continued, "We're going to have to go back in. So we'll cut open the top, take the metal plate out and pull the two halves of your brain apart to try to get to him. Obviously, there are all kinds of risks involved. We can't guarantee that we'll be able to get the tumour out – and it will have an impact on the rest of your brain." He explained that it was impossible to reach the tumour without disturbing the parts of my brain that functioned, and it would almost certainly affect my vision, speech and motor skills. Pretty much everything I relied on as an actor.

Suddenly, Shirlie spoke. This was a very different Shirlie from the woman who had been in that room with me 18 months ago. "I don't think we want to do that," she said, calmly, as though she was simply telling a waiter she didn't want any dessert. "There must be another way. I think we should get a second opinion."

"Shirlie!" I felt so embarrassed and awkward that I'd forgotten my world was ending. "You can't *say* that! He's a doctor. He knows what he's doing." I couldn't believe it. Doctors were the smartest people I knew. Professor Crockard did an extremely difficult job, and he did it brilliantly. He wasn't some cowboy builder who'd just given a quote on a conservatory.

Shirlie remained calm. "I'd just like to find out what our options are," she said politely.

Looking back, I can see that my reaction was a little bit strange. She wasn't rude to Professor Crockard, she was warm and courteous. I think I saw a tiny glimpse of teenage Shirlie – the punky girl who wasn't afraid of being cheeky to a teacher.

On our way back to the car, I was still feeling slightly shaken up. "I don't think there *are* other options, you know," I whispered, nudging her. "He knows what's best."

Shirlie simply smiled and said a phrase I'd heard her say millions of times. "Leave it with me."

Over the next few days, I fretted about the upcoming operation and the recovery. I'd been so lucky to survive the first time. Could I possibly do it again? This was much more serious, after all. It might take even longer than nine hours. And what if they got the tumour out but it caused more general brain damage? I wouldn't be able to be the dad I wanted to be. All I wanted was to take care of my family, but I'd be even more dependent on them. The awful thoughts went round and round in my head. I should have been thinking positively, not filling my brain with more sadness and negativity. The little fella had a *lot* to answer for.

Meanwhile, Shirlie was constantly on the phone, making all sorts of mysterious calls. She was in touch with Yog all the time – I could tell when it was him because her voice softened and she'd sound like a teenager – or she'd be using a very serious, adult voice and using words like "neuro" and "benign". Eventually, I received a mysterious phone call of my own.

Immediately, I knew I was being called from a hospital. I could just about make out bleeps and squeaks, the dull hum of wheeled equipment, the sound of a series of fast footsteps.

"Mr Kemp, my name is Professor Black." It was a surgeon Yog had found. "I've been having a look at your scan, and there's something I'd like to try," suggested the man on the phone. He was a doctor in America, pioneering a new kind of tumour treatment. Rather than cutting into the area where the tumour was located, he was using lasers to destroy the active part of the tumour and shrink it down. He'd only operated on malignant tumours before. Benign ones have a different kind of composition, so he wasn't sure it would work. He was hopeful though. "Now, at the moment this treatment is very new, and there's only one machine in the world that can do it," he explained.

Automatically, I assumed this meant a trip to see Professor Black in America. Yog, who'd been calling every single doctor and medical expert he could find, had told me he would send me anywhere in the world for treatment and sort everything out. "I've got this – please don't worry," Yog had said. He'd already been kinder and more generous than I'd ever imagined a friend could be.

To be honest, it made me feel strange. I was utterly touched, and I knew it was ultimately a sign of just how much he loved Shirlie. He would have done absolutely anything for her – and he did. Also, money was a real worry at that time. Neither of us was working, Shirlie had gone bankrupt and we'd reorganised our finances so we'd be able to cope if I did die. But an international flight would have been a real stretch. I don't know how we would have managed to pay for an operation in America.

There was some pain there for me, too. Yog's amazing, generous gesture reminded me I wasn't in a position to do those things for the people I loved any more. I'd grown up with no money and, when money had come into my life, I hadn't cared about chasing it. Earning it was very exciting, but only because it gave me the chance to be generous with my mates and show them how much I loved them. Not that long ago, I would have spent any amount of money and flown any distance to be by Shirlie's side. Now, I could barely afford to buy her a bunch of flowers.

"I understand you live in North London," Professor Black continued. "The stereotactic radiation machine is at St Bart's." A whopping seven miles away – just half an hour in a black cab. At least Yog didn't have to cover that!

Shirlie and I went to the hospital to find out a bit more about the procedure. I would be measured for a Perspex box, which would be placed over my head while I went inside the machine. Two lasers would be aimed at the specific location of the tumour and shrink its corona – the centre of the problem. The whole operation would take 20 minutes.

Days ago, I'd been remembering the way it felt to wake up after a nine-hour operation, groggy from opioids, surrounded by medical staff and struggling to regain consciousness, knowing I had many nights in hospital ahead of me. Now, I was so shocked I wanted to laugh. I'd worried that I could be in an operating theatre for *days*, yet, in theory, I could be in and out in 20 minutes. If it went well, maybe I'd be home in time for *EastEnders*!

Obviously, the operation still had an enormous amount of risk attached. No one had ever treated a tumour like mine using this method. The technology was very new and, although the procedure had a good success rate when it was used on malignant tumours, it hadn't been tested widely. I knew I was going to be a medical guinea pig. We had no idea what could happen if the operation went wrong, or how we'd cope.

I understood my options were limited. I could go back to Professor Crockard and have a lengthy, invasive operation that would take me months, maybe years, to recover from. I could leave the second tumour to grow and let it kill me. Or I could put my head in a box and let the doctors shoot lasers at it. Lasers sound so normal now, but at the time they were still a thing of sci-fi. It wasn't just that this experimental option seemed as though it might be best for me and my family in the long run. When you're a big kid at heart, you're *always* going to pick the lasers.

At this stage, in my head, my heart and the public eye, I was still "Martin Kemp: brain tumour". My illness was defining my life, and I was fed up with it. When the first tumour was removed, I was happy to be open about it. After all, my experience was an unusual one, and at first I didn't mind the fact that everyone knew about it. Usually, when you're going through something difficult, it helps to share the news, making the burden easier to bear. But when it came to dealing with the second tumour, I couldn't face the thought of being in the papers again.

I knew if I told too many people what was going on, I'd get a permanent new newspaper caption. "Martin Kemp: brain *tumours*", plural. If I was ever going to get better and manage to act again, I'd have to win an Oscar and go into space to collect it before I could shake off the label. So I kept it in the family. Shirlie, Yog, our parents and the doctors knew, but that was it. Of course, Harley and Roman knew that "Daddy has a poorly head", but no one wants to worry their kids. With them, we focused on the idea that the clever doctors were going to make me better.

In the run-up to the operation, I tried really hard to keep a low profile. I avoided going to any of the places where Shirlie and I could get papped. Everyone who knew what was going on was good at keeping quiet about it, and the plan was simple. On the day, all we had to do was drive to Bart's and get the job done. Of course I was nervous – but I was a little bit excited, too.

Facing the first operation had been overwhelming, terrifying and bleak. When I'd been wheeled into the operating theatre 18 months ago, I'd only known about my tumour for about 72 hours. I was filled with dread, heading for the unknown, and trying not to think about the fact that the operation could kill me. This time, it was two completely different people who drove to the hospital. Compared with the last occasion, we were almost cheerful, thinking to ourselves, *Let's get this mess over with once and for all.*

Looking through the window at the familiar, soft grey London sky, I thought about Shirlie. The last time we'd made this journey, she'd been in a state of shock. I remembered how vulnerable she'd seemed to me, and the unspoken silence between us. The way she'd tried desperately to hide her own panic and pain – and how I'd struggled to contain my feelings, not wanting to make her deal with my fear and sadness as well as her own. The woman beside me now looked exactly the same – she was still my angel, my pin-up, the girl I saw on *Top of the Pops* and fell in love with. But I knew she had grown up. Shirlie had faced an impossible challenge and won. She'd managed to live with so much fear and practical and emotional pain, and she'd fought those things with love. She hadn't just looked after Harley, Roman and me – she'd made a home for us. Somehow, she'd found the strength to stick the world back together after it had fallen apart. Seeing Shirlie's vulnerability was what made me fall in love with her, but seeing her endless, undefeatable strength took my breath away.

We arrived at the hospital and took care to park in a place where we'd be tucked away. We'd covered ourselves up with the usual collection of hats, scarves and glasses, partly because we didn't want to be seen, and partly because I felt self-conscious about my strange, swollen body. I knew there was usually a bit of waiting around and moving from place to place, so I was surprised when I went straight into one of the doctor's offices.

A young doctor with an RAF moustache put a Perspex box on my head and secured it around my neck. "Great!" he said. "It fits perfectly. Now, wait here for a bit. Someone will come to collect you shortly."

I'd assumed the box would go on at the last minute, but I suppose this would give me time to get used to it. I could pretend to be a weird humanoid robot from the future. I just had to make sure I didn't breathe too much and get it all steamed up.

Eventually an older man in a white coat arrived to take me to the stereotactic radiation machine. "Great, it looks like you're all ready," he said. "Get in the wheelchair – we don't have far to go."

We went down a corridor, wheels squeaking against the linoleum floor, neon strip lights crackling and catching the corners of my box, giving my face an eerie glow. Then down another one, and another one, and... hold on... Why were we going outside? The porter wheeled me right out into the middle of Smithfield in broad daylight.

In the 90s, this part of London was starting to get trendy. We were surrounded by City types, getting some fresh air and a quick sandwich, and media darlings on their way to long liquid lunches. And there, in the middle of it all, for any passing tourist or office worker to see, was Martin Kemp, Spandau bassist, Hollywood actor, husband of Shirlie from Pepsi & Shirlie, right outside a hospital, in a wheelchair, with a big, mad box on his head. There was nowhere to hide. You can't exactly put a baseball hat on over a massive box. If the paparazzi spotted me, they would have a field day. I had to laugh.

Mercifully, the porter managed to wheel me into the operating room without attracting too much attention. I definitely received the odd funny look, and at one point I was convinced I was recognised. A young girl on the street gave me a polite smile and I politely raised my hand to wave back as if everything was normal, but I think her smile was more out of pity than recognition.

I'd been distracted by my journey to the operating room, but as I came close to the machine, I started to feel nervous. Just because my head wasn't being cut open this time, it didn't mean it wasn't dangerous. Last time, I'd been completely unconscious, but this time I'd be able to see everything. I'd been reassured about how precise the operation would be, but I was still scared that where the laser hit the tumour, the corona would spread out into the good parts of my brain. I was anxious and my heart raced as if I was climbing into a boxing ring. *Okay, let's do it*, I said to myself.

Still, through my fear, I felt a glimmer of positivity coming back. I'd made it this far. This wasn't about the tumour any more. This was about my family, especially Shirlie, and honouring their kindness, patience and generosity. I didn't know whether the operation would work, but I knew I was incredibly lucky to have the chance to try. I said a little prayer to the universe – well, less of a prayer, more of a "wish me luck!" – and we started. In 20 minutes, my life could be on a completely different path.

Except, after 10 minutes, the machine broke down.

While I wasn't supposed to be moving my head, it was hard not to laugh. It was almost like a scene from *Carry On Doctor* – I half-expected Babs Windsor to burst through the door and ask if I'd like a lovely pair for lunch. There I was, psyching myself up for this serious operation, only to be foiled by creaking technology.

"Well, we haven't used this machine very often, it's still quite new," said a nurse, apologising for the delay.

Looking back, I don't know why I didn't panic or freak out. I suppose that deep down, I'd wondered whether this solution was too good to be true. I was so used to things going wrong that I was able to take it in my stride.

They fired a second time, the machine picked up where it left off, and 20 minutes later, the tumour had been zapped. Even though I was trying not to get my hopes up, it was hard not to start thinking about the future. After my first operation, I'd struggled with depression. It had been so hard to stay positive and optimistic, because I couldn't do any of the things I loved to do. But now, it looked as though there could be a little light at the end of the tunnel. One day, I was going to go on holiday with Shirlie, Harley and Roman, and I'd be the first in the pool. We'd go back to LA Maybe I'd play with the band again. But more than anything else, I wanted to act again.

It's nearly 25 years since Professor Black and Dr Alan Crockard saved my life by cutting away and zapping those two brain tumours. And I will always be in their debt. Over the years I have tried to pay some of it back by raising money for more machines, visiting hospitals and speaking to patients who are being treated for brain tumours. I know that the technology is developing so quickly, and that's fantastic – but human interaction is such an important part of recovery, too.

I can speak to patients about their worst fears because they were *my* worst fears. I was so scared I'd never get better, and that I'd never be able to live the life I'd loved again. I know how difficult and dark life seems when you're trying to recover. When I was diagnosed I had no one to look at and say, *If they came through it, so can I.* No one to give me hope or faith in a recovery. So I wanted to put myself out there, telling as many people as I could, *Look it happened to me, and I came through the other side.* If I can, I want to give people hope. It reminds me that I can never take anything for granted.

My illness changed me. Before that first operation, I was a kid. I felt as though I was going up and nothing could stop me. Countless opportunities were coming my way, and everything seemed to be getting bigger and better. But I never gave myself a moment to truly appreciate what was happening in my life. Because I was young and ambitious, I was always looking towards the future, and wanting more. I thought that was what success felt like. Then it felt as though I lost everything. The home we were going to raise our children in. The security I'd tried to establish for my family. The career that didn't only allow me to provide for the people I loved – it fulfilled me and defined me, too.

Now, I'm not just grateful for my recovery, I'm grateful for that period of illness. It's turned me into a kinder and more compassionate man. I've a lot more time for people. When I was younger, I could be impatient. I was so caught up in my own life that I rarely paused to consider what other people were doing or feeling, or to think about the fact that they might be going through a painful emotional journey. Now, if I'm finding someone difficult, I always think about what may be happening in their life, behind the scenes.

It's humbling to realise we have so little control over so many of the major events in our lives. I used to think that hard work was one of the most important things in the world, and that we would all be rewarded for our graft. Now I know that life-changing events, good and bad, are usually a result of pure chance. They come out of the blue, and they give us an opportunity to see who we really are.

There's no doubt in my mind that I wouldn't have survived without Shirlie at my side. I know that not all couples would have been able to make it through the events we endured. When you subject a marriage to an enormous amount of pressure, it's bound to change shape. It's a test of strength, and it's entirely understandable that some people collapse under the strain. But we found a strength in each other that we didn't know existed.

When we met, we were a tabloid couple and we lived in an exciting world, but our love became even stronger when life became painful and real. I suspect that lots of "showbiz couples" don't make it because the extraordinary becomes ordinary. If your life is all about premieres and parties, nothing feels special. You're going to start taking the high points for granted, and it's only a matter of time before you take each other for granted, too. After getting through my illness, we will never, ever do that. You don't worry about getting tables in posh restaurants or being invited to particular parties after going through an experience like this.

I think Shirlie's instincts have always been to protect, nurture and love. When we fell for each other, all I wanted to do was take care of her. But when she had to look after me, it made us equals. It isn't that I owe her everything – there's a balance. We're a team. She's never made me feel that I need to repay her for the way she looked after us all, during my illness, and that's because she didn't just do it for me. She did it for all of us.

Now, I know that every single success I have is Shirlie's, too. And when Shirlie does well, I feel just as proud and excited as I would if something great had happened to me. But love is about sharing everything – it makes success twice as good, and pain and failure half as bad.

I still have the tumour. After the surgery, it started to shrink and darken. Now, it's a piece of dead skin floating in my brain. It reminds me that I'll never be "normal" again. I'll always have epilepsy and mild dyslexia. I'll always know there's a chance another tumour could turn up. But I'm glad. I don't want to be normal. I want a reminder of how precious my health is, and how lucky I am.

Weirdly, the experience has turned me into a bit of a daredevil. You may think that nearly dying makes you incredibly cautious, but it's made me into a person who snatches opportunities with both hands. I'm lucky, because I get asked to do all sorts of weird and wonderful TV jobs. When Roman was 15, we filmed a show called *The Dangerous Book For Boys* and flew old WWII Spitfire training planes. Roman was a little bit nervous at first, but after a few goes on a flight simulator, he took to it like a duck to… well, to the air, I suppose! It was utterly exhilarating. It was such a precious moment of freedom, and I was so happy to be able to share it with my boy. When you've spent so long worrying that you're going to die, it forces you off the sofa and out into the world, ready to embrace everything that comes your way. Every part of my world makes me feel lucky to be alive.

16

Steve Owen and Me

Martin

"Great, thanks for coming in, Martin. We'll be in touch."

I must have heard that sentence, or some version of it, over a thousand times in my lifetime. And it feels as though it means over a thousand things. If you're an insecure actor, you can try to interpret it, play it back in your mind and drive yourself up the wall, trying to crack the code.

Sometimes, someone will say it and mean, "We're about to offer you the opportunity of a lifetime." And sometimes it means, "We will *never* see you again." To be honest, when I heard it from the *EastEnders* executive producer Matthew Robinson, I was certain it was the second one and that he was too polite to say, "Don't let the door hit your arse on the way out."

Finding the door and *leaving* the audition was a bit of a challenge, let alone turning up and remembering my lines. At that point in my life, I was a complete mess. My brain tumours had left me with a complicated legacy. I wasn't myself. I didn't even look like myself. The steroids I'd been prescribed to bring down the inflammation had left me heavy and swollen. Remembering anything was a challenge. I could just about manage to remember Shirlie, Harley and Roman's names and the street where I lived. But my ability to memorise lines had vanished.

As an actor, it doesn't matter what you look like or how talented you are. If you don't have your memory, you've lost your most important tool. And my other major problem was another symptom of my recovery – spatial dyslexia.

Because the tumours had been sitting so heavily on my brain, key pathways had become confused and were still in the process of building new pathways. My brain couldn't always give the right signals to my body, which meant I constantly confused right and left.

* * *

But actors need to move, and the joke gets old pretty quickly. Also, leaving an audition is a little bit like going on a date. When you walk away, you're hoping the other person is looking at you, and you want to leave a lasting, strong impression. Even if you know you've nailed an audition, you're going to scupper your chances if you say "thanks very much!" and then walk into a wall.

The trouble with this particular audition was that I needed this job so badly. I needed any job. The stakes were high, and the opportunities weren't coming my way.

After the success of *The Krays*, Gary and I had been invited to go out and audition for acting jobs in Los Angeles. The film had been a cult hit in the States, and it caught the attention of lots of directors and producers. It meant that loads of exciting opportunities were coming our way – but it also meant that I was constantly away from home.

I'd go out for about four weeks at a time, because I couldn't face leaving the family for much longer. If I wasn't staying in George's house, I'd stay at a hotel called Le Parc in West Hollywood, weirdly a hotel I used to stay in with Spandau if we were playing a show in LA. In the band, we'd take over an entire floor, and the biggest room would be the party room, where we'd have a big bash after we played. I'd had so much fun with the band in California. We were constantly busy, and sometimes it felt as though you never had a second to yourself. But I'd have given anything to be back with the band during those LA auditions.

Sometimes, I'd be staying in the old party room, but it would just be me alone, either trying to learn my lines or speaking to Shirlie on the phone, running up huge bills. It was probably the loneliest time of my life. It seemed ironic. I was living the sort of life that sounded like a dream come true when I was a kid. Not only was I getting to act all the time, which I loved, but I was in Hollywood. I was working in the movies, but I just felt anxious and homesick.

In a way, it helped that Gary was out there with me, in the same position, but I couldn't help comparing myself with him. We'd spent our lives working together and working alongside each other. In the past, I'd been happy to just tag along. He was always the ambitious, driven, focused one, and I was the laid-back little brother, open to any opportunities that came my way. But in Hollywood, he was getting roles in huge blockbusters. He was starring alongside Kevin Costner and Whitney Houston in *The Bodyguard*, and I was appearing in the NBC *Movie of the Week*. Don't get me wrong, I was delighted to get the NBC job, and I was really proud of the work. It was going out to 50 million people and I wanted to do a brilliant job. But life in Los Angeles was so competitive. All I wanted to do was work, and auditions were difficult. Quickly, I realised it didn't matter how hard I tried to learn my lines or look the part. Everywhere you go in LA, you see hundreds and thousands of people who are more talented *and* better-looking than you. It's the land of the most beautiful people in the universe.

Before I was ill, LA was challenging but I loved it. Being out on my own for work sometimes took its toll, but when I was with Shirlie, Harley and George, beside the pool, feeling the sunshine warming my skin, it was the most glorious place on earth. And slowly, I was starting to break through. My hard work was paying off. My showreel was growing, the parts I was being offered were getting bigger, and I'd even mastered a decent American accent, which makes it much easier to get jobs. Then I came home, ended up in hospital and didn't work for four years.

The thing was that I *needed* to work, and I needed to act. Psychologically, it was very important to me. From that moment at Anna Scher's school, when I stopped being the shyest 11-year-old boy in the world, acting was the space where I could find my personality and work out who I was. When I was ill, I felt completely lost. So many of the key parts of my identity, being an actor, a performer and a provider for my family, had been taken away. I longed to act again, because I longed to express myself and get out of the pit of depression that I found myself in. And practically speaking, we needed an income.

Shirlie was at home, looking after two little children. When I was right in the middle of my illness, the "Pepsi & Shirlie" company had been declared bankrupt. We'd sold our house by the Heath, the place I'd been so proud of and so excited to raise my family in – and downsized to a much smaller house in Muswell Hill. We'd lost absolutely everything, and we'd cut back as much as possible to prepare for the worst-case scenario. If I died, and left Shirlie to bring up Harley and Roman, I wanted to be able to give them as much security as possible.

Money is funny. Gary and I had both grown up with next to nothing, and suddenly had access to absolutely everything. It can be very difficult to keep a sensible head on your shoulders when you're playing stadiums and staying in lavish hotel suites – when not that long ago you were getting up in the night to pee in a bucket because you were too scared to go out in the dark and use the outdoor toilet. Spandau was a juggernaut, and we were all being looked after – other people made the big money decisions and sorted out our smallest bills. But it seemed strange that we'd gone from being kids who thought nothing of jumping on planes to America, and running up thousand-pound phone bills, to worrying about paying the mortgage each month.

I suppose I wanted to run before I could walk. It seemed to be taking me so long to get better from my illness. I felt frustrated, impatient and scared that I'd never get another job again. So, desperate to prove myself, I flew back to LA.

It was far too soon though. My auditions were disastrous. I could barely remember a single line, and I was in a vortex that was sucking me in and spitting me back out. One of the hardest things was the lack of sympathy I encountered. No one was patient, or even friendly, really.

Brain tumours aren't contagious, but people treated me as though I had leprosy. LA is a city where everyone is obsessed with perfection, and as soon as anyone realised what I'd been through, they didn't want to know me. I remember going to an exercise class and noticing everyone was backing away. You'd think I'd been possessed by the devil by the way other people behaved.

At the time, I was staying at George's house. I couldn't afford a room at Le Parc and I was trying to save some money. I was sleeping in Anselmo's old bedroom. Anselmo Feleppa was George's first boyfriend, who died in 1993. George was back in London, but just being in his house made me feel safe. Life felt tougher than ever, and every single audition went badly. But there was something comforting sleeping in Anselmo's old room.

One restless night, I had a surprise visitor. I woke up to feel a warm hand in the middle of my back. At first, it was startling, then it was profoundly comforting. Very clearly, I heard Anselmo's voice in my ear. He'd always spoken softly and beautifully – instead of yelling for attention, he made sure you were really listening to him. He said, quite simply, "It's all going to be OK," and then he was gone. The tension eased out of my body and I was filled with a feeling of deep peace. I shut my eyes and drifted off to sleep.

The memory of Anselmo's words came to me. I had to ring Shirlie and tell her what happened. It felt so emotional and intense that I burst into tears. Shirlie, who had at that point been up for hours with the kids, was a little sceptical. "Are you sure it wasn't just a dream? Jet-lag?" she suggested. But as time passed, I felt sure it was an old friend offering support and comfort when I needed it most.

The strangest part of all was that Anselmo was right. A couple of days later, I had a message asking if I could come back to London for another audition. The producers of *EastEnders* wanted to see me. Could I prepare for a meeting?

Now, deep down, I knew this was another job I wasn't ready for. There's a cliché about actors with a lot of truth to it. If someone asks us if we can do something, we'll say, "Sure! Of course!" even if we don't have a clue. If we get the job, we can just teach ourselves how to do it, whatever "it" is. Do you think everyone who gets cast in the musical *Starlight Express* knows how to rollerskate? Of course not. They want the work, and if they can learn lines in a day, they can learn how to deliver the lines on four wheels.

Before I was ill, I was cast in a Disney movie called *Aspen Extreme*, playing a German ski instructor.

"Can you ski?" I was asked at the audition.

"Of course I can ski!" I replied. Well, how hard could it be? If I was given the role, maybe I could hit the beach and try to build a dry slope out of sand.

When I was given the part, I was chuffed – and I'd completely forgotten about my white, snowy lie. Shirlie and I flew out to Aspen. On the first day of filming, the actors lined up. There were about six of us playing ski instructors. *I'll just watch what the others are doing and copy them,* I thought to myself. It turned out, though, that not one of us knew how to ski.

Eventually, the skiing scenes were all performed by stunt doubles – and I was given my own ski instructor for about four weeks. By the end of the shoot, I was flying down the slopes. If I could learn how to ski, I could learn how to act again. Even though I felt as though I was at rock bottom, I could feel a glimmer of my old confidence returning.

The *EastEnders* role wasn't just a job, either. It was a scheme George had cooked up. He knew I was desperate to get back to work and that not having an income was scary and frustrating. He'd been endlessly generous and kind to all of us during my recovery, but he understood something crucial – that, to recover fully, I needed to feel as though I was establishing some independence and moving on. George got in touch with Michelle Collins and they got me an audition for *EastEnders*. OK, George had been addicted to the programme for years and tuned into every episode. I've often thought it was *EastEnders* that kept him in London.

Michelle was a series regular, and George asked her to arrange a meeting with Matthew Robinson, the producer. Everyone I knew kept telling me not to do it. Back in the 90s, the TV landscape was very different, and even though 20 million people were tuning into *EastEnders*, there was a real snobbery about it. People thought you could never play Hamlet if you'd been in a soap.

"What about *The Krays?* Your CV? Your career? You've been in Hollywood!" they'd say.

Firstly, I thought they were being ridiculous. This was an iconic show with a vast audience. If you were in *EastEnders*, you got to act all the time and be part of an evolving storyline. It was a brilliant challenge and a truly great opportunity for any actor. Secondly, well, what *about* my career? I wasn't in a position to pick and choose or turn any work down. The work was scarce, the stakes were high and, most of all, I owed this to my family.

After that first audition, I knew I'd been truly appalling. I wouldn't have hired me. I'd stepped into that room and let my anxieties get the better of me. All I'd wanted was to do a good job, but the harder I tried, the more my brain struggled to work. I stumbled and fluffed my way through it with little belief.

The next few days at home were hard. The depression was starting to swallow me up. My life had been filled with so much love and happiness, I'd experienced some truly golden days. But maybe I'd used up all my luck. I was desperate to do right by Shirlie, Harley and Roman. What would happen to us all if I couldn't work?

Still, windows of opportunity are funny things. Sometimes, you spot them from a long way away, and you have to climb up a wall to get to a distant, metaphorical skylight. Sometimes, it's a French window of opportunity – it's enormous, it's unmissable and someone turns the handle, swings it open and ushers you straight through. That's what happened here. I had the luckiest break of my life when I needed it the most.

Matthew Robinson got back in touch with my agent. "Martin was absolutely *awful*," he said. "I think we need another go. Could he come back in and do the audition again?"

It is very, very rare that you get a second chance to do anything like this. But the second chance was exactly what I needed. The first time around, I'd made such a mess of things because I was so nervous. Entering the audition room, I'd pictured my worst fears and they'd all come true. When I came back, I knew it couldn't possibly go that badly twice, so I relaxed. I knew Matthew had seen me at my absolute worst, so the pressure was off.

The lines came right into my head when I needed them. For the first time since my operations, I could feel my brain working with me. It was my ally, not my enemy. Even though I was nervous and lacking in confidence, as the meeting went on, I started to realise that I'd probably get the part. I knew, because I recognised the feeling that I always have when things are going well – not excitement or pride, but relief. My future had felt so scary and uncertain. If I bagged this job, I was going to be OK.

How could I possibly thank George enough for everything he'd done for me? I knew I'd never be able to repay him – but he had a pretty good idea of how I could.

"Here, take my blue jumper to work," he said one day, giving me a bundle of wool.

"Thanks. Um, why?" I asked. Was cold weather forecast for Elstree?

"It's not for you, it's for Steve Owen," said George. "Wear it for me one day on camera – that way, I can have a walk-on part in *EastEnders*. You know it's always been my dream!"

There's no doubt about it – Steve Owen helped me get

better. He's a character who inspires and provokes people in lots of different ways, but I'll always love him. When I started on the show, the two of us were poles apart. But as I learnt how to function, I borrowed all kinds of tips and tricks from him.

Ever since I was a kid, I'd been curious about charisma, what it was and how it worked. How it was a magnetic force that attracted people. Well, Steve had charisma to spare. Even though he murdered Saskia, people loved his vulnerability. Steve was able to get away with all kinds of sketchy schemes because he had so much confidence and charm. In real life, when I started, I was lacking that confidence, but spending time as Steve helped me to let it grow. My brain was so raw and still in the process of reshaping itself, so I think it was inevitable that I took on a little bit of Steve. Even now, when I'm walking into a party, or going into a room where I don't know anyone, I channel him – not the violence or the dodgy dealing, but the charm.

Mind you, not everyone loved Steve – even though it seemed that everyone felt as though they knew him. One day, I was walking down Tottenham Court Road when I heard a voice yelling, "Steve Owen!"

And from out of nowhere a man ran up to me and punched me in the chest as hard as he could. The punch completely winded me and I couldn't get a good look at him as he ran away. I was standing on Tottenham Court Road, doubled over, trying to get my breath back. It took me a couple of days to get over the shock.

Ultimately, you have to be philosophical about that sort of thing. No one wants to get hit, but it's incredible to play a character who evokes such an extreme response in people. I could completely understand why someone might want to hit Steve Owen.

Steve had become one of the most recognisable faces on TV. The show went out to nearly 20 million people three times a week. I was in a supermarket once when a little old lady in front of me turned around and stared. "I *knew* it was you," she said, eventually. "I recognised you from the sound of your breathing."

To be honest, my favourite critics, and the ones I care the most about, are Harley and Roman. When she was little, I think Harley struggled with the idea of me being on TV. It was difficult for her when we went out as a family. She didn't want lots of people rushing over to speak to her dad, and she found it hard to deal with the fact that so many people felt as though they knew me.

Because filming was quite intense, we didn't have as much time to spend together as a family as we would have liked. During my illness, Harley was used to having me at home all the time, playing in the garden every day. I loved being with my family all day long. Suddenly, I wasn't at home all the time *and*, when we were together, there were lots of other people vying for my attention.

Roman was the complete opposite. Even though he was too young to watch *EastEnders* when I was on it, he was really proud that his dad was on the show. We still tease him about something that happened during his first year at school, when the local fire station came to the playground to put on a demonstration.

One of the firemen brought out his hose and said, "This is 100ft long, it sprays hundreds of litres of water every second and can put out a building that's caught fire in minutes."

Roman leapt to his feet. "You may think that's impressive," said Roman to the crowd of his school friends. "Well – my dad is *Steve Owen*!"

I have nothing but fond memories of my time on *EastEnders*. Getting that job was one of the luckiest opportunities of my life. Working always feels like a privilege, but this was an extra special one. *EastEnders* is a show that belongs to everyone, and being Steve Owen reminded me that working in entertainment comes with a lot of responsibility. I was entering millions of living rooms every single week, and that meant being at the top of my game. I'm really proud of the work I did, and really grateful to

George, Michelle and Matthew for taking a chance on me and giving me back the confidence I'd lost over the previous years.

Most of all, I'm grateful to Shirlie. She's the one who was endlessly patient with me. She would go through my lines over and over and over again, while my brain was piecing itself back together. She was the one who always had confidence in me, when I had none in myself. Although I was becoming like Steve Owen in lots of ways, she made sure that, at home, I was still Martin. At work, I was making drama, but when I finished for the day, I had no more drama to deal with, because I knew I was coming back to a place that was always calm and quiet. Well, as calm and quiet as any place can be when you have two little kids running around. Without Shirlie, there could have been no Steve.

Then in the year 2000, I won a National Television Award for my work on *EastEnders* and I dedicated it to Shirlie.

After they called my name – other than thanking Shirlie, I barely remember my speech – we slipped out of the Royal Albert Hall and sat on the edge of a fountain, holding hands. We didn't have to say anything. A few years ago, we'd both been so scared that I was going to die. Winning the Most Popular Actor award was a real pat on the back. And it was a pat on the back for all my family, who had helped me through all those awful years – the way they willed me better, supported and most of all believed in me. As you grow older, you realise success isn't something you deserve, it's something you earn. Going through those awful dark times has made me appreciate it all so much more.

17

Empty Nests and Later-Life Adventures

Shirlie

Confidence is a funny thing. Growing up, I never felt completely relaxed in my own skin – I was constantly anxious and self-conscious. But every so often, I'd feel something shift. I've never been the sort of woman who could walk into a room and want to be the centre of attention, but sometimes, when I was doing something I truly loved, I'd forget myself and become so absorbed in the task at hand that I'd forget to worry about how I looked or who was watching me.

Dancing with my dad, or helping Tracey with the horses, I'd feel a real sense of flow – and I'd be so connected with my work that I'd have a chance to escape my worries and fears. Later, I experienced it when I was dancing with George. I loved performing because I had a job to do. Not just entertaining an audience, but making sure my friend looked good and felt good. I think that's why I had stage fright so rarely. When I had a task, and knew I was able to complete it, I experienced a blissful absence of anxiety.

In many ways, this is how I feel about being a mum.

When I was pregnant with Harley, I felt blissfully happy because I'd been longing for that moment for years. It never occurred to me to worry about what could go wrong, or what lay ahead, because I felt so connected with a primal purpose. Perhaps this is why the labour took so long. I'd made things so relaxing for baby Harley that she didn't want to come out.

It took me a little while to get used to motherhood, partly because I'd assumed I'd know what to do straight away. It made me very anxious to discover that sometimes I'd make mistakes and I didn't have all the answers. But when Roman was born, I was overjoyed. I'd worked out what I was doing – or rather, I'd worked out that no parent ever *really* knows what they're doing. And I had everything I'd ever wanted: a home with Martin and our two beautiful, brilliant babies.

Harley and Roman's childhood was often a real struggle. Their first memories are of Martin's illness and that period when we were desperately attempting to make ends meet. But even so, I have so many happy memories of their early years and what it was like to be a new mum. Parenting gave me purpose. When you have two little children to run after, you're constantly busy, and once again, I was in that glorious state of flow. I loved it because I didn't have any time to worry about how well I was doing. I was completely focused on keeping them alive. Perhaps because of the shock of Martin's brain tumour, I didn't spend too much time worrying about how well they were doing, or how they were developing. If they could be happy and healthy, that was a gift. Everything else was a bonus.

Nothing brings me more joy than expressing unconditional love, and every day, I get to show my children just how much I love them. When they were little, if they had problems, Martin and I usually knew exactly how to fix them. Don't get me wrong, the early years were hard work. Every parent knows how it feels to collapse into bed, not knowing whether you're dreaming, or hallucinating from sheer tiredness, only to be woken up about 20 minutes later by a tiny person who wants to tell you they've wet the bed or they have some urgent questions about why the sky is blue. We were broke, knackered and overwhelmed – but those were some of the happiest days of my life. I've sung and danced in front of hundreds of thousands of people – but there's no audience like a two-year-old and a five-year-old begging for an encore of 'Twinkle Twinkle Little Star'.

For me, the hardest part of parenting has been letting go. Nothing has made me more proud than watching Harley and Roman making their own way in the world – but it broke my heart a little bit, too.

It became apparent very quickly that our children were both driven, focused and creative in their own ways. It would have been easy to overdo things and push them as soon as they showed signs of promise. But Martin and I agreed that we needed to give them plenty of room to explore and experiment. Martin has always said he loves working because he has so much fun doing it. The dream we had for both of them was that they would eventually find jobs they loved so much that they felt like hobbies. I think lots of parents go the other way, and their talented children find themselves forced into hobbies that feel like jobs.

When Harley became interested in photography, I was delighted – but I knew I needed to give her the room to work out what her style was. When she and Roman were little, I loved involving them with my own photography, and they were some of my first models. Just for fun, we'd all drive out to the countryside and have an adventure. At the time, I loved getting them to dress up as Victorian children, and they were happy to oblige. I think this sparked off Harley's interest. If nothing else, maybe it's what made her decide that she wanted to be behind the camera – anything was better than standing in front of it, wearing Victorian clothes!

Having hated school, Harley decided she didn't want to go to university. I remembered just how miserable I'd been at school, and I had a lot of sympathy for her. Back in the 60s and 70s, no one really cared about how children were feeling. We were all expected to put up and shut up. "Your school days are the best days of your life!" said the grown-ups. That's a phrase that has only ever made me feel worse. Imagine being scared, anxious and miserable all the time, and being told that those are your "best days". I was terrified about what was to come.

In the way that learning about alternative healing opened my eyes to the alternative ways to treat our bodies and minds, becoming a mother made me realise there are plenty of great ways to get an education beyond the accepted norm. So, as soon as I realised Harley felt the way I did, I decided to think about my own childhood and what would have helped me when I was struggling.

When I was ready to leave school, I'd gone to Sussex with Tracey. At the time, it seemed like the perfect opportunity – I didn't want to learn in a classroom, I wanted to learn in the paddock. But when Harley was 16, I finally understood why my mum had been so devastated when I left home. I looked at my little girl, and part of me couldn't believe that I'd put my own parents through that. I wasn't completely happy about the idea of Harley going to London by herself for a day trip. I knew that supporting her independence was the right thing to do, and that she'd have to leave one day. But I was delighted when Martin had his studio brain-wave. Harley could learn how to be a photographer in her own time, at her own pace, and she wouldn't be going anywhere for a while.

As always, the years flew by, and my baby girl had become a skilled, confident and experienced young woman. Her work was in demand and she was ready to move out. And I was devastated.

What made it very hard for both of us was the fact that it wasn't an easy decision for Harley, either. My daughter and I are incredibly close because we're so alike. And I knew there was a part of Harley that would never be ready to leave home. At the time, it seemed like the right thing to do, though. A few friends were setting up a house-share, and as she was doing so much work in London, it made sense for her to be a bit more central. It was a very logical step, and I wanted Harley to go out and have the time of her life. I thought that I might be devastated for a week or two, and then I'd be able to process it. But nothing could have prepared me for how much I was going to miss her.

Harley and I are two of a kind: very sensitive and very private. Our good friends are our family, and our family are our best friends. When we love someone, we let them in, but you really have to earn our trust and loyalty. Roman is much more open and gregarious, like Martin – I knew that when the right moment came, he'd love living in London in his own place. But I was worried that Harley would be horribly homesick. She reminded me of myself, and I remembered being her age and the way I'd fall apart and move back in with my mum whenever Martin was on tour.

I had what I called Wendy Craig moments, as in *Butterflies*, where I was wandering around aimlessly looking for a purpose. It's that inevitable transitional phase that I'm sure lots of parents go through when their children become young adults and want to find their own way in the world. Although it's a great thing, you can't help but feel you're no longer needed. Suddenly, life had no schedule to stick to, no more school drop-offs, football practice and dance lessons. The world seemed to get a little bit smaller and little bit quieter.

But the reality was bittersweet. Harley moved in with a group of girl friends, and they all got on like a house on fire. (Happily, that was just a metaphor – the building stayed safe and stable during their tenancy.) She'd ring up and tell us what a brilliant time she was having and how much she loved her new life.

Martin was delighted. I think he'd been a little worried about how Harley would manage on her own, because he knews how Harley's mind worked – just like mine. He knew that in the end, moving out would be great for Harley's confidence – and he thought she'd take to it much more quickly than I was expecting her to.

Martin was right. (Incidentally, that's how a marriage lasts as long as ours has done. When your partner is right and you are wrong, you need to put your hands up and admit it.) We're both so proud of Harley for being able to stick it out and, most importantly, she's proud of herself. Since she moved away, she's achieved so much, and I think that's because enjoying her independence has boosted her confidence. She knows she's capable of going through all kinds of situations and that she can cope.

If I'm honest, however, I'm *still* finding it hard. I don't think anyone ever talks about the challenges of being a parent with grown-up children. In some ways, going through that situation with Harley prepared me for what it would be like with Roman – but Roman has always been so independent and outgoing that I think I'd been preparing since the day he was born. It was Martin who struggled when Ro moved out, and it was my turn to be there for him.

We both adore both of our children equally, and we cherish their similarities and their differences. But they will both tell you they have very different relationships with the two of us. Martin and Roman have always bonded over football, and Harley and I over photography and music.

The thing about children, teenagers especially, is that if they want to confide in you, they don't usually want to sit down and have a deep and meaningful conversation. They'll do it stealthily, under the pretext of something else, when you're talking about camera lenses, or a tense moment in an Arsenal match. While I've always been aware that I have a strong, pragmatic, masculine streak, I think there's something about the way that boys and girls bond, too. Girls and women are expected to share their feelings with each other – and boys and men are told to express themselves in different ways.

When Harley moved out, I fell apart. I felt as though I'd lost one of my best friends. We still spoke and saw each other all the time, but the house felt so empty. It didn't make sense. I'd walk into the kitchen, singing, expecting her to join me on the chorus – but the house stayed quiet. Or I'd think I heard her voice, and rush into a room, but it was just the radio.

Because Harley was my firstborn, we'd been through so much together. She taught me how to be a mum, because she needed my love and care, and because she's so nurturing and maternal. She loved to dance, and often she would break into dance and get me to do it, too. The music would come on in the kitchen, and she would teach me all her new body-popping moves. That laughter, that spontaneous moment when we were in our home, dancing, took me back to dancing with George in his bedroom and with my dad.

Harley had a big energy and a presence that, when she moved away from the family home, left an emptiness. I desperately missed the noise. I knew there would be no more raves in the kitchen. What I love most about Harley is that she inspires me, she's a hardworking and talented woman, and I'm so proud I created a stronger female than me. Martin and Roman missed her, too – but they were usually bonding over the football when Harley and I were gossiping over tea in the kitchen.

It was a weird time. I needed to be needed, and everyone needed me a little bit less. It brought back some of the grief I'd experienced when Martin's parents died. I lost my mum when I was 43, while Harley and Roman were teenagers. She was 71 and had gone into hospital to be fitted with a new nebuliser for her asthma. During that week, she rapidly deteriorated and we were told that she was dying. This was a terrible shock, especially because we weren't prepared to say goodbye. It brought back those same fears I had as a five-year-old: mums can't die.

Because the Kemps, Frank and Eileen, died days apart in January 2009, we were all stunned to lose them both so quickly.

Soon after my mum died, we realised my dad had vascular dementia. We didn't realise it while she was alive because he'd always been eccentric, and their relationship was so dysfunctional that she didn't connect with him emotionally. But now that we were face to face with my dad, we noticed he would do strange things. One time, he poured washing-up liquid on the carpet because he said it was crawling with ants. He would constantly ring me up, saying, "Where are you? Someone is at the door."

Realising your parents need help is hard for children, as you become aware of how vulnerable they are. And the feelings of guilt and *"Am I doing right by them?"* are greater than ever. Eventually, we found a home for my dad, but sadly one day he fell and broke his hip. I received a phone call telling me he had fallen and had been taken to Watford General Hospital. By the time I arrived, he was in a room ready to have hip surgery and was very confused.

My dad had never said he loved me, even though in action I felt it. And I had never said "I love you" back. The day before, I'd been chatting to Pepsi, and she told me that I should tell him I love him. I brushed this off, thinking I didn't feel comfortable doing this.

But on that day in the hospital, looking at him lying there, I had Pepsi's words swirling in my head. And then just like that, as awkward as it felt, I simply said, "I love you."

He looked up at me, and quietly said, "I love you, too. Give my love to all."

I left the room as they took him away, and he died on the operating table. That was the last time I saw my dad, and I've been forever grateful that I said those three words.

When it came to my children leaving home, I hadn't understood how much I loved looking after them and having them around. Even though I'd grown up in a noisy, chaotic house, and longed for quiet and calm, I'd learnt to love that feeling of having a house full of life. I'd just about got used to the fact that I'd never walk into a room and see Eileen curled up on the sofa, looking for the remote – and now there was another empty space where Harley was supposed to sit.

My menopause added a layer of complication to everything as well. I'd struggled with my periods all my life, so you'd think I'd be delighted for that chapter to be over. But going through the menopause was worse than going through puberty in reverse. I always felt sensitive and horribly hot. It reminded me of being on those dreadful fertility drugs when I was trying to conceive Harley. I used to be able to dance on stage for hours without breaking a sweat. Suddenly, I was waking up in the night, having soaked the bed sheets. I constantly felt oversensitive, physically and emotionally.

Martin has always been very tactile and, when he saw how sad I was about Harley, he just wanted to cuddle me until I felt better.

"Martin, get off!" I'd cry, as he reached for me. "I feel as though I'm on fire!"

It's a strange thing to say, but for every hurdle you overcome there is another one waiting for you. This was a very different sort of challenge. I had to work out who I was.

* * *

Every weekend, our house had been full of teenage boys, gathered in the den, watching the football. Roman's friends had always accepted Martin as one of their own, and he'd got on with them easily, talking about sports and music. When Roman left, his friends stopped coming over. Martin hadn't realised that socialising with that group had been such a huge part of his life until it didn't exist any more when Roman left home.

I was heartbroken for Martin, and I missed my little boy, but it redefined the parameters of our relationship. Suddenly, it was just the two of us, together again, and we had to learn how to simply slow down and be with each other. We weren't pouring all of our energies into the kids and what they were getting up to. It was time for us to reconnect with each other. We had to remember how we started, and we needed to reconfigure our relationship in a way that reflected everything we'd been through. From pop stars to parents, from Bushey to Beverley Hills and back again.

A couple of years ago, Martin received a call about a TV show – they wanted him to be on a rally driving team with Roman, going through south-east Asia, from Thailand to Vietnam. Martin was desperate to do it.

"It will be great fun," he said to me, "*and* they're going to give us a beautiful classic car. Imagine!"

Roman was a big part of the draw. His show on Capital was doing really well, and the producers were keen to get him on board – but he couldn't get the time off work. So Martin asked me if I fancied getting in the car with him.

"I don't know that it's really my sort of thing," I said. "The heat, the noise, the stress – it will be me and you, cooped up in a car for ages. I don't think I'll be much good at it."

At the time, my confidence was at a real low. Having been battered by the menopause, I felt strange and self-conscious. I don't like the limelight on a good day, when I've been to the hairdresser. Just thinking about it made me feel sweaty and stressed.

Martin was persuasive. "I think you'll be great, Shirlie," he said. "It's a chance for us to spend some time together and go on a real adventure. Let's give it a try. I think if you didn't have a go, you'd always regret it."

Over the years following his recovery, Martin had developed a bit of a daredevil streak. I think that supporting him through his illness had made me more cautious – and more anxious. I'd gone from being relatively carefree to being much more of a worrier. We'd lost everything, but somehow managed to find a new normal. I was scared to discover what else could go wrong.

I think Martin had much more of a survivor mentality. He'd been to hell and back, and he saw every weird and wonderful request as a gift – an opportunity. He'd been fully focused on his career and was ambitious to achieve as an actor. Now, he was open-minded and enthusiastic about everything that came his way. The more he embraced these unexpected new opportunities, the more he was offered. Flying around with Roman in tiny WWII planes? Bring it on! Swimming through ice in the Arctic? Why not! And while I worried about him, I couldn't help but be touched by his positivity.

So Martin managed to talk me into it. I'd never been to that part of the world, and I longed to see Cambodia. Also, if I'm honest, I was *slightly* concerned about Martin's driving. He's a real petrolhead, and I knew that if I took the wheel, I wouldn't be worrying about us getting back in one piece.

"I'll do it – as long as you leave the driving to me," I said.

When we arrived in Thailand, we couldn't wait to see the car. I thought of my dad, and the huge, vintage American beasts he used to drive, and fantasised about Chryslers and Cadillacs. Waiting to be shown our car, we spotted a beautiful bright yellow Mini.

"That's a lovely one," I said to the producer. "What are we driving?"

She gestured to the Mini. "This *is* what you're driving."

We didn't know whether to laugh or cry. The car was gorgeous, but Martin is over 6ft tall. When he gets into a Mini, his knees end up next to his ears.

To get the recording equipment in, the car had been pretty much stripped out, so it was bare, apart from our hard seats. At the time, I had a bad back, so I had to be padded up to be able to sit down and drive without being distracted by the pain of my slipped disc.

We were following a tulip map, which is typically used in rally driving. It's more like a set of instructions with arrows than a traditional map, and while it's useful for when you're driving off road, it's a bit of a shock when you're used to an AA Road Atlas. The car was fitted with a device that looked a little bit like a taximeter, and we were supposed to push it as we followed the map, so we could record our progress. Unfortunately, because Martin was far too big for the car, he kept knocking it with his knee and putting us back at zero. Combined with the Thai heat and the rudimentary air con – an open window – it wasn't just a test of our driving, but a test of our marriage, too!

One night, early on, I had a vivid and disturbing dream. Waking up, I dashed to the bathroom, my heart pounding and my face burning. I was very, very sick.

Martin was worried. "Shirlie, what's wrong? What's going on? Do you think it's something you ate?"

I shook my head. "No, it's fear. I don't think we should drive today. I had a premonition that we crashed. I don't think it's safe."

My dream had been scarily clear – we'd flipped the car over and rolled down a hill. It was so vivid that I could smell the dust and grass as we tumbled over and over. I'd never been so frightened that I'd thrown up before, and I thought it made sense to listen to my body.

Martin tried to calm me down. "Look, it's new, that's all. You're in an unfamiliar place, of course you're anxious. There's jet-lag, there's the heat. But there are loads of people here to look after us. Everything is going to be fine."

After a chat with the producer, I decided to have a go. Maybe I was just being paranoid.

It was speed test day. We were driving in some old farmland, along a really muddy road surrounded by paddy fields. We really did feel as though we were in the middle of nowhere, surrounded by nothing but rice fields and sky. It looked beautiful, but it made it very hard to see where we were going. It didn't help that Martin's competitive streak had been aroused. OK, *our* competitive streak. Noel Edmonds and his wife Liz had been making some really fast times, and my anxiety was briefly forgotten. We were going to win this challenge!

We sped along, Martin's knee knocking the device and rendering the tulip map useless. It was OK for a while – the path was straight and clear, even though it was hard to see thanks to the red dust everywhere. Suddenly, we were heading for a huge tree. I don't know how fast we were going exactly, but I'd floored the accelerator pedal. If I slammed the brakes on, we'd still hit it. What could I do? I had to think fast. Before my brain knew what my hands were doing, I was turning the steering wheel as hard as I could – and, in seconds, we were reliving my dream. For one surreal moment, we were flying up into the air. Then we were tumbling, over and over.

The crash was deafeningly noisy. My senses were overloaded, and I was overwhelmed by the sound of hot metal scraping and crumpling. So when we finally stopped, the silence was eerie. I was still clutching the steering wheel, but it was upside down. And so was I. The feeling rushed back into my skin, and I breathed in and out, touching my fingertips to my throat. *I'm alive,* I thought. *I'm alive.*

The silence was shattered by a croaking noise coming from beside me. "Fuckin' 'ell," went the noise. "Fuckin' 'ell, fuckin' 'ell, *fuckin' 'ell."*

Martin was screaming with pain. He'd instinctively grabbed onto the flimsy roof when we started rolling – and now the entire weight of the car was trapping his arm.

Still mic'd up, I opened my upside-down door and hopped out of the car, calling for help. I had no idea where the crew were – or how long we'd need to wait for a doctor to find us.

"Help! *Help!"* I screamed, while trying, and failing, to lift the car off Martin's arm. Suddenly, I had a scary thought. The car was full of petrol. Was it about to blow up?

A couple of local farmworkers rushed over to help. I'm sure they were confused and quite frightened by this mad blonde woman yelling like a banshee, but they were incredibly kind. Unfortunately, they didn't realise what was happening with Martin's arm, and they started trying to roll the car the right way up, which made things worse. Luckily, they were nearly as small as me and didn't make much progress. All I could think about was Martin's arm. Was it broken? What if he could never play bass guitar again?

Miraculously, the location scout arrived with two brilliant Swiss doctors, and we managed to release Martin and get him out of the car, just before his epilepsy kicked in. At that point, I felt weirdly calm. This was almost exactly as it had happened in my dream. Martin was hurt, but no one had died and the medics were here.

When you're very anxious, it's sometimes a strange relief when the worst possible thing happens. Because I felt like I'd predicted the worst of it, I felt strangely relaxed. It helped that the two doctors were magnificent. We rushed Martin to a local hospital, and they more or less took it over, installing their own portable equipment. Mercifully, nothing was broken, and thanks to their quick thinking and expertise, the nerves in Martin's arm were fine, too.

Understandably, Martin had gone into shock. It was over 35 degrees outside, but he was shivering. While he was lying under a thick, brown blanket, I phoned home to talk to Harley and Roman.

"Now, please don't worry," I said, which is a pointless way to start a sentence, because as soon as you hear it, you start worrying. "Me and your dad have had an accident during one of the challenges. We flipped the car, but we're completely fine. Your dad hurt his arm, but he's been checked over and he's going to be OK. I think we may come home, though. We're both pretty shaken up."

Not for the first time, Roman surprised me. He's much wiser than I am. If the situation had been reversed, I would have been chartering a flight for him and dashing to the airport. But Roman was weirdly calm.

"Mum, you know what?" he said. "I reckon you should both keep going. The worst is over. You'll probably have a much better time now you know you've survived this. And I think that when you look back on it all, you'll be so proud of yourself for sticking it out. You'll never forgive yourself if you come home."

Listening to my son was spooky. This is exactly what we'd taught him. Never give up. Even when things get tough, and scary, you have to stick it out. It's the best way to grow. Roman is a living example of the values that he's been raised with, but I never thought he'd be teaching those values back to me. And I knew that if he'd been able to come on the trip with Martin, he wouldn't have let the crash hold him back.

It was completely worth it. Reaching the end of the challenge felt like a huge achievement, and we were rewarded with stunning scenery. When we reached the Vietnam coast and saw the sea sparkling in the distance, I felt as though a huge weight had been lifted off my chest. It helped that the

Mini had been declared unsafe, so we completed our journey in a Nissan Qashqai. Not nearly as groovy, but much more comfortable. We'd been chugging along these dark, dusty trails. Finally, figuratively and literally, we saw the light.

Our experience was strange and scary, but it was brilliant, too. After decades of marriage, Martin and I needed to be reminded that we could still discover new things about each other, and getting out of our comfort zone was a fantastic way to do that. I definitely don't recommend getting into a car accident as a way of giving your relationship a boost – but it did bring us closer together. It reminded us that we're both vulnerable and fallible, and that we still have plenty of adventures to come. Roman was right, as well. Surviving the experience was a huge confidence boost, and helped me work through some of the self-doubt and anxiety that had descended during the menopause.

I think the only downside was that when the show was on TV, some viewers fell over themselves to make jokes about women drivers. "That's what happens when you let your wife take the wheel!" joked one Twitter user to Martin. "You should have been driving!" I think we all know the answer to that. If I'd been in the passenger seat, we would have been going at 250 miles an hour – and we would definitely have hit that tree.

18

Close Encounters
with Friendly Ghosts

Martin

Luck is a funny old thing. On the one hand, I firmly believe you make your own luck. It's up to all of us to find opportunities and be open to new, exciting possibilities. I'm sure that a combination of optimism and gratitude is what keeps life interesting and ensures that good fortune will keep coming your way.

Or to put it another way, there is some spiritual guide, a heavenly presence that has taken that hand and is leading you through a complicated maze.

Ever since I was a little kid, running from the shadows in the basement, I've believed in the supernatural. When I was about 12, just after we moved to Elmore Street, I had the first paranormal experience I can remember.

Our brand new house didn't open straight out onto the street. We had a little front garden and a gate that opened out onto the pavement. I remember my mum getting excited about how posh it was. I'd been used to looking both ways, carefully, before walking out onto the busy road, but Elmore Street was a little bit quieter. The street was largely residential, and it was rare to get much traffic – especially in the mornings when I was on my way to school.

One morning, I left the house thinking about the day ahead, seeing my friends and probably what was on telly the night before, when I heard a voice in my ear, as if someone was talking to me. It wasn't an outside sound or even a thought in my head. It was a voice talking to me directly, as though they needed to tell me something really important. It was a man's voice, clear and deep, pitched slightly lower than my dad's. The voice seemed to speak slowly, as if it wanted to make sure I wasn't going to be scared. Still, I sensed some urgency. It simply said, "Go back inside the house."

This was *weird*. I wasn't in the habit of hearing strange voices, and for a second, I paused, my hand on the latch of the gate. I started to walk back towards the front door, trying to make sense of what had just happened, when I heard an almighty bang.

A Ford Cortina had careered into the space between two cars parked in the road. The exact space where I would have been standing if I hadn't heard the voice. The driver got out and ran, abandoning the vehicle. I didn't know what to do. I went to school as normal, and I think my mum reported the car wreck to the police. At the time, I was a child and I had no idea how to deal with what had happened to me. I couldn't explain it. People would think I was crazy. Someone – or something – had stopped me from finding myself in between those cars.

Around a year later, Steve, a school friend of mine, became fascinated by Ouija boards and ghost-writing, where you let your mind drift away and the pen moves by itself in the same way the Ouija glass moves. His dad had died a few years earlier, and he and his mum were still living with shock and grief. In certain parts of North London, some old Victorian and Edwardian ideas and values lingered long after the era had ended, and his mum had a kind of Victorian fascination with the gothic. Some days, after school, I'd go to his house and, with his mum, we'd attempt to communicate with the spirit world. We were always hoping to hear from his dad.

It was about 4.30 in the afternoon and I remember the sunlight trying to peep through the curtains, illuminating the room just enough to reveal the dust motes dancing through the air and the gleam of heavy, silver photo frames. The house smelled of an English garden, with faded notes of rose, lavender and tea. It felt comforting – not dissimilar to my own house, but maybe a bit more affluent.

We sat around a dark wooden table, watching the glass spin around the old-fashioned Ouija board, spelling out "A MESSAGE FOR MARTIN". The room felt a little cooler, and I could feel goosebumps rising on my forearms. Steve nudged me.

"Let's see what it says," I muttered, trying to sound calm as the glass picked up pace.

"I AM YOUR GUIDE. MY NAME IS LEN."

My heart was hammering in my chest. I said my goodbyes and raced out of the house. I nearly didn't bother to put my shoes on, I was so desperate to get home. I was only 10 years old, and this was frightening stuff. I'd just been messing about. Who was Len? Why was he guiding me?

For a few days, I didn't tell anyone. I lost my appetite and, even for a shy kid, I was quieter than usual.

My mum and dad were worried. "What's up?" asked my dad. "Has something happened? You don't seem yourself."

"Whatever it is, you can tell us," added Mum. "Don't worry if you're in some sort of trouble. We can help."

I knew my mum would have gone crazy. Deep down, she was quite religious and believed that if there's good then there's evil, and if there's God then there must be a devil. I knew I was going to upset her, but I pushed the words out and finally told her about the strange message from "Len".

"I don't even know anyone called Len!" I added, indignantly.

My dad went a whiter shade of pale and my mum clutched a hand to her heart and threw a look over to my dad. My dad was silent, but my mum spoke in a relaxed tone that made me feel safe, the way she always did when she told me that everything was going to be alright.

"Len was one of the foremen at your dad's print-works," she explained. "He died a few years ago. He knew all about you and Gary. Dad was always talking about you and saying how proud he was of his boys."

Once I'd managed to get over my fears, I decided I loved the idea of being guided by Len. I still think it's Len who managed to save my life and stopped me from standing in the space that car had crashed into. I believe there must have been thousands of tiny moments when Len was looking out for me over the years. And he wasn't the only one.

Being "visited" by Anselmo, just after my illness, was a huge comfort. Maybe it was just a dream, but I'll never forget how comforted I felt by the sense of his presence and the warmth of his hand on my back. I like to think that sometimes ghosts show up and make themselves known in a direct way, and sometimes they manifest unexpectedly.

One night, I was staying at my parents' house. At the time, Shirlie and I were in our very first apartment in Highbury, but Shirlie was away on tour and I was staying with my mum and dad. It was getting late, so everyone went to bed. I was back in my old cosy bedroom, asleep as soon as my head touched the pillow – but I was startled by a strange nightmare. It was so vivid that I could have been back upstairs with my family. I was in the living room, and I could see my dad on his chair. Everything else was black. It was as if Dad was in a play, on a theatre stage, illuminated by a spotlight, with every other detail of the room cast in shadow. In my dream, Dad suddenly and dramatically turned a very pale grey and slumped forwards. I *knew* he was having a heart attack.

A knock on my bedroom door woke me up and pulled me out of my dream. It was my mum, standing there grey-faced and shaking. I leapt out of bed and went over to my mum.

"Martin," she said, on the verge of tears. "Your dad's had a heart attack. Call an ambulance!"

I was able to calm Mum down, and look after my dad, while we waited for the paramedics to arrive. It was only as we were following the ambulance to the hospital that I realised my nightmare had come true. I didn't tell Mum, but I realised that the eerie premonition had been a good thing. I'd had the dream for a reason. It was to keep me calm and focused so I could cope and think quickly enough to get Dad the help he needed. I don't know whether that was Len looking out for me again, but on that occasion, it meant Dad survived.

One night, I was in Steve Strange's flat with Gary, Billy Idol and his girlfriend. Steve was in his green-velvet Robin Hood costume, Billy was in his Rocker Boy leather and I think Gary and I were in a medieval combination of robes, scarves and feathers. We were trying to look like wandering minstrels.

You can picture the scene. Crammed into a tiny front room, sitting in the dark, are some of the most eccentric musical icons of the 80s, dressed to the nines, trying to contact some ghosts, and feeling a little bit the worse for wear. We were watching the board intently. Suddenly, the glass started flying around the board, stopping on letter after letter, finally spelling out the letters "DON'T MOVE".

Don't move? We jumped out of our skins. Billy's girlfriend screamed and Gary leapt up 3ft in the air, pulling on my shirt. We were all trying to pile out and get into the hallway, when the curtain pole holding the heavy velvet curtains flew across the room towards us. No one said anything for several minutes.

Then Steve spoke. "I've been trying to get my landlady to replace those for ages," he said. "I don't think they've even been *cleaned* since the First World War."

It's been a long time since I've used a Ouija board, but the ghosts keep popping up. A few years ago, I was filming an episode of *Marple* in a very old house in Hertfordshire, not far from where we live now. Shirlie is fascinated by houses and, when we stopped filming for lunch, I decided I wanted to explore, so I could tell her what I'd found.

I knew that all kinds of people had lived in that house, and there were so many stories to discover – not just grand lords and ladies, but generations of servants, too. I'd even heard rumours that the house was full of priest holes. Around the 16th century, members of the Catholic Church were being persecuted by the monarchy. If priests wanted to worship and help other Catholics to do so, they had to hide and preach in secret. Priests' lives were saved by these hiding places, often in walls and under floorboards. I'd heard that some even had tunnels to chapels and churches, so it was definitely worth a look.

I didn't run into any secret priests, but I did have a strange encounter on my way up the stairs. Walking through the grand front entrance and into the lobby, I was dressed for the early 1950s, and I was feeling a little warm in my thick three-piece suit.

Then out of the corner of my eye, I saw a very young woman in a black dress, with a white apron and matching cap. I had the impression that her apron was freshly starched. Her dark hair was pulled into a bun. I thought she glanced at me and then looked away very quickly, but I was too shaken to look directly at her. After a split second, I braced myself to look back, but she had vanished.

It seemed silly, but I felt a little bit shaken up. Would I tell my friends in the cast, Dawn French and Paul McGann, about what I'd just seen – or would they laugh at me? Had I imagined it all? It had only lasted for a couple of seconds. Had I simply wanted to see the ghost? Maybe I needed to sit down with a cup of tea for a minute! I was trying to get my breath back when I saw a man at the bottom of the stairs. He was dressed in a black suit with a black shirt and no tie.

"Hello!" he said, waving in greeting. "I've come to spend the night here, and I don't know where I'm supposed to go."

He explained that he was a medium and he'd been invited to stay at the house and watch out for any paranormal activity. It was supposed to be one of the most haunted buildings in Britain. Even though he was the perfect man to tell, I wasn't quite ready to say what I'd seen. I wasn't sure that I believed it myself. I made it through the rest of the day and saved the story to tell Shirlie when I arrived home that night.

Ever since her awful trip to China, Shirlie has been terrified of ghosts. I think the experience of the possessed band member on the plane really got to her. When I took her to the south of France to recover, she was convinced that ghosts were lurking in the shadows in every chateau we stopped at. Shirlie doesn't get scared very easily, and I know this anxiety was partly a symptom of her post-traumatic stress. All I ever want to do is comfort her.

Do I really believe in ghosts? I certainly believe that we leave an energy behind us, a force that can't dissipate, that floats in the ether... but who knows?

When I was younger, I felt as though I was very much in the driving seat when it came to my career and my life. Even though supernatural occurrences have played a part in my life since I was very young, the arrogance of youth means you believe you're the one who's in complete control of what's happening to you. Now I'm older, I know better. I realise that no one experiences as much good luck as I do without getting more than a little help. The world moves in mysterious ways.

I know that something or someone put Shirlie in my path, and I do know that we've been looking after each other ever since, and having her by my side makes life magical. When you have a love that grows, evolves and gets stronger all the time – a love that can survive so much change, drama and tragedy – you realise that love is anything but ordinary. It's so powerful that it must be a little bit supernatural.

I know Shirlie believes we were put here for each other. Something bigger than us was up there, making sure we were placed in each other's paths. It doesn't matter how sceptical and cynical you may be – I firmly believe that the world is a kinder, happier place if we make peace with the fact that quite a lot of it is beyond our control. I appreciate every single moment simply because I'll never stop realising just how lucky I am to be around. After all, I may have had plenty of near-death experiences, but I'm not quite ready to be a ghost just yet.

19

The Last Christmas that Broke our Hearts

Shirlie

"Mum! Mum! The van is here. They're coming! I knew it would be today."

It was tradition for Roman to keep watch from an upstairs window. He was on Christmas patrol. Just like in the adverts, the arrival of a special van meant the holidays were coming – and even though Roman was 25, he was as excited as he was when he was a tiny toddler seeing snow for the very first time.

This was a Harrods van – and every year, George's closest friends would see that glossy green vehicle parked outside their house and know it was time for the Christmas festivities to begin. The hamper had arrived.

George's generosity is legendary. Over the course of his lifetime, he helped countless strangers, as well as constantly doing what he could to look after his friends and family. He loved being lavish, and he was a firm believer in luxury and fun. To him, wealth wasn't about status – but he wanted everyone around him to have as good a time as possible. This was never more true than at Christmas, which was his favourite time of year.

The hampers seemed magical – they were bottomless. Every time we thought we must have pulled everything out, Harley or Roman would reach in and unwrap another treat. Countless bottles of champagne, boxes of chocolates, an array of cheeses, peaches in brandy – every single year, I felt as though I was a Dickensian heroine who had reached the end of the story and found her happy ending. George was no Scrooge, but if he could, he would have run to every butcher's in the country, asking for "the biggest turkey in the window" so he could give it away. He knew I loved the ceremony of Christmas meals, so, as well as delicious food, the hamper would always contain beautiful pieces of crockery and crystal-cut glasses.

Standing in the kitchen, I felt my heart swell with love. Together, our friends and family had made it through another year, and I was so proud of them all. I thought of Harley, making the art she loved, and Roman, with his success as a broadcaster. Martin and I had created a happy family. It hadn't always been easy, but we'd worked through hard times, and we had so much to celebrate and feel joyful about. And George had always been part of the family, too.

It had been a long time since we were those eager kids who just wanted to dance and mess about. Between us all, we'd muddled our way through world tours, near-death experiences, children, grief, shamanic healing sessions, bankruptcy, career changes and eye-watering fame. I was starting to realise that the quiet times were the ones I needed to treasure. It had taken Martin and me a long time to adjust to our big changes. Our parents weren't around any more, and our children were ready to make their own homes and lives. But I was excited about embracing the next chapter. I didn't have any big Christmas wishes. I had everyone and everything I needed. All I could ask for was the continuing happiness and health of the people I loved.

Feeling a little sentimental, I texted George. *Hampers just arrived, thank you so much! Christmas starts now! XXX*

He replied straight away. *Great! Are you and M around on Boxing Day? Going to have some people over. Would love to see Harley and Roman, too, if they're around? X*

Every year, George would host a party at Christmas time, and every year, it was the stuff of lavish legend.

"Shirlie, will you come early?" he'd ask. "I want you to see my tree before everyone arrives."

George put a huge amount of effort and energy into the decorations. He liked to have a theme, but like everyone, he had a few traditional bits and pieces he'd picked up on his travels and felt very sentimental about. He lived in a beautiful home in Highgate, but he always wanted his houses to seem cosy, not grand or showy. This meant his decorating made me feel as though I was in a woodcutters' cottage, in a fairy tale. He loved to have a tall, bushy, ceiling-grazing tree – and once the party room was full of friends, tree, candles and cocktails, there wasn't room to move.

Of course, in some ways, George marks the official start of Christmas for millions of people. He may not have been able to send Harrods hampers to everyone – but you only have to hear the first two bars of 'Last Christmas' to start feeling festive. I still can't quite get my head around the fact that the video is still played several times a day, every year, all over the world. No matter where I am or what I'm doing, my 2-year-old self is running around setting the table, decorating the tree and getting caught up in a snowball fight!

Luckily, I love the song. And George did, too. I think he was genuinely deeply proud of the fact that he created a piece of work that so many people adored and continue to listen to. All George wanted to do was make music that lifted people up. Lyrically, 'Last Christmas' may not seem like his most profound song – but it's all about love and loss. There are so many ways to enjoy it and connect with it. The melody is beautiful, and it evokes so many happy memories in people who associate the first time they heard it with friends and family, parties and fun. But it's also a song about missing people, and the way that love makes us extremely vulnerable.

I miss George every day – but spending Christmas without him feels especially painful. Still, filming the video for 'Last Christmas' is one of my favourite memories ever.

In November 1984, a huge group of us flew out to Saas-Fee in Switzerland. We hadn't filmed a video on location since we'd gone out to Ibiza for 'Club Tropicana'. Usually, making music videos wasn't nearly as much fun as it looked. You'd spend a lot of time waiting around, taking hours and hours to film something that only lasted for a couple of seconds, and feeling like the least important person for miles around. I only had to whisper something to Pepsi for a director to bellow, "Quiet on set!" It was like being at school. I'd go to sleep and dream that someone was shouting at me to be quiet on the set.

This was something else.

I'd been skiing once, on a school trip when I was a teenager, and I hadn't particularly enjoyed it. I'd loved the snow, but we seemed to spend most of our time squashed onto a coach or hovering outside the communal showers waiting for the water to get warm. Switzerland looked like a storybook, and Pepsi had never seen so much snow. In London, you may get the odd flake, but it always goes grey before it has a chance to settle. This was like jumping into a Christmas card.

Cars are banned in Saas-Fee, so the atmosphere feels completely different from anywhere else – calm, quiet and restful. There's nothing but the soft sound of snow falling and the delicious, dull crunch as your foosteps thud into the soft, frosty ground beneath you. At least, that was what it was like before Wham! arrived.

George and Andrew had gathered a gang of their best friends to cast in the video. We had a few models with us – George's love interest was a model called Kathy. She was absolutely beautiful and did a fantastic job, but I felt a little bit sorry for her. She'd come to Switzerland to work, but she was surrounded by people who wanted to party. They weren't in the video very much, but Pepsi and I had a couple of model boyfriends, too. Lots of people think that Martin is in the video – he isn't, but my model boyfriend was a bit of a Martin lookalike.

Our friends Dave and Johnny came along, too. Andrew knew them from rugby, and they were an established part of our gang. They were brilliant fun, and well known for making mischief. We filmed for about four days, and every day, they made us laugh until we all ached. But chaos reigned. I think Kathy would have loved a little more quiet on set. As soon as we arrived at our gorgeous hotel, there was a stampede for the bar, with Andrew's rugby friends leading the way. George turned pale under his tan. "What have I done?" he mouthed at me. It felt a bit like being on another school trip – only a luxury one. It was definitely going to get out of hand.

Pepsi and I were slightly more innocent. While everyone else was knocking back as many drinks as they could order, we were in heaven because we'd discovered we could order hot chocolate to our rooms. The best thing of all was in the rooms themselves. We had duvets! I'd *never* seen one before. Back in the UK, they were a real luxury, and most of us had scratchy nylon sheets and blankets. I couldn't get over the fact that the duvet was so soft and warm and yet so light. All alone, I squealed with glee and slipped under the covers, hugging myself. Suddenly, I heard a knock at the door. Feeling a little bit self-conscious, I straightened my clothes, stood up and composed myself. It was Pepsi, completely cocooned in her duvet.

"Shirlie, we *have* to take these home!" she cried. "I mean, they're really bulky, but they're so light. I'm sure we can squash them in somehow."

We're all really familiar with the famous shot of George, looking moody and gorgeous while he looks out from under an enormous, luxurious furry hood. According to the story we're acting in the video, you're supposed to think he's sad because he's thinking about Kathy and how she left him after their romantic, happy Christmas in 1983. But George's smouldering gaze may be a result of him feeling *slightly* grumpy.

Andrew's crazy friends had started a snowball fight, and it got out of control quite quickly. I was happily joining in and running around, until someone smacked me in the eye with a snowball. Even though it was an accident, I stormed off the set in tears until I dried myself off. That's the thing about snowball fights – when they're filmed, they look like they're great fun. Then you get a face full of snow and you remember that they're pretty violent.

Poor George had it even worse than I did. Our lovely hairdresser Kathleen had spent hours and hours giving him a perfect blow-dry, setting his hair so it fell in gorgeous, soft golden waves. Then the lads started pelting him with snow. On one side, his hair was still perfect – like a thoroughbred horse's flaxen mane and tail. But on the other, his hair was absolutely soaked, plastered to his scalp and forehead in tiny ringlets. Even the hairdresser couldn't fix it completely – so wardrobe had to find a hood to hide his hair. At least it protected him from more snowballs.

I think the video gave the boys an opportunity they needed. In a very short space of time, the pressure from being in the band had built up. As they became more and more famous, work became more and more serious. Ultimately, this was right for George. Every one of us knew he was enormously talented and had to do everything he could to use his gift. But filming 'Last Christmas' gave us all a last chance to be together and have fun. We were capturing the magic of dancing together in George's bedroom.

Still, George definitely had a vision for the video. We were working with director Andrew Morahan. George had said he wanted to create a Christmas-themed version of 'Club Tropicana' – a video that had been hugely fun to shoot. I don't remember much of the filming process, but I'll never forget how exciting it was to visit Ibiza for the first time.

Like Switzerland, Ibiza was an extremely romantic setting. It's changed so much now, but back then it was rural and lush. The hotel where we filmed the video, Pikes, was famous – and it's become even more famous since it had the starring role in 'Club Tropicana'. The late owner, Tony Pike, was an amazing man. He was sweet, generous and funny – and the only man I've ever seen in real life who would actually do a cartoonish double-take if he saw a girl in a bikini. All day long, he was surrounded by some of the most beautiful women in the world, and he never stopped appreciating them. I think he must have been one of the happiest people I'd ever met.

George and I arrived at Pikes a few days early because we wanted to work on our tans so we would be nice and brown for the video. We overtanned in the 80s, so it was more of a burnt-crisp brown. Lying on our loungers by the pool, I noticed George, who was always a great talker, suddenly became unusually tongue-tied. I became aware that he was feeling uncomfortable, and I started to worry he'd done something really bad and couldn't tell me. He seemed scared to say the words that were clearly on his mind. He looked me in the eyes, almost searching for me to speak on his behalf. I was trying to find space in my head to be open for whatever he had to tell me. He was my friend, and whatever it was, I needed to be there come what may.

"Shirlie, there's something I've needed to tell you for a while," he said. "I think I'm gay."

"What do you mean?" I asked gently.

"I think I could fall in love with a man," he said quietly.

I let out a big sigh of relief. But then I was hit with a massive wave of sympathy, because he had to struggle to tell me, someone who was his best friend, about who he really was.

"I haven't told Andrew yet, I'm worried how he might react," George continued.

I was still sitting there speechless, in shock that someone had to live that long and be afraid to say who they really are. "But what about your parents?" I asked. "Do they know?"

"No, they can't know, Shirlie."

"But they love you," I said. "What's the problem with that, George? They love you whatever." He looked at me so seriously with his big eyes, and I could tell this was something he was protecting them from. "I'll tell your mum for you if you want," I offered.

"No, you don't understand. My mum would worry so much. I couldn't live with that."

Aids was sweeping through the gay community at the time, so as soon as he said this, I understood what he meant. It wasn't the fear that he was gay that worried him, it was more that his mum would be constantly worried about him. We had our own reality and no one else knew. Andrew didn't know, and it was just George and me in our zone, safe for now.

"I've got to tell Andrew, what do you think he'll say?" George asked me.

"I don't think he'll be bothered, he loves you. Now please could you pass me the sun lotion?" It was such a big moment for George, I wanted to bring him back to the lightness we were used to. It doesn't make any difference to me.

Later that evening, we decided we would tell Andrew the next day and would both be there. I was glad George was finally free and I could get him back to being that light, happy boy I knew. From that day on I became even more protective of him.

Years later, I was at the famous Serpentine Summer Party, full of the most stylish and beautiful people on the planet – famous faces, designers and what felt like the elite of London all gathered in the park, posing and checking to see who was the best dressed – when I spotted Sadie Frost walking towards me. "This is my friend Matthew Williamson, and he'd love to say hello," she said, introducing this guy with a lovely big smile. As we started chatting, he instantly confessed that he was a big Wham! fan when he was younger and said that he used to have a Wham! poster on his bedroom wall. He then laughed and said, "I had to tell everyone I was in love with you, Shirlie, but really l loved George." We both started laughing, though for a second I was disappointed I wasn't the love of his life – but once again it made me think how hard it is and was for young gay men to open up, especially in their teens, and I guess this was exactly what George must have gone through too.

All I knew was that I loved my friend and I wanted him to be happy. These men were living through a time when homophobia was common. Being gay had been illegal until the end of the 60s, and gay people still had very few rights. I think my gay friends had a special level of understanding and compassion towards anyone who struggled with shyness and anxiety and who longed to express themselves creatively. After all, they knew exactly what that felt like.

Still, I think that was why George couldn't tell many people. In the early 80s, any gay public figure faced a great deal of difficulty, and there was a lot of societal pressure to stay in the closet. But I don't think George ever kept it quiet for the sake of his career. He simply didn't know how to tell his mum and dad.

Filming 'Club Tropicana' was hugely bonding, and 'Last Christmas' had that same energy. I think the reason people love both of those videos so much is that under all of the 80s gloss, polish and camp, you can see a group of friends genuinely having a brilliant time.

But my last Christmas with George, in 2016, was a Christmas that never really happened.

After the hampers arrived, the family settled in for the holidays. We knew the next couple of days would be quiet and cosy. Just the four of us on the 25th, and then the drive to George's on Boxing Day. Christmas Day itself started badly though. I'm not much of a drinker, but we have a tradition – Martin will pour Harley and me a glass of champagne to drink as we open our presents, before Christmas lunch. I was a little tipsy, but not dramatically so – at least, I didn't think I was until the kitchen was engulfed in grey smoke. Something smelled *awful,* too. It was as though the bin had exploded.

"Sprouts!" I screamed, as I realised there was no water in the steamer. They'd gone grey and ashy, as though they'd been cremated in the pan. Poor Martin loves Brussels sprouts, but that year he only saw them when they were flying out of the window. I had to get rid of everything to put the fire out, and tossed the charred pan out onto the lawn to cool down.

Then, at the end of the meal, when everyone had left the table, there was another fire. Someone must have knocked over a tea light, and in a matter of seconds, everything was blazing, including the dining table, which was made of wood. Everyone helped to put the fire out, but it felt like a bit of a crappy Christmas. *I suppose I'll be looking for a new table in the January sales,* I thought, grumpily, looking at the charred tabletop. We all went downstairs to the TV room to cheer ourselves up with a Christmas film. I didn't care what we watched, I was ready for a little nap.

I'd left my phone upstairs, not wanting to be distracted by it while I was with my family. That morning, I'd called or texted everyone I wanted to wish a Happy Christmas, and I didn't think there was anyone else to speak to. So I didn't hear my phone ringing as I drifted off to sleep. I woke up after the film had finished and padded upstairs to the kitchen to get a glass of water. I was still feeling a bit groggy – I wasn't completely awake yet. My phone was close to the sink, on the countertop, and it was buzzing and flashing crazily. I had many, many missed calls from George's sister, Melanie.

My heart sank a bit. *She's calling to cancel tomorrow,* I thought. It must have been too short notice to sort out the caterers, or something. Knowing George, he'd gone overboard with the invites, and poor Mel was worried that 200 people were going to descend on her in Hampstead, and she'd have to make thousands of turkey sandwiches. Never mind, maybe we could have them over for lunch before New Year. I yawned, thinking I'd ring Mel later, or maybe just text and tell her not to worry.

Then I saw I had an incoming call from George's PA. *That's really odd,* I thought. It was only a party – this seemed to be a lot of fuss and panic. And why hadn't George called or texted? Still feeling slightly bleary-eyed and dazed from sleep, I slid my finger over the screen to pick up.

"Shirlie, are you… I'm so sorry. Are you sitting down? Are you on your own?"

I took a deep breath. "No, no, I'm just in the kitchen. Martin and the kids are downstairs." What was going on?

"Oh, Shirlie, I don't know how to tell you this. It's George…"

Then the world went black.

I have no memory of the rest of the conversation. The shock kept hitting me in waves. I felt as though I was going to be sick. Was I still asleep, having a horrible nightmare? They must have made a mistake. George just couldn't be dead. We were seeing him tomorrow.

Adrenaline coursed through my body, making me shaky. Holding onto the walls, I made my way back downstairs to tell Martin, Harley and Roman. They were laughing and joking, looking Christmas-Day cosy, lounging on the sofas while the TV blared brightly in the background. They turned around to look at me, startled. Later, Martin told me he'd never seen anyone looking as pale and shaken as I did.

"It's George," I told them, my voice faltering. "He's died." Then I sank to my knees and wept.

It didn't make any sense at all. My beloved best friend. My gorgeous Yog. On Christmas Day, his favourite day of the year. The more I tried to take it in, the less sense it made. I felt like an injured animal. I couldn't move, I couldn't speak, I could only curl up and howl. It wasn't just my loss – he'd been one of Martin's very best friends, too. He was Roman's godfather. Harley and Roman had known him for all their lives. He'd been their biggest cheerleader, constantly applauding them and encouraging them. I thought of a time in the 90s when I'd taken Harley to see him at Wembley. She'd seen the tens of thousands of adoring fans, all screaming with joy to see George on stage. He wasn't a pop star to her – he was her uncle. "Mum," she asked. "How do all of these people know him?"

I knew my family were as shocked and as devastated as I was. We were united in our grief. But usually, I'd be the one pulling everyone together, trying to comfort them, putting the kettle on and attempting to make sense of the awful news. I couldn't do it this time. I couldn't speak or breathe properly, I was crying so hard.

That night, I curled up and sobbed into my pillow as Martin held me. Eventually, I cried myself to sleep. It's all thanks to George, and what he did all those years ago, that I had Martin beside me to comfort me.

"I'm here," Martin whispered. "I'm right with you."

Martin has never been afraid to cry, and he's usually much weepier than me – but that night, he was my rock. I think lots of people are very frightened of strong emotion – we're told to bottle things up, and we feel uncomfortable when we see other people in the throes of grief. Martin has always understood it's really important to express our sadness. He was really brave for me during that time.

We were woken up at 3am when Martin's phone went off. I managed to get back to sleep again – but Martin was hassled by a non-stop stream of TV and radio people. The news was public, and anyone who had his mobile number was calling him, trying to get a comment. Yet the worst was still to come.

It was Boxing Day, and still dark outside, and we were both reeling from the awful news about one of our best friends. It was horrible. What can you say about the loss of someone you've loved so much? How can you be expected to share some of your most raw and painful emotions with the world?

The next day, we were like a pair of zombies. Harley and Roman were absolutely incredible. They didn't try to restore any sense of normality – but they were quiet when I needed quiet and kept me company when I felt overwhelmed.

"It just seems so unreal," said Roman, thoughtfully. "It's bizarre to be surrounded by... *Christmas*, when this has happened."

"You're right," I said. "I think we need to take the decorations down."

We kept ourselves busy that day, taking ornaments off the tree, putting things away in boxes. I think we all felt so utterly numb. Every so often I'd forget what was happening, and I'd catch myself thinking about how we'd better stop and get ready to go to George's party. All day long, the phone rang, but I couldn't even manage to speak to my friends and family. Harley took charge and even rang Pepsi in St Lucia, because I could barely bring myself to talk. At first, Pepsi assumed that Harley was ringing to say "Happy Christmas" – it took poor Harley a little while to get the awful news out.

Harley also spoke to Melanie for me. I'd known George's big sister for as long as I'd known George. She was only three years older than him, but she was extremely maternal. Their mum, Lesley, had died in 1997, and I think Mel had naturally found herself taking on that mothering role – they were a very loving, nurturing family.

As our tree became emptier and emptier, I found myself saying, "I think I need to go and see Mel."

As soon as the words were out of my mouth, I felt a little scared and selfish. Mel must be completely heartbroken. She needed as much support and looking after as I did – but I longed to be mothered by her, and to hug her tightly. Would she want to see me? Was she being hounded by people, too?

"Mum, I think she'd really love to see you," said Harley. "Do you want me to drive you round to Hampstead?"

Mel lived in George's old house, a place where we'd celebrated so many Christmases together. It was filled with happy memories. Grief is so strange – I knew it would be almost unbearably painful to be in that space, filled with ghosts, knowing I'd never hear George's laugh again or feel his head resting against my shoulder when we curled up on the sofa. But it was the place where I'd feel closest to my old friend. Just the idea of being in his home soothed me slightly.

At the time, Martin was starring as Sam Phillips in *Million Dollar Quartet,* a musical about an impromptu recording session that happened between rock 'n' roll legends at Sun City studio. There was a performance scheduled for Boxing Day.

"I don't want to leave you," said Martin. "But I can't let anybody down."

"It's OK, I think you need to do this," I said.

If I was with Melanie, Martin knew I was being looked after – and I knew that Martin was still in a state of shock and struggling to process the news. For him, work has always been a safe space. Going to the theatre and inhabiting a different life for the evening would give him some room and respite from what was going on.

The press kept calling. Even on the journey to Mel's, it was impossible to listen to the radio. The entire world was in mourning for our friend, and Harley, Roman, Martin and I were all experiencing so many confusing emotions. In one way, we felt so proud of George. He was such a talented man – a true musical genius. Millions of people all over the world had fallen in love, recovered from heartbreak, danced at their weddings and healed, while listening to his songs. It's no wonder that everyone felt as though they knew him. He'd helped people through the most significant moments of their lives, and his fans had a deeply personal relationship with him.

But it was alienating, too. A lot of the time, we didn't recognise the man being described on TV and the radio. There was so much hurtful speculation about what had happened to him – and why. George Michael was a megastar. Yog was our friend. We weren't sad about never seeing him in concert again or hearing a new album. I was devastated because I'd never hear him sighing happily after the first sip of tea or cackling when *EastEnders* became a bit melodramatic.

His job never defined him, in our eyes. Of course, his soul and his spirit were at the centre of his work – but it didn't matter what he did. George could have been an accountant or a baker, he still would have been the friend who brought Martin and me together, the one who held me up and put me back together when Martin was sick, the person I'd laughed with, grieved with and grown up with.

It didn't help that George had been going through a very hard time in the year before he died, and that people kept asking me about whether I'd been expecting him to die so young. It was just an awful question. George had been a huge part of my life since I was a teenager – of course I didn't think about this or expect it. We'd been through so much together, good and bad. Nothing can prepare you for losing someone you're that close to.

The next few weeks passed in a blur. I was still so shocked and sad that I don't remember very much – although Martin and I were constantly turning down requests to speak to the press. One breakfast TV show asked if I'd report live from his funeral, which would have been funny if it wasn't so macabre.

Another thing that made me laugh a little bit happened after I was at Mel's. I was on my way home when Harley rang to say there was an odd man hanging around outside the house.

"He looks a bit weird, Mum," she said. "I don't know what he wants, or how to get rid of him." Like me, Harley is very wary of people intruding. She was the one who hated Martin being on TV when she was little – she gets very self-conscious and loves privacy. Thankfully, we live in an area where there's a little gatehouse by the entrance with a security guy.

"What do you mean?" I replied.

"I think he's from *The Sun*," she said.

"I'll call the security guy."

When I called him, he said, "Mrs Kemp, I am sorry there is someone outside. Mrs Kemp, it's George Michael's son."

What? I was grieving this huge loss and had someone outside my house claiming he was George Michael's son?

Flanked by Harley, I couldn't believe it. Was this a part of George's life I didn't know about? But it turned out Harley was right and he was from *The Sun* after all. We were a little bit shaken up, but we managed to giggle about it later. It's strange how even during your darkest points, you can still find things that make you laugh.

Anyone who has lost someone they love very much will know that the period between their death and their funeral is agonising. I've always felt as though I'm in a state of limbo during this time. It's impossible to fully accept what has happened when you haven't said a proper goodbye. I remember how hard it was when my mum died – it was in the winter, so there was a big delay. We had to wait for three weeks to bury her. With George, it was three months.

The Last Christmas that Broke our Hearts

During any year, the period after Christmas is a difficult one for many of us. I thrive in the sunshine, and even when the days are beginning to get slightly longer and lighter, I struggle with the endless grey. That year, it felt as though spring would never come. It reminded me of the awful winter when Martin became ill for the first time. I remember staring out of the window, looking at barren branches and dark skies. Everything outside reflected what was going on inside my head.

The awful thing about grief is that the only thing that makes it any easier to bear is the passing of time. During those months, I felt as though I was going backwards. Every so often I had a day when I started to understand what happened. I was never going to see my friend again. And I felt so lucky to have known him, and so grateful for every single joy-filled moment and memory that he brought me. Then, the next day, I'd wake up, and feel just as overwhelmed with despair as I did when I received that first awful phone call.

We live in a world where no one wants to talk about death and dying, even though it's going to happen to all of us. I think the tabloid interest in George's death was partly because everything he did – and quite a lot of things he didn't do – would inevitably end up in a newspaper. But perhaps it was also partly because people wanted reassurance. George was exceptional in so many ways, and I think lots of people needed to believe that he'd led an exceptional lifestyle.

Everyone wants to believe they're too healthy and too "normal" to die in their 50s. We all want to think our friends and family are safe from harm because they follow the rules. "Wild" pop stars dying young are the exception that proves the rule and makes sense.

Death makes people feel frightened, and grief makes other people feel extremely uncomfortable. They want to rush you through it, yet it's not something that can be fixed or changed. I think grieving for George – and I am *still* grieving – has changed me. I can be quite practical or pragmatic. If someone has a problem, I want to resolve it and make them feel better. Now, more than ever, I realise our feelings need space to grieve, and we need time to heal. Luckily, Martin, Harley and Roman were all very intuitive about this. We found the room to grieve together.

I'd always been very careful about how and where I spoke about George, and I became even more protective of his memory after he died. But in February 2017, Andrew, Pepsi and I were asked to talk about George at the BRIT awards.

Pepsi flew in from St Lucia, and Andrew came up from Cornwall, which sometimes seems almost as far away. Together, we were able to put together a tribute, explaining just how much George meant to us, and what a big role he'd played in our lives. After Wham!, Andrew had done lots of other things and retreated from the public eye – we were in touch, but we hadn't stayed especially close. Life gets in the way. And although Pepsi and I spoke all the time, I didn't get to see her as often as either of us would have liked, so we had a bittersweet reunion. It felt wonderful for the three of us to be back together – but so painful to be reunited for such a tragic reason.

Still, the BRITs was the perfect place for us to honour our friend. In front of an audience of music fans, we were able to celebrate the work of a man who has defined pop. George made it fun, he made it emotional and he's still touching people with his music every day.

Speaking about him gave me a chance to remind the world of the George I want them to remember. Not the megastar, or the troubled tabloid gossip king, but the sweet, fun-loving, and astonishingly talented boy I used to dance with when I was a teenage girl. The boy who loved music and lived for it, who wanted to inspire people in the way he was inspired by his own musical heroes. The boy who brought so much love into my life, and into the lives of everyone who knew him.

The last time I saw George, we had a strange conversation. He'd come over for a cup of tea and a catch-up – we'd not properly spent time together in a little while and it felt overdue. It started in the usual way. We gossiped, and he wanted to hear all about what Harley and Roman were up to – but we ended up talking late into the night about the meaning of life and about our lives. It reminded me of the way we talked when we first met, with George exploring his ideas and emotions thoroughly and thoughtfully.

The lovely thing about our relationship was that I could ask him *anything.* He would never shy away from weird subjects or uncomfortable ones, and we were always very open with each other. Still, I don't know what it was that made me ask him, "Do you *like* being famous? I know it's difficult, in lots of ways, but have you enjoyed it? Are you glad that you're doing what you do?"

I still remember George's grin, a Cheshire cat beaming over the back of the sofa.

"Yeah," he said softly. "I *am* glad. I've had a really good time."

It was 2am. I caught sight of the time and yawned. "It's really late. I've got to go to bed. I've got stuff to do tomorrow."

"Are you kicking me out?" he said, pretending to be indignant. "OK, OK. I'm off."

Feeling a bit sleepy, I walked out of the front door with him and watched him get into his car, before waving him off.

The Last Christmas that Broke our Hearts

This may be the last time I see him, I thought, before shuddering. Why would I think something as strange as that? What was wrong with my brain? I must be tired.

Hindsight is strange, and when you combine it with grief, it's easy to leap to all sorts of odd conclusions. There's no way I could possibly have known I was going to lose my best friend when he was still so young and had so much more that he wanted to do. I still can't work out why that thought crossed my mind, or why my prediction came true. But even though I miss him every day, I was so lucky to have George in my life for so long. And in the way I believe that meeting Martin wasn't a happy accident – someone, somewhere, sent him to take care of me – I believe that about George, too.

George made my life better in every way. That's true for every single one of his friends, and for every fan who loved him. Maybe we were all just incredibly fortunate to have George on earth for as long as we did. He endured some dark, difficult times. Still, remembering our last conversation brings me comfort and joy. Even when life was really hard for him, he could find ways to be happy. He's still the most generous person I've ever known – but after forcing me to meet Martin, that last conversation is the most precious gift he ever gave me.

20

Making Sweet Music Together

Martin

For a long time, work and marriage were two aspects of my life that I wanted to keep completely separate. When I first met Shirlie, I was always longing for a bit of time off so I could be with her. If you're in a band like Spandau, there's a danger that work could take over. Similarly, later, when I was filming *EastEnders*, the days were long and demanding.

I've always been aware that I have workaholic tendencies. I'm a grafter, like my dad, but I'm lucky enough to love what I do. Still, I've always been careful to come home, leave my job at the door and shut it behind me. Being with my family is the most precious part of my life, and I've always wanted to make sure those boundaries hold up. Over the years, I've had plenty of offers to take on different projects and get Shirlie involved, but we've always said no. She feels uncomfortable when she's in the limelight, and more importantly, we want to concentrate on being together when we're both at home. We don't want to let the outside in.

But something changed. Not long after we'd filmed *The Road to Saigon* together, I was asked to record an album of retro swing music. I'd just appeared as Billy Flynn in *Chicago,* and I loved the idea of doing something old-fashioned and cool. After all, I loved Frank Sinatra and the Rat Pack. The idea of paying homage to some of those idols really appealed to me.

As always, Shirlie was enthusiastic and supportive. When we needed some female vocals for 'You Make Me Feel So Young', I didn't think twice about asking her.

"Are you sure?" she asked. "I'd love to have a go, but it's been a while – when did you last hear me sing?"

I laughed. "This morning, when you were listening to Roman on the radio. It's up to you, but let's give it a try. You'll be great."

We went to the studio, and Shirlie blew everyone away. She opened her mouth, and Doris Day came out! I think that because we were in there together, we felt incredibly relaxed.

The producer loved it, too. "I think we may need to rethink the album," he said. The record company came back straight away after hearing it, and said, "Let's do a full set of duets."

I loved the idea, but I still felt full of trepidation. "Shirlie, I'd love to make an album with you, but – are we mad? Will people think this is bizarre?"

Shirlie felt the same way. "I know what you mean. As soon as the idea came up, I was so excited, but now I feel a bit self-conscious. Let's talk to Harley and see what she thinks."

There was no way our eldest would sign off on anything that made us look like idiots. Harley has a finely tuned nonsense-meter. We knew there was no point recording an album unless we made something excellent. Harley is a gifted singer, songwriter and musician. Her standards are high.

We pitched it to her and sang 'You Make me Feel so Young' in the kitchen to a backing track. "So, what do you think?" I asked, waiting for her to start laughing at us.

Her eyes lit up. "Oh, that sounds fantastic. Go for it. It's going to be amazing!"

Harley ended up writing two songs on the album: 'Like We Used to Do' and 'When We're Apart'. Shirlie worked with her on the second one, and those songs have a really special resonance for me. I can't quite believe how talented my girls are, and seeing Harley's creativity inspire Shirlie made me feel quite emotional.

In fact, the whole process was hugely emotional. Shirlie and I had pretty much grown up on stage, spending our teens and 20s singing about love, loss, desire and heartbreak. Of course, we'd thought about each other when we'd sung those songs, but singing to each other, and making a record, had a really special resonance. I'm so proud of the music we've made because you can hear how much we love each other in every single track.

It's one thing to sing about love when you're younger, when you have less life experience to base the emotion on. And when I fell for Shirlie, I thought I knew everything there was to know about love, because my feelings were so intense and dramatic. Yet singing those love songs as a nearly 60-year-old man, I had a chance to reflect on the fact that I'd known the love of my life for over half my life. Sometimes, love was intense, dramatic and passionate – most of the time, though, it was simply filled with happiness and laughter.

In the early days, we'd flown around the world to be with each other, we'd gone to banquets and boat parties, and we'd had our picture taken at premieres. But our favourite place to be was at home, on the sofa, cuddling up in front of the fire, with Poppy the dog trying to wriggle in between us, like the world's cutest gooseberry. Or in the kitchen, with Harley and Shirlie riffing off each other while Roman and I clutched our sides.

In that recording studio, listening to Shirlie singing her heart out, I saw hundreds, maybe thousands, of different Shirlies. I saw the glamorous, grown-up woman before me, stylish, blonde and beautiful. I saw the mother of my children, the brave warrior who had gone into labour and brought our family into the world. I saw the person who had loved me and poured absolutely all of her energy into taking care of me and making me better when I was staring death in my face. I saw the frightened, vulnerable, shell-shocked girl who had been to hell and back in China, the one I longed to hold and protect. But more than anything else, I saw Shirlie, the *Top of the Pops* vision in white, the most stunning woman in the world, the face that had haunted every one of my dreams since I first saw her on screen.

Every single one of those songs means many different things to us. But I think 'A Nightingale Sang In Berkeley Square' is our favourite. It reminds us both so clearly of that very first night we spent together. Ours is a London love story, and I feel so lucky to be surrounded by so many happy memories every time we're in the capital. Of course, we were brought together by our very own nightingale – George. The only slightly bittersweet part of making the album was knowing how much he would have loved it, if he'd been around to hear it. Of course, he would have liked to have been the one to think of it!

The thing about the best love stories is that they're not just about two people. When I fell for Shirlie, there were moments when we were completely cocooned in love, and it felt as though we were the only two people in the world. But as we both got older, we realised it takes a village to write a love story. George may have given us the paper and pen, but so many people came up with the words. My mum and dad, who loved each other so much and showed me that passion and romance need to be coupled with honesty, decency and kindness to make love last. Harley and Roman, who make my life better every single day. For years, I didn't think I'd ever be ready for fatherhood, but it's the best thing I've ever done. When you have a family, you realise you'll never run out of love. It keeps on multiplying, expanding to fill the space it's in. I love my children more than I ever thought possible, and I love Shirlie even more than I dreamt I could. Watching the way she embraces motherhood has been truly magical. She's the most loving person I've known, and I can see her in her element.

Quite honestly, I have no idea about what may be written on the next page – grandchildren! I know that Shirlie and I would both absolutely love for that to be the next stage of our journey. Still, if life has taught us anything, it's that you can never guess what's around the corner.

Life has a way of taking us by surprise. We've had some shocks, and we've made it through grief, drama and heartache. But, more often than not, the surprises have been happy ones. We've never encountered any problems we couldn't handle, and we've been blessed with joy more times than we can count. I just know that when Shirlie and I are together, there's nothing we can't do. And every morning when I wake up beside her, I feel the same as I did on that first morning waking up in that small hotel, just off Berkeley Square, not knowing what the day will bring.

Postcard 1 (front/address side)

39300 | Wetterhorn | Bergstation First
Bergrestaurant | Eiger

Colour Photo by Gyger, Adelboden

Printed in Switzerland – Imprimé en Suisse

Thor E. Gyger
- Adelboden -

I =

LOVE =

= YOU

S. KEMP

MUSWELL HILL
LONDON N.10
ENGLAND

Postcard 2 (message/address side)

Geisha
Highly trained professional entertainer of Japan is seen with
a formal greeting posture, Kyoto.
Geisha (ou le Danseurse) à Kyoto
Tipicas bailarina de Kyoto

563

POST CARD

AIR MAIL

PUBLISHED BY NBC (NIPPON BEAUTY COLOUR) INC. JAPAN

NBC

芸妓／京都
西陣や友禅の豪華な衣裳をつけた芸妓さん。新年のあいさつ
をする美しいひとみのおもだちは、こぼれるように美しい。

Photo : Hiroshi Mizobuchi   Printed in Japan

HELLO
SHIRLIE WAS RIGHT
THE FLIGHT MAKES YOU
FEEL ILL, BUT. ITS
NICE BEING HERE,
EVERYBODY IS SO POLITE
IT TENDS TO DRIVE YOU
MAD.
BE BACK
SOON LOVE
MARTIN

THE HOLLIMANS

BUSHEY, HERTS

ENGLAND

Epilogue
What We've Learnt About Love
Shirlie & Martin

Martin

The funny thing about love is that the more you know, the more you realise you have left to learn. Love isn't static. Well, life isn't, so how could it be? Just when you think you have everything figured out, there's a surprise in the post. I truly believe that these surprises make love last. When I met Shirlie, I was a kid, a young boy of 20. The guys I knew told me you needed to have as much fun as possible before you settled down. Well, the day I met Shirlie was the day the fun really started. And "settling" has never been on the table.

Still, even though periods of our life together have been totally chaotic, Shirlie is the one who makes me feel at peace. She has a real aura of love. It doesn't matter what's troubling me, or worrying me, she shows me how to work things out. I could be in the middle of an earthquake and, as long as I was with Shirlie, she would help me to find calm.

To be honest, I don't think I can take much credit for the fact that I've been married for as long, or as happily, as I have. I think a tremendous amount of luck has been involved. But I do believe it's important that I know exactly how lucky I am. Every single day, I find something to feel grateful for. I've seen other relationships falter and fail for lots of different reasons, but mainly because the gratitude isn't there. For me, the bedrock of love is friendship, and you can't have one without the other.

My life with Shirlie has been filled with fun, fortune and great windows of opportunity. When you're constantly getting exciting offers, it's easy to take them for granted – and, worse, believe you're entitled to them. It's not just about remembering to stay down to earth, but about knowing yourself, and knowing what luck looks like.

My parents taught me and Gary that if we had a chance to succeed, we had to grasp it, even if we couldn't predict what may lie ahead. But also, we were taught not to define ourselves by the result. If you stay grateful, you remain open to the unexpected. And the unexpected can bring the most exciting things. Is it luck or is it fate? I'm not sure I need that answered. I just know Shirlie and I will be together all our lives, and I am so happy. No one else but me is lucky enough to have a Shirlie.

What Martin has learnt...

Long-distance love can be deeply romantic – you need time to miss each other. And although it's never been easier to stay in touch, it may be fun to stay off Skype and send postcards instead… just once in a while.

Know your strengths. Shirlie is the admin queen and travel ninja, and I let her get on with it, bowing to her superior powers.

If you're missing someone, it's never too late to phone them – and they're never too far away.

Try not to bring your work home with you, but always be open to a good collaboration.

Be careful when you're offloading on your partner. They know when you're worried, and they'll worry some more. Know when it's time to stay strong for each other.

There's no right way to be a parent – because every kid is different. The only way to do a good job is to listen.

If you wear your heart on your sleeve, your emotions won't ever build up and get the better of you. Say "I love you" freely, not just because you want to hear it back. If a movie's sad, let yourself have a proper weep. A good cry often leads to a great laugh.

It's important to be able to give your children good advice. It's even more important to be able to listen when they have advice for you.

Shirlie

Martin has shown me that I'm capable of great strength and great vulnerability – and that the two things aren't really that far apart from each other.

I adore music and dancing and jokes – and long before I'd known it was even possible to meet him, there was a strong pull guiding me towards Martin.

Quite honestly, if Martin had played games, or even been a little bit shy, I wouldn't be here writing this today. I fell for him hard because I recognised his love – he loved me in exactly the same way my mum did, making me feel nurtured and safe. Safe isn't the same as boring – it's trusting someone totally and knowing there's no one else you'd rather be with. When you're with them, you never doubt them and you never doubt yourself.

Looking back has brought me an enormous amount of perspective. I realise I've done so many things I never thought were possible, such as looking after everyone when Martin was ill. And I've spent weeks worrying about things that turned out to be fine in the end. I was so scared I'd never have a baby. Then I was so scared I wouldn't be a good mum. Sometimes I'm pragmatic and Martin is the worrier, and sometimes we switch. Still, the important thing is that we always listen to each other, and we never tell each other that we're wrong to worry. I appreciate that Martin always makes an effort to be happy and positive, too. He's the first to see the bright side of any situation, and that makes him a pleasure to be married to. No matter how anxious you are, it's important to try to stay optimistic for each other when you can.

Making love last can be difficult – but sometimes, it feels very, very easy. People ask us *how* we've stayed married for so long, but they don't ask us *why* we've been married for so long. And I think that question produces a more interesting answer.

We've been married for this long because Martin is my all-time favourite person. He's still the boy on the cover of a magazine to me, but he's also the man who makes my heart leap when I hear his key in the door. He's the first person I want to share my news with, good and bad. If something has made me laugh, I want to tell Martin first. Quite simply, he makes every single day better.

What Shirlie has learnt...

Love existed long before Instagram. It's fun to share family life, but remember that you sometimes need to stay out of the spotlight to keep your relationship strong.

When it comes to love, your best friends usually know what's best for you.

The secret to a good marriage is to make sure you have a dog. So when you have an argument, someone can always take the dog out for a walk. Just make sure your dog is a good counsellor and can listen.

When you fall in love with someone, you're not the only person who can spot how special they are. If they're talented, the rest of the world may see that and fall in love with them, too. If you let yourself get jealous, you'll feel unhappy. Learn to share – up to a point.

If you're getting married, you don't need to have a big, dramatic, fancy wedding. But you do need to make sure you've organised some transport to the venue.

There's no point loving someone unless they're kind. Good looks, success and a sense of humour are nice – but you can never regret being too kind.

Being bored is bliss. When you're 20, you think boredom is a fate worse than death. When you're nearly 60, and you've experienced illness, grief and bankruptcy, you realise boredom is a blessing.

Don't worry too much about parenting. If your children are some of your favourite people to spend time with, you've done a great job.

Embrace change. No matter how difficult or frightening a new project feels, it's always an opportunity to walk through a new door.

Trust in fate. No matter how strange, silly or far-fetched an idea may seem, if you can imagine it, it can happen.

Open your heart up as wide as it can go. Love changes us all for the better, and when you realise how much love you're capable of, you'll realise you can transform people's lives by sharing that love.

Acknowledgements

Thank you to Harley and Roman for being the family we always dreamed of. You have given us so much happiness, we are honoured to be your parents, and we love you both more than you could ever imagine.

Also we would like to thank Ajda Vucicevic for making this possible; Issy Lloyd, Laura Colman and everyone at Insanity for looking after us so well; and Daisy Buchanan for bringing our story together.

And a big thank you to all our friends and family. We love you dearly.

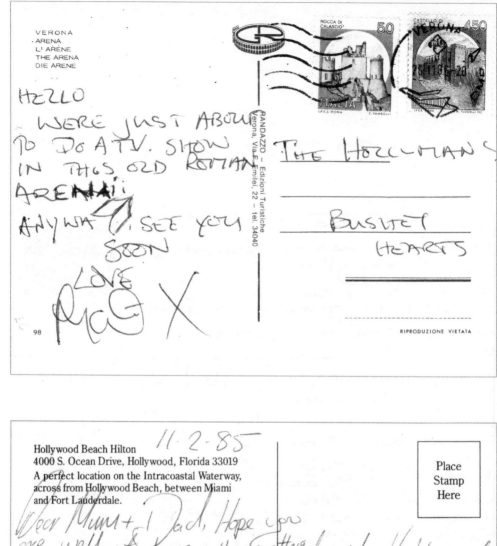

VERONA
ARENA
L'ARENE
THE ARENA
DIE ARENE

RANDAZZO – Edizioni Turistiche
Verona, Via E. Emilei, 22 – tel. 34040

ITALIA

HELLO
- WE'RE JUST ABOUT
TO DO A T.V. SHOW
IN THIS OLD ROMAN
ARENA!!
ANYWAY SEE YOU
SOON
LOVE
MAT X

THE HOLLIMANS
BUSHEY
HEARTS

98

RIPRODUZIONE VIETATA

Hollywood Beach Hilton
4000 S. Ocean Drive, Hollywood, Florida 33019
A perfect location on the Intracoastal Waterway,
across from Hollywood Beach, between Miami
and Fort Lauderdale.

11·2·85

Place
Stamp
Here

Dear Mum + Dad, Hope you
are well at home + the weathers
ok. Well here I am Miami,
didn't want 4 days in dallas
So we flew here for 2 days
its not all that nice, thousands
of old people, but its hot. Martin
phoned me + he wants me to see
him in Brussels So I might fly
there for one day then I'll be
home on the 20th? So I'phone you
Lots of Love Shirli XX
XXXXXX XXX

Mr + Mrs Holliman
BUSHEY
HERTS WD23BG
ENGLAND

Dear Mom + dad, (from SYDNEY)
Hope alls well at home, well
arrived safely (long flight though)
Its nice to see Martin
+ Australia, I still love it here
+ would like to live here.
We went on a big
boat yesterday had
lunch + Champagne
So I'm enjoying myself.
Please phone Siobhan +
ask her to phone Jackie at
Martins office (about
China) I will stay in
Australia untill April.
So take care.
Lots of Love Shirlie xxxxxx

Mr + Mrs HOLLIMAN

BUSHEY, HERTS

ENGLAND

WD2 3BG